T0214643

Communications
in Computer and Information Science   1281

Lu Qin · Wenjie Zhang ·
Ying Zhang · You Peng ·
Hiroyuki Kato · Wei Wang ·
Chuan Xiao (Eds.)

Software Foundations for Data Interoperability and Large Scale Graph Data Analytics

4th International Workshop, SFDI 2020
and 2nd International Workshop, LSGDA 2020
held in Conjunction with VLDB 2020
Tokyo, Japan, September 4, 2020
Proceedings

 Springer

Editors
Lu Qin (iD)
University of Technology Sydney
Sydney, NSW, Australia

Ying Zhang
University of Technology Sydney
Sydney, NSW, Australia

Hiroyuki Kato
National Institute of Informatics
Tokyo, Japan

Chuan Xiao
Osaka University
Osaka, Japan

Wenjie Zhang
The University of New South Wales
Sydney, NSW, Australia

You Peng
The University of New South Wales
Sydney, NSW, Australia

Wei Wang
The University of New South Wales
Sydney, NSW, Australia

ISSN 1865-0929   ISSN 1865-0937   (electronic)
Communications in Computer and Information Science
ISBN 978-3-030-61132-3   ISBN 978-3-030-61133-0   (eBook)
https://doi.org/10.1007/978-3-030-61133-0

This Springer imprint is published by the registered company Springer Nature Switzerland AG
The registered company address is: Gewerbestrasse 11, 6330 Cham, Switzerland

Preface

This volume gathers the papers presented at the Second International Workshop on Large Scale Graph Data Analytics (LSGDA 2020) and the 4th Workshop on Software Foundations for Data Interoperability (SDFI 2020), held in Tokyo, Japan, on September 4, 2020. The LSGDA and the SFDI workshops continued the series of annual workshops which have previously been held in Macau, China (2019), Kyoto, Japan (2018 and 2019), and Fukuoka, Japan (2019), respectively. The Second LSGDA workshop was organized by the University of New South Wales, Australia, in cooperation with the University of Technology Sydney, Australia. The 4th SFDI workshop was organized by the National Institute of Informatics, Japan, the University of New South Wales, Australia, and Osaka University, Japan.

Unfortunately, due to the escalation of the COVID-19 pandemic, and the anti-COVID-19 regulations in Japan and the rest of the world, the planned onsite conferences in Tokyo had to be reformatted. The workshops were held online as virtual conferences featuring live and semi-live presentations during the same period of time.

The LSGDA and the SFDI series of workshops have served as international forums for researchers, practitioners, and PhD students to exchange research findings and ideas on the crucial matters on large-scale graph data analytics and data interoperability, respectively. The LSGDA 2020 and the SDFI 2020 workshops continued this tradition and featured original research and application papers on the development of novel graph analytics models, scalable graph analytics techniques and systems, data integration, and data exchange.

The program of the LSGDA 2020 included three invited keynote talks, given by Prof. Chengfei Liu (Swinburne University of Technology, Australia), Prof. Da Yan (University of Alabama at Birmingham, USA), and Prof. Weiren Yu (University of Warwick, UK). The program of SFDI 2020 included three invited keynote talks, given by Prof. Koiti Hasida (The University of Tokyo and Riken, Japan), Prof. Rui Zhang (The University of Melbourne, Australia), and Prof. Kazutaka Matsuda (Tohoku University, Japan). The call for papers for LSGDA 2020 welcomed original unpublished research and application experience papers on graph data model, storage, indexing and query processing techniques, graph mining techniques, techniques for distributed graph analytics, graph visualization techniques and system interfaces, dynamic and streaming graph data analytics, spatial-temporal graph analytics, AI techniques for graphs, machine learning techniques for graphs, and vision papers to survey the area of graph data analytics as well as describe the future research directions. The call for papers for SFDI 2020 welcomed original unpublished research and application experience papers on software foundations for data interoperability, including data integration, data exchange, distributed collaborative systems, and applications in real-world systems such as data markets. The two workshops collectively received 38 submissions with authors coming from 10 countries. Each paper was evaluated through single-blind review by at least three members of the Program

Committee (PC). The reviewers were assigned after careful consideration of all potential conflicts. Papers were not assigned to PC members originating from the same affiliation or having any known conflicting interests. After the review process, papers with consistent negative evaluations were rejected, whereas papers with mixed ratings (positive and negative) were additionally evaluated by program chairs prior to the meeting, in which all the papers and final decisions regarding them were thoroughly discussed. The evaluation process resulted in the selection of 15 papers (acceptance rate of 39%), which were accepted for presentation at the conferences and publication in this joint proceedings.

The original research results presented in this volume concern well-established fields such as graph data model, storage, indexing and query processing techniques, graph mining techniques, techniques for distributed graph analytics, graph visualization techniques and system interfaces, dynamic and streaming graph data analytics, spatial-temporal graph analytics, AI techniques for graphs, machine learning techniques for graphs, similarity query processing techniques, solutions to data exchange and data integration, heterogeneous data management, and distributed data management. The research results feature vision papers to survey the areas of graph data analytics and data interoperability as well as describe future research directions. The volume also includes three papers for the keynote talks of LSGDA 2020.

Finally, we express our deep gratitude to the members of the Program Committees of the two workshops for their time, comments, and constructive evaluations. We would like to thank everyone from the Organizing/Steering Committees for their time and dedication, which helped make the conferences successful. We are also grateful to the authors and all the participants who truly made the conferences successful, even within the short time frame we had to reorganize the workshops due to the COVID-19 outbreak, we managed to face the new reality and hold the conferences virtually from a safe distance.

September 2020

Lu Qin
Wenjie Zhang
Ying Zhang
You Peng
Hiroyuki Kato
Wei Wang
Chuan Xiao

LSGDA 2020 Organization

General Chair

Xuemin Lin   University of New South Wales, Australia

Program Committee Co-chairs

Lu Qin   University of Technology Sydney, Australia
Wenjie Zhang   University of New South Wales, Australia
Ying Zhang   University of Technology Sydney, Australia

Program Committee

Witold Abramowicz   Poznań University of Economics and Business, Poland
Anil Pacaci   University of Waterloo, Canada
Bolin Ding   Alibaba Group, USA
Chuan Xiao   Osaka University, Japan
Chunbin Lin   Amazon Web Services, USA
Donatella Firmani   Roma Tre University, Italy
Huasong Shan   JD.COM, USA
Jiafeng Hu   Google, China
Jianye Yang   Hunan University, China
Lijun Chang   The University of Sydney, Australia
Matteo Lissandrini   Aalborg University, Denmark
Rong-Hua Li   Beijing Institute of Technology, China
Sergey Pupyrev   Facebook, USA
Stefano Leucci   University of L'Aquila, Italy
Verena Kantere   National Technical University of Athens, Greece
Vijil Chenthamarakshan   IBM AI Research, USA
Weiren Yu   University of Warwick, UK
Xiang Zhao   National University of Defense Technology, China
Xin Cao   University of New South Wales, Australia
Yuanyuan Zhu   Wuhan University, China
Zhaonian Zou   Harbin Institute of Technology, China

Organizing Committee

Dong Wen   University of Technology Sydney, Australia
You Peng   University of New South Wales, Australia
Kai Wang   University of New South Wales, Australia

SFDI 2020 Organization

Steering Committee

Zhenjiang Hu   Peking University, China, and NII, Japan
Makoto Onizuka   Osaka University, Japan
Masatoshi Yoshikawa   Kyoto University, Japan

Program Committee Co-chairs

Hiroyuki Kato   NII, Japan
Wei Wang   University of New South Wales, Australia
Chuan Xiao   Osaka University, Japan

Program Committee

Yang Cao	Kyoto University, Japan
Muhammad Aamir Cheema	Monash University, Australia
Yuyang Dong	NEC, Japan
Raul Castro Fernandez	University of Chicago, USA
Torsten Grust	University of Tübingen, Germany
Sheng Hu	Hokkaido University, Japan
Verena Kantere	National Technical University of Athens, Greece
Sebastian Maneth	University of Bremen, Germany
Parth Nagarkar	New Mexico State University, USA
George Papadakis	University of Athens, Greece
Jianbin Qin	Shenzhen University, China
Lu Qin	University of Technology Sydney, Australia
Yuya Sasaki	Osaka University, Japan
Toshiyuki Shimizu	Kyoto University, Japan
Massimo Tisi	IMT Atlantique, France
Jiannan Wang	Simon Fraser University, Canada
Xiang Zhao	National University of Defense Technology, China
Wenjie Zhang	University of New South Wales, Australia
Erkang Zhu	Microsoft, USA
Kostas Zoumpatianos	Harvard University, USA

Contents

Large Scale Graph Data Analytics

Attribute Diversified Community Search

Chengfei Liu$^{(\boxtimes)}$, Lu Chen, Rui Zhou, and Afzal Azeem Chowdhary

Swinburne University of Technology, Melbourne, Australia
{cliu,luchen,rzhou,achowdhary}@swin.edu.au

Abstract. Discovering communities that naturally exist as groups of fine-connected users is one the most important tasks for network data analytics and has tremendous real applications. In recent year, community search in attributed graphs has begun to attract attention, which aims to find communities that are both structure and attribute cohesive. Whereas, searching a community that is structure cohesive but attribute diversified, denoted as attribute diversified community search, is still at preliminary stage. In this paper, we introduce our recent effort for discovering attribute diversified community. In fact, for different applications, the needs of attribute diversification for modelling the community are quite different. We introduce three attribute diversified community models in which attribute diversification takes different roles for presenting objective, query requirement, and constraint. We also discuss major techniques for speeding up the attribute diversified community search.

1 Introduction

Graphs have emerged as a powerful model for representing different types of data, such as social networks and collaboration networks. In these graphs, discovering communities that naturally exist as groups of fine-connected users is one the most important tasks for network data analytics and has tremendous real applications. Nevertheless, most of the previous studies [1,4,5,10,24,29] have focused on finding communities from a graph without considering attributes. As such, the returned communities may miss out important attributes describing a variety of features of real applications. Recently, community search in graphs having attributes called attributed graphs has begun to attract attention [6,7,11,15,20,28]. These works endeavour to find communities that are both structure and attribute cohesive. Besides, there are also a few works [18] that aim to find communities which are attribute diversified among them. However, a study for community search that takes serious consideration of structure cohesiveness but attribute diversification within a community is still at preliminary stage.

In this paper we focus on introducing our recent works for attribute diversified community search, including three attribute diversified community models in which the attribute diversification takes different roles for presenting an objective, a query requirement, and a constraint.

© Springer Nature Switzerland AG 2020
L. Qin et al. (Eds.): SFDI 2020/LSGDA 2020, CCIS 1281, pp. 3–17, 2020.
https://doi.org/10.1007/978-3-030-61133-0_1

Maximizing Attribute Diversification. Discovering a community with members as diversified as possible has numerous applications. One example is building a team for group brainstorming to address a cognitive bottleneck of idea generation. Group brainstorming shall engage diversified individuals to collaborate by communicating and sharing ideas in groups, where diversified individuals can substantially broaden the knowledge base available for idea generation and the social engagements among the individuals allow the creative effort to be aggregated. Other examples are: gathering socially connected experts of different marketing fields to brainstorm a marketing session of different new products, selecting a panel of concerted engineers with different technological expertise for reviewing and testing different products to show the collective information pool of the panel, etc. For these applications, since they target community members for innovations and there are evidences that maximizing diversity leads to creativity [22], the desired community would be preferred to maximise the attribute diversity of its members [9].

Attribute Diversification with Specific Requirement. For some applications, the diversification requirements could be specific. Let us consider a real event happened in 2019. A small town in Australia was devastated by the severe bushfire, which results in at least 11 damaged properties and 33 people injured. The town needs community spirit to rebuild. This naturally arises the needs of several activities with diverse demands. A group needs to be formed urgently to react on the disaster, with at least 3 members having expertise in building temporary accommodations, 5 doctors, 4 psychologists, 2 members having the expertise in community support, etc. Each member may contribute to as many skills as possible in this kind of group. Due to damaged properties, a construction team also needs to be built for rebuilding these properties, with members having different skills, such as at least 2 architects, 11 members handling masonry, 5 members dealing with welding, etc. Due to the intensive labouring, each member may contribute at most 2 skills in this kind of construction teams since multi-tasking may lead to multi-failing. Due to the disaster, people may suffer a lot mentally. To help relief psychological pressure from these people, it would be great to organize an improvised music show to soothe them, which needs to discover musicians to form a band. The found musicians may be able to play multiple instruments. However, since they perform as a band, each of them shall focus on a single instrument. From these examples, it is clear that, apart from social cohesiveness and spatial closeness requirements, an effective community model for impromptu activities with diverse demands should allow people to express specific diversification requirements including: 1) collective capabilities of the group w.r.t. a particular skill, e.g., at least 3 members have expertise in building temporary accommodation; and 2) capacity of each member on maximum contribution the member can make, e.g., at most 2 skills in a construction team. This motivates us to study how to find an attribute diversified geo-social group with specific diversification requirements [8].

Attribute Diversification as Constraint. Some applications would like to find a community that exhibits certain level of attribute diversification but has members with social relationships as cohesive as possible. For instance, assume that we need to find a group of organisers for organising a conference. To make the organisation smooth, the organisers are expected to communicate and collaborate with each other extensively. The more that organisers identify with each other, the more likely they are to believe that they hold similar goals for successfully organising the conference. On the other hand, to make the conference accept various ideas, we also expect that the organisers would jointly share a variety of domains. Similar applications include promoting a product through commonly associated experts of difference domains, team formations for maximising productivity, etc. Motivated by these applications, we introduce a novel community model that considers attribute diversification as a constraint while maximising the structure cohesiveness as the primary searching objective.

Road Map. The rest of this paper is organized as follows. In Sect. 2, we introduce and discuss basics for attributed graphs. In Sects. 3, 4, and 5 we discuss our recent attribute diversification community search works. We discuss the related works and conclude this paper in Sects. 6 and 7.

2   Preliminaries

In this section, we first formally introduce the commonly used community cohesiveness metrics and attributes diversification metrics.

An attributed graph is denoted as $G = (V, E, A)$, where $V(G)$, $E(G)$, A denote the set of vertices in G, the set of edges in G, and the set of attributes in terms of *keywords* respectively. Each vertex $v \in V(G)$ is attached with a set of attributes $A(v) \subseteq A$. Given $v \in V(G)$, $deg(v, G)$ denotes the degree of v in G and $N(v, G)$ denotes the neighbours of v in G. A triangle in G is a cycle of length 3. A triangle induced on vertices $u, v, w \in V(G)$ is denoted as $\triangle_{uvw}$ and when these vertices are not specified we omit the subscript. Given a subgraph $H \subseteq G$, $Tri(H)$ denotes the set of triangles in H.

2.1   Social Cohesiveness Metrics

Coreness. Coreness is defined according to the degree of every vertex.

Definition 1. k-core subgraph. *Given a subgraph $H \subseteq G$, an integer k, H is called k-core subgraph if for every $v \in V(H)$, $deg(v, H) \geq k$ and such maximum k is called the coreness of H.*

Intuitively, a k-core is a subgraph in which vertex has at least k neighbours. A k-core with a large value k indicates strong internal connections over vertices. A k-core is maximal if it cannot be extended.

Trussness. Trussness is defined based on the number of triangles each edge is involved in a graph. In general, given a subgraph $H \subseteq G$, we use $\triangle_{uvw}$ to denote a triangle, a cycle with length of 3, consisting of vertices $u, v, w \in V(H)$.

Support. The support of an edge $e(u,v) \in E(H)$, denoted by $sup(e, H)$, is the number of triangles containing e, i.e., $sup(e, H) = |\{\triangle_{uvw} : w \in N(v, H) \cap N(u, H)\}|$, where $N(v, H)$ and $N(u, H)$ are the neighbours of u, v in H correspondingly.

Minimum Subgraph Trussness. The trussness for a subgraph H is defined as an integer k that is 2 plus the minimum possible support for edges in $E(H)$. That is, the minimum subgraph trussness defines that for every edge $e \in E(H)$, the number of triangles in which e participates shall be no less than k - 2.

Definition 2. *c-truss constraint. A subgraph H satisfies c-truss constraint if the trussness of H is c, and c is connected.*

Intuitively, if H satisfies c-truss constraint, the vertices of an edge in H have at least c-2 common neighbours in H, every vertex in H has no less than c-1 neighbours and at least c-1 edges have to be deleted in order to make H disconnected. The communication cost of H is at most $\lfloor \frac{2|V(H)|-2}{c} \rfloor$. A H with a large value c indicates strong internal social relationships over vertices.

2.2   Attribute Diversification Metrics

Diversity for Two Vertices. Given a pair of vertices, $u, v \in V(G)$ with attributes $A(u)$ and $A(v)$, a diversity function is defined as $div((u, v)) = 1 - \frac{|A(u) \cap A(c)|}{|A(u) \cup A(v)|}$.

Average Based Diversity. Given H, the attribute diversification of H is measured by $avgDiv(H) = \frac{\sum_{(u,v) \in H} div((u,v))}{|V(H)|}$.

We will introduce detailed attribute diversification metrics when introducing the specific models.

3   Discovering a Community Maximizing Attribute Diversity

In this section, we introduce an attribute diversified community search work [9] that aims to find a community maximizing the attribute diversity. We first introduce the community model and search problem, then discuss the search framework and optimizations, respectively.

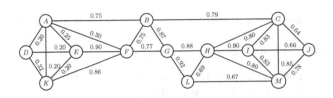

Fig. 1. Graph with edge diversity

Algorithm 1: basicADC(H)

---

1 $H^* \leftarrow \phi$;
2 basicEnum (H);
3 **return** H^*;
4 **Procedure** basicEnum *(H)*
5 | $H' \leftarrow k$-core(H);
6 | let $\mathcal{H}'$ be the set of connected component in H';
7 | **foreach** $h \in \mathcal{H}'$ **do**
8 | | **if** $avgDiv(h) > avgDiv(H^*)$ **then**
9 | | | $H^* \leftarrow h$;
10 | **foreach** $h \in \mathcal{H}'$ **do**
11 | | **foreach** $v \in V(h)$ **do**
12 | | | basicEnum $(h \setminus \{v\})$;

3.1   Problem Definition

Attribute Diversified Community. We propose the attribute diversified community model, using k-core and average based diversification metric.

Definition 3. Attribute diversified community. *Given a subgraph $H \subseteq G$, an integer k, H is defined as an attribute diversified community if H satisfies the following constraints simultaneously:*

- *Connectivity: H is connected;*
- *Structure Cohesiveness: H is a k-core subgraph;*
- *Maximizing Average Diversity: for $avgDiv(H)$, H is $argmax_{H'}$ $\{avgDiv(H')|H' \subseteq G\}$;*

Accordingly, given G and an integer k, the research problem we focus on in this paper is as follows.

Research Problem. *Find the subgraph $H \subseteq G$ that maximises $avgDiv(H)$.*

Example 1. To briefly show the results of the above problem, we discuss the example shown in Fig. 1. For the attribute diversified community search problem with $k = 2$, the result is the $\{B, C, F, G, H, I, J, L, M\}$ induced subgraph with diversity of 1.44.

3.2   Search Framework

For ease of understanding, we first show the basic enumeration used in the branch and bound algorithm. Algorithm 1 shows the basic enumeration that derives the optimum result. Initially the input of the algorithm is G. By recursively calling itself, Algorithm 1 tries all possible subgraphs of G if the subgraphs may contain the optimum result and checks if there is a feasible solution in the current recursion. If there is a feasible solution h in the recursion and the feasible solution is greater than the current optimum one H^*, H^* is updated to h.

Search Space Reduction. Algorithm 1 also applies space reduction optimisations based on the observations as follows.

Observation 1. *The optimum result can only be contained in a connected k-core of G if it exists when the enumeration starts.*

Observation 2. *During the recursion with an input H, the optimum result can only be contained in a connected k-core of H.*

With the observations, when a recursion starts, Algorithm 1 first reduces the input to the maximal k-core, which would transform the input into a set of maximal connected k-cores. Algorithm 1 only tries combinations in each connected k-core. As such, the search space can be reduced significantly.

3.3   Optimisations

Upper Bound Based Pruning. The idea is that we estimate the upper bound of the average edge diversity of the current search branch. If the upper bound is smaller than the diversity of the optimum result found so far, we terminate the search branch.

Next, we will propose three upper bounds.

Upper Bound Based on Core Property. We firstly show an upper bound for a connected k-core based on core property. The upper bound for h is defined as follows.

$$ubcore(h) = \frac{\sum_{(u,v)\in E(h)} div((u,v))}{k+1} \tag{1}$$

The upper bound based on core property would only be tight when h contains an optimum result with size close to $k + 1$. However, it has limited pruning effectiveness when h contains large-size results. Next we study tight bounds for arbitrary h.

Maximum Average Diversity in a Core. Given a connected k-core h, this bound is defined as follows.

$$ubavg(h) = max\{avgDiv(h')|h' \subseteq h\} \tag{2}$$

Lemma 1. *ubavg(h) is an upper bound for h.*

Approximate Maximum Average Diversity in a Core. The computational cost of $ubavg(h)$ is high. It would take $O(|V(h)|^3)$ if using the algorithm in [13]. However, there is a simple but effective approximate algorithm [3] that can achieve $\frac{1}{2}$-approximation with complexity $O(|E(h)|)$. As such we can use the approximation algorithm to get an at least $\frac{1}{2}$ $ubavg(h)$ value first and then multiple it by 2 to derive a slightly loose bound, denoted as $apxubavg(h)$. In implementation, $ubcore(h)$ and $apxubavg(h)$ are prioritised as they are cheap.

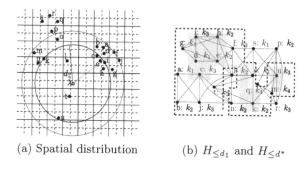

(a) Spatial distribution   (b) $H_{\leq d_1}$ and $H_{\leq d^*}$

Fig. 2. Running example

Search Order. For each connected k-cores that cannot be pruned, we sort them in non-increasing order according to their upper bounds. By doing this, we can heuristically find communities with large average diversity as early as possible. This would make the upper bound based pruning more effective.

4 Discovering Attribute Diversified Geo-Social Group with Specific Requirement

In this section, we tackle the problem of finding an attribute diversified geo-social group with the given specific diversification requirements [8]. We first introduce the query, model and search problem. Then the novel search framework is discussed. After that, the optimizations for speeding up the search are introduced.

4.1 Problem Formulation

Data. We consider an undirected graph data $G = (V, E)$ with network structure, spatial attribute and textual attributes. For each vertex $v \in V(G)$, v has a piece of location information expressed as latitude and longitude denoted as $(v.x, v.y)$, and has a set of keyword attributes denoted as $v.A$.

Since our proposed group model would satisfy minimum keyword, capacity and social constraints while optimizing spatial closeness, we name the proposed model as MKCSSG. Our proposed geo-social model is introduced as follows.

We formally define the query for searching MKCSSG.

Query for MKCSSG. The query Q for MKCSSG consists of a social parameter c (an integer), a set of keywords φ, keyword parameters P (a set of integers), r (an integer), and a location λ (latitude and longitude).

Minimum Keyword and Capacity Constraints. Given a set of query keywords $\varphi = \{k_1, \ldots, k_{|\varphi|}\}$, $P = \{\rho_1, \ldots, \rho_{|\varphi|}\}$, r, and S, MKCC is defined below.

Definition 4. *Minimum keyword and capacity constraints*, MKCC. S satisfies MKCC if there is a $v.A' \subseteq \varphi \cap v.A$ for every $v \in V(S)$ such that:

- *Capacity constraint:* $|v.A'| \leq r$,
- *Minimum keyword constraint (MKC):* $\forall\ k_i \in \varphi$, $|V(S_{k_i})| \geq \rho_i$, where $V(S_{k_i})$ is the set of vertices such that for each $v \in V(S_{k_i})$, $v.A'$ contains $k_i \in \varphi$.

Searching Objective. Now, we formalize the spatial closeness for MKCSSG and the research problem.

Spatial Closeness. Given a query location λ, we consider a distance function to measure the closeness between λ and an MKCSSG S as:

Definition 5. *Spatial closeness.* $dist(\lambda, S) = max\{\|\lambda - v\| | v \in V(S)\}$,

where $\|\lambda - v\|$ denotes Euclidean distance between v and λ.

Definition 6. (P, c, r, d)**-truss.** Given $Q = \{\lambda, P, \varphi, c, r\}$ and a distance threshold d, a subgraph $S \subseteq G$ is a (P, c, r, d)-truss, if it satisfies all the conditions: 1) S satisfies MKCC, 2) S satisfies c-truss constraint, 3) $dist(\lambda, S) \leq d$.

Research Problem. MKCSSG search. Given $Q = \{\lambda, P\ \varphi, c, r\}$ and G, return (P, c, r, d)-truss S^* so that there is no (P, c, r, d')-truss S' with $d' \leq d$.

Example 2. An example dataset is shown in Fig. 2, where Fig. 2(a) shows locations for vertices of graph data in Fig. 2(b). Let the query be: $Q = \{\lambda, P = \{2, 2, 2\}, \varphi = \{k_1, k_2, k_3\}, c = 4, r = 1\}$. $\{d, e, f, g, h, i\}$ induced subgraph S^* is the optimum result for Q for this dataset. S^* satisfies social constraint, i.e., every edge in $E(S^*)$ involves no less than 2 triangles. S^* satisfies MKCC. That is, it firstly satisfies capacity constraint, i.e., every vertex contributes to at most one keyword in φ, where $d.A' = \{k_1\}$, $e.A' = \{k_2\}$, $f.A' = \{k_3\}$, $g.A' = \{k_1\}$, $h.A' = \{k_2\}$, $i.A' = \{k_3\}$. Then it satisfies MKC, i.e., with the A' for each vertex (those underlined), the keyword vertex frequency for every query keyword is no less than 2. Last but not least, among all groups satisfying the constraints, S^* is the closest one to λ and the most distant vertex (to λ) in S^* is f.

4.2   Search Framework

We firstly introduce some definitions.

Definition 7. *d radius bounded graph.* Given a query location λ, a subgraph H and a distance threshold d, d radius bounded graph, denoted as $H_{\leq d}$, is the subgraph of H induced by vertices of H with distance to λ no greater than d.

We would like to highlight an instance of d radius bounded graph, d^* radius bounded graph, $H_{\leq d^*}$. $H_{\leq d^*}$ has the property below. There is no $H_{\leq d'}$ such that $H_{\leq d'}$ contains MKCSSG and $d' < d^*$.

Optimum Search Space. We refer $H_{\leq d^*}$ as optimum search space since it is just large enough to contain MKCSSG for the query.

The Framework. MKCSSG search framework consists of two stages: expanding stage and reducing stage. During the expanding stage, it intends to quickly identify $H_{\leq d}$ that is just sufficiently large to contain the optimum search space $H_{\leq d^*}$ by exploring $H_{\leq d}$ that progressively gets larger, in which it determines the existence of a subgraph satisfying all constraints. For the reducing stage, to get the optimum result, it attempts to progressively remove the vertex that is the most distant to λ in S^*. The last survived (ρ, c)-truss during the vertices removing process is the optimum result.

4.3 Optimizations for Expanding Stage

Expanding Strategy. We first define an expanding invariant as follows.

Definition 8. Δ *size invariant. Let* $\{d_1, d_2, \ldots, d_i\}$ *be the series of radius for defining d radius graphs, for any two consecutive d, d', we define Δ invariant as* $\Delta = \frac{|E(H_{\leq d'})|}{|E(H_{\leq d})|}$, *in which $\Delta > 1$ must hold.*

The Strategy. The strategy applied for the expanding stage is to maintain Δ size invariant over any two consecutively evaluated $H_{\leq d}$, $H_{\leq d'}$. Applying Δ invariant for expanding stage guarantees two nice properties below. Now, let us show the tight bound that is guaranteed by applying the proposed expanding strategy.

Initial Expanding Range. Intuitively, if the initial search range is close to d^*, the total amount of subgraphs that has to be evaluated to approaching $H_{\leq d^*}$ is less. This motivates us to study a lower bound of d radius subgraph.

Definition 9. $H_{\underline{\leq} d}$. *A subgraph $H_{\underline{\leq} d}$ of H is a lower bound d radius subgraph of $H_{\leq d^*}$ if it satisfies conditions: 1) $H_{\underline{\leq} d}$ is connected, 2) $H_{\underline{\leq} d}$ satisfies minimum keyword constraint and 3) there is no $H' \subseteq H_{\underline{\leq} d}$ such that H' satisfies the first two constraints and $dist(\lambda, H') < dist(\lambda, H_{\underline{\leq} d})$.*

Checking (ρ, c)-truss in d Radius Subgraph. To simplify the discussion, for any two consecutive $H_{\leq d}$ and $H_{\leq d'}$ with $\frac{|H_{\leq d'}|}{|H_{\leq d}|} = \Delta$, let us introduce a new notation $H_{d' \backslash d}$ to denote the subgraph of $H_{\leq d'}$ induced by vertices appearing in edges of $E(H_{\leq d'}) \setminus E(H_{\leq d})$.

We propose two techniques to speed up (ρ, c)-truss checking below.
Lazy (ρ, c)-truss checking strategy. Given $H_{\leq d}$, we only apply (ρ, c)-truss checking on any subgraph potentially containing (ρ, c)-truss, defined as ρ potential subgraph below.
ρ *potential subgraph $P_{\leq d}$*. A subgraph $P_{\leq d} \subseteq H_{\leq d}$ is defined as ρ potential subgraph if it is connected, satisfies minimum keyword constraint and is *maximal* within $H_{\leq d}$.

The Strategy. Since a (ρ, c)-truss should reside in $P_{\leq d}$, we propose lazy (ρ, c)-truss checking strategy that applies (ρ, c)-truss constraint checking on every $P_{\leq d}$ in $H_{\leq d}$ only instead of the entire $H_{\leq d}$.

Union with Existing Truss. To avoid graph traversing for checking minimum keyword constraint and connectivity after updating trussness, we propose a solution below. Firstly, we maintain every maximal connected c truss subgraph in every $P_{\leq d}$, each of which is attached with keyword vertex frequency. Secondly, after $P_{\leq d}$ is expanded to $P_{\leq d'}$, we update the maintained c-truss subgraphs if applicable. Although this approach cannot update trussness for existing truss subgraphs precisely, it is sufficient and efficient to check the existence of (ρ, c)-truss in $P_{\leq d'}$. As such, minimum keyword constraint and connectivity checking for truss subgraphs can be performed simultaneously and incrementally.

4.4   Optimizations for Reducing Stage

We will maintain a minimum spanning forest for S (the result of the expanding stage) augmented with aggregated keyword vertex frequency. Notice that initially, every spanning tree in the forest satisfies minimum keyword constraint. After an edge is deleted from S, one of the two cases below may happen.

Case 1: the deleted edge is not in the forest. The remaining subgraphs are still connected and each connected subgraph still satisfies minimum keyword constraint.

Case 2: the deleted edge is in the forest. In this case, one of the tree in the minimum spanning forest is cut into two trees, which may lead to one of the following subcases.

Subcase 1: cannot link the cut trees. We cannot find a replacement edge from the remaining S to link the two trees, which means the subgraph referred by the two trees becomes two disjoint subgraphs. We update keyword vertex frequency for each of the cut tree. After the update, we safely prune the cut tree from the maintained spanning forest if it does not satisfy minimum keyword constraint since they cannot contribute to MKCSSG.

Subcase 2: can link the cut trees. If we can find a replacement edge, the subgraph referred by two cut trees is still connected. We link the two trees with the replacement edge. Keyword vertex frequency remains the same.

To efficiently maintain the above index, we borrow the idea from [14]. Given S, every edge in $E(S)$ is associated with a level progressively increased as edges are deleted, which is equivalent to progressively partitioning S hierarchically. Edges with high level refer to a more restricted part of S. In contrast, edges with low level refer to a more general part of S (super graphs of the high level subgraphs). As such when deleting an edge with a certain level, we do not need to consider any edge with lower level as a replacement edge, which elegantly reduces the search space for finding a replacement edge.

4.5   Optimizations for Keyword Constraint Checking

We will show that MKCC checking for a set of vertices S, query keywords $\varphi = \{k_1, \ldots, k_{|\varphi|}\}$, $P = \{\rho_1, \ldots, \rho_{|\varphi|}\}$ and r can be reduced to an instance of the min cut problem.

The Instance of Maximum Flow Problem. We construct the flow network N based on φ, P, r and S. N consists of different types of nodes below. For each keyword in φ, we create a keyword node. For each vertex in S, we create a vertex node. Additionally, we create a source node s and a sink node t. The edges and capacities for N are as follows. For each vertex node n, we create an edge from s to n with capacity of r. For each keyword node n' representing k_i, we create an edge from n' to t with capacity of ρ_i. In addition, there is an edge between a vertex node n and a keyword node n' (from n to n') if the keyword attributes of n representing vertex contain the query keyword represented by n', and the capacity between n and n' is set to ∞.

Lemma 2. *S satisfies MKCC if there exists a min cut for N whose T part contains the node t only.*

We adopt preflow–push (push-relabel) algorithm to solve the min cut problem. As such, the time complexity of MKCC checking for MKCSSG search is shown below.

MKCC checking complexity for the expanding stage. This part can be bounded by $\mathcal{O}\left((1 + \Delta^3 + \frac{1}{\Delta^3 - 1}) \times |V(H_{\leq d^*})|^3\right)$, assuming $|\varphi| \ll |V(H_{\leq d^*})|$. As discussed previously, by letting $\Delta = 2$, the time complexity becomes the minimum, $\mathcal{O}\left(|V(H_{\leq d^*})|^3\right)$.

MKCC checking complexity for the reducing stage. This part can be bounded by $\mathcal{O}\left(|V(H_{\leq d^*})|^3\right)$ as well, by taking advantage of the preflow-push algorithm.

5   Discovering a Community with Attribute Diversification Constraint

In this section we introduce an attribute diversified community search work that focuses on finding a community maximizing the structure cohesiveness while maintaining the attribute diversity to a certain level. The community model is discussed firstly. Then the solution vision is introduced.

5.1   Problem Formulation

We formally define the *subgraph diversity* below.

Definition 10. Subgraph diversity. *Given a subgraph $H \subseteq G$, we define its subgraph diversity as:*

$$\tau(H) = min\{div(u, v) | \forall u, v \in V(H), u \neq v\}$$

Definition 11. (k, τ)-**core.** *Given a subgraph $H \subseteq G$, a pairwise vertex diversity threshold τ, H is a (k, τ)-core if H satisfies the following constraints simultaneously: 1) H is connected, 2) $\forall v \in V(H)$, $deg(v) \geq k$, 3) $\tau(H) \geq \tau$.*

Research Problem. *Most cohesive diversified community search.* *Given an attributed graph G, a user given attribute diversity threshold τ, find a (k, τ)-core $H \subseteq G$ such that there is no (k', τ)-core H' with k' greater than k.*

5.2 Solution Vision

We introduce a definition and an observation as follows.

Definition 12. Diversity Subgraph. *Given a subgraph diversity threshold τ, let D denote a new graph named as diversity graph with $V(D) = V(G)$ and $E(D) = \{(u, v) \mid div(u, v) \geq \tau \ and \ u, v \in V(G)\}$.*

Observation 3. *Given a (k, τ)-core H, the $V(H)$ induced subgraph of D is a complete subgraph (i.e., a clique).*

We are ready to discuss the vision of our proposed algorithms.

Baseline. The baseline algorithm enumerates all maximal cliques of D using the state-of-the-art clique enumeration algorithm. When a maximal clique C is generated, it runs core decomposition for $G(C)$. If the largest core number of $G(C)$ is greater than the largest k of the (k, τ)-core found so far, then $G(C)$ contains the best (k, τ)-core found so far. After evaluating all the maximal cliques in D, the optimum result is found. The correctness of the baseline algorithm is clear since the vertices in a most cohesive (k, τ)-core must be resident at one of the maximal cliques in D.

Core Based Heuristic. To speed up the baseline, we consider a core based heuristic: vertices in a large core will be considered prior to the vertices in a small core. Using this heuristic, we may terminate the search quite early, i.e., let k be the largest k for (k, τ)-core found so far, if the core number of the current explored vertex is smaller than k, then we can terminate the search.

Advanced Heuristic. The core based heuristic just considers prioritising vertices that are structurally promising. Since the definition of the (k, τ)-core considers both the structure and the attribute properties, a heuristic that prioritises vertices that are promising from both structure cohesive and attribute diversified perspectives would be better. We propose a novel index denoted as KD-Index to help us identify the vertices that are promising from both the structure cohesive and the attribute diversified perspectives. To make the index general for different τ, we pre-compute promising vertices for different diversity thresholds. When a query τ is given, we evaluate the precomputed index that is just smaller than τ for speeding up the search.

Better Local Enumeration Order. The advanced heuristic provides an overall search order. However, when evaluating each promising subgraph, the local search order can be further optimised for speeding up the search. We propose to use the degeneracy order when evaluating vertices in a promising subgraph, which can nicely bound the search depth of the promising subgraph to the degeneracy of the subgraph. The degeneracy of the subgraph is much smaller than the total number of vertices contained in the subgraph.

6   Related Work

Community Search in Attributed Graph. In [18], Li et al. propose a skyline community model for searching communities in attributed graph. Zhang et al. propose (k, r)-core community model that considers k-core and pairwise vertex similarity [28]. Fang et al. propose a community model that is sensitive to query attributes. In [16], an attributed community model is proposed by using k-truss for capturing social cohesiveness and the resultant community shall contain attributes similar with query attributes. In [12,23], community models considering spatial closeness are studied. The works above would find communities with users having similar attributes while our work find communities with users having diversified attributes. In [6], a parameter-free contextual community model is studied. Community models considering influence are studied in [2,17,19]. In [2,19], the authors use max-min objective function, which aims to find influential communities where scores are defined on vertices.

Community Detection in Attributed Graph. Works including [21] consider graph structure with LDA model to detect attributed communities. Unified distance [30] is also considered for detecting attributed communities. In [30], attributed communities are detected by using proposed structural/attribute clustering methods, in which structural distance is unified by attribute weighted edges. Xu et al. [26] propose a Bayesian based model. In [15], Huang et al. propose a community model considering attributes based on an entropy-based model. Recently, Wu et al. propose an attributed community model [25] based on an attributed refined fitness model. Yang et al. [27] propose a model using probabilistic generative model.

7   Conclusion and Open Problems

In this paper, we introduce our recent works on attribute diversified community search. Based on the detailed real application scenarios, different attribute diversified community models are introduced where the attribute diversification takes the roles of objective, query requirement and constraint. For each of the community model, the search framework as well as major optimizations for speeding up the search are discussed in great detail.

Although we have made a fair effort for discovering attribute diversified communities, however the study is still at preliminary stage. We conclude by introducing an open problem for attribute diversified community search.

How to effectively model and efficiently search top-r attribute diversified community considering both inter and intra attribute diversifications?

Acknowledgments. This work is jointly supported by the ARC Discovery Projects under Grant No. DP170104747 and DP200103700.

References

1. Batagelj, V., Zaversnik, M.: An o(m) algorithm for cores decomposition of networks. arXiv preprint cs/0310049 (2003)
2. Bi, F., Chang, L., Lin, X., Zhang, W.: An optimal and progressive approach to online search of top-k influential communities. PVLDB **11**(9), 1056–1068 (2018)
3. Buchbinder, N., Feldman, M., Naor, J., Schwartz, R.: A tight linear time (1/2)-approximation for unconstrained submodular maximization. In: Annual Symposium on Foundations of Computer Science, pp. 649–658 (2012)
4. Cai, G., Sun, Y.: The minimum augmentation of any graph to a k edge connected graph. Networks **19**(1), 151–172 (1989)
5. Chang, L., Yu, J.X., Qin, L., Lin, X., Liu, C., Liang, W.: Efficiently computing k-edge connected components via graph decomposition. In: SIGMOD, pp. 205–216 (2013)
6. Chen, L., Liu, C., Liao, K., Li, J., Zhou, R.: Contextual community search over large social networks. In: ICDE, pp. 88–99. IEEE (2019)
7. Chen, L., Liu, C., Zhou, R., Li, J., Yang, X., Wang, B.: Maximum co-located community search in large scale social networks. PVLDB **11**(10), 1233–1246 (2018)
8. Chen, L., Liu, C., Zhou, R., Xu, J., Yu, J.X., Li, J.: Finding effective geosocial group for impromptu activities with diverse demands. In: SIGKDD. ACM (2020)
9. Chowdhary, A.A., Liu, C., Chen, L., Zhou, R., Yang, Y.: Finding attribute diversified communities in complex networks. In: Nah, Y., Cui, B., Lee, S.-W., Yu, J.X., Moon, Y.-S., Whang, S.E. (eds.) DASFAA 2020. LNCS, vol. 12114, pp. 19–35. Springer, Cham (2020). https://doi.org/10.1007/978-3-030-59419-0_2
10. Cohen, J.: Trusses: cohesive subgraphs for social network analysis. National Security Agency Technical Report 16 (2008)
11. Fang, Y., Cheng, R., Chen, Y., Luo, S., Hu, J.: Effective and efficient attributed community search. VLDB J. **26**(6), 803–828 (2017). https://doi.org/10.1007/s00778-017-0482-5
12. Fang, Y., Cheng, R., Li, X., Luo, S., Hu, J.: Effective community search over large spatial graphs. PVLDB **10**(6), 709–720 (2017)
13. Gallo, G., Grigoriadis, M.D., Tarjan, R.E.: A fast parametric maximum flow algorithm and applications. SIAM J. Comput. **18**(1), 30–55 (1989)
14. Holm, J., De Lichtenberg, K., Thorup, M., Thorup, M.: Poly-logarithmic deterministic fully-dynamic algorithms for connectivity, minimum spanning tree, 2-edge, and biconnectivity. J. ACM **48**(4), 723–760 (2001)
15. Huang, X., Cheng, H., Yu, J.X.: Dense community detection in multi-valued attributed networks. Inf. Sci. **314**(C), 77–99 (2015)
16. Huang, X., Lakshmanan, L.V.: Attribute-driven community search. PVLDB **10**(9), 949–960 (2017)
17. Li, J., Wang, X., Deng, K., Yang, X., Sellis, T., Yu, J.X.: Most influential community search over large social networks. In: ICDE, pp. 871–882. IEEE (2017)
18. Li, R.H., et al.: Skyline community search in multi-valued networks. In: SIGMOD, pp. 457–472. ACM (2018)
19. Li, R.H., Qin, L., Yu, J.X., Mao, R.: Influential community search in large networks. PVLDB **8**(5), 509–520 (2015)

20. Li, Y., Sha, C., Huang, X., Zhang, Y.: Community detection in attributed graphs: an embedding approach. In: AAAI (2018)
21. Nallapati, R.M., Ahmed, A., Xing, E.P., Cohen, W.W.: Joint latent topic models for text and citations. In: SIGKDD, pp. 542–550. ACM (2008)
22. Wang, H.C., Fussell, S.R., Cosley, D.: From diversity to creativity: stimulating group brainstorming with cultural differences and conversationally-retrieved pictures. In: CSCW, pp. 265–274. ACM (2011)
23. Wang, K., Cao, X., Lin, X., Zhang, W., Qin, L.: Efficient computing of radius-bounded k-cores. In: ICDE, pp. 233–244. IEEE (2018)
24. Wen, D., Qin, L., Zhang, Y., Chang, L., Chen, L.: Enumerating k-vertex connected components in large graphs. In: ICDE, pp. 52–63. IEEE (2019)
25. Wu, P., Pan, L.: Mining application-aware community organization with expanded feature subspaces from concerned attributes in social networks. Knowl.-Based Syst. **139**, 1–12 (2018)
26. Xu, Z., Ke, Y., Wang, Y., Cheng, H., Cheng, J.: A model-based approach to attributed graph clustering. In: SIGMOD, pp. 505–516. ACM (2012)
27. Yang, J., McAuley, J., Leskovec, J.: Community detection in networks with node attributes. In: ICDM, pp. 1151–1156. IEEE (2013)
28. Zhang, F., Zhang, Y., Qin, L., Zhang, W., Lin, X.: When engagement meets similarity: efficient (k, r)-core computation on social networks. PVLDB **10**(10), 998–1009 (2017)
29. Zhou, R., Liu, C., Yu, J.X., Liang, W., Chen, B., Li, J.: Finding maximal k-edge-connected subgraphs from a large graph. In: EDBT, pp. 480–491. ACM (2012)
30. Zhou, Y., Cheng, H., Yu, J.X.: Graph clustering based on structural/attribute similarities. PVLDB **2**(1), 718–729 (2009)

Parallel Mining of Frequent Subtree Patterns

Wenwen Qu[2], Da Yan[1(✉)] (iD), Guimu Guo[1], Xiaoling Wang[2], Lei Zou[3], and Yang Zhou[4]

[1] The University of Alabama at Birmingham, Birmingham, USA
{yanda,guimuguo}@uab.edu
[2] East China Normal University, Shanghai, China
wenwenqu@sei.ecnu.edu.cn, xlwang@cs.ecnu.edu.cn
[3] Peking University, Beijing, China
zoulei@pku.edu.cn
[4] Auburn University, Auburn, USA
yangzhou@auburn.edu

Abstract. Mining frequent subtree patterns in a tree database (or, forest) is useful in domains such as bioinformatics and mining semi-structured data. We consider the problem of mining embedded subtrees in a database of rooted, labeled, and ordered trees. We compare two existing serial mining algorithms, PrefixTreeSpan and TreeMiner, and adapt them for parallel execution using PrefixFPM, our general-purpose framework for frequent pattern mining that is designed to effectively utilize the CPU cores in a multicore machine. Our experiments show that TreeMiner is faster than its successor PrefixTreeSpan when a limited number of CPU cores are used, as the total mining workloads is smaller; however, PrefixTreeSpan has a much higher speedup ratio and can beat TreeMiner when given enough CPU cores.

Keywords: Tree · Parallel · Frequent pattern mining · Prefix projection

1 Introduction

Frequent patterns are substructures that appear in a dataset with frequency no less than a user-specified threshold. A substructure can refer to different structural forms, such as itemsets, sequences, trees and graphs. Frequent pattern mining (FPM) has been at the core of data mining research for over two decades [3], and numerous serial mining algorithms have been proposed for various types of substructure patterns. The mined frequent substructures have also been widely used in many real applications. For example, FG-index [5] constructs a nested inverted index based on the set of frequent subgraphs, to speed up the finding of those graphs in a graph database that contains a query subgraph; while [8] uses frequent subgraphs as features for classifying labeled graphs modeling real-world data such as chemical compounds.

ⓒ Springer Nature Switzerland AG 2020
L. Qin et al. (Eds.): SFDI 2020/LSGDA 2020, CCIS 1281, pp. 18–32, 2020.
https://doi.org/10.1007/978-3-030-61133-0_2

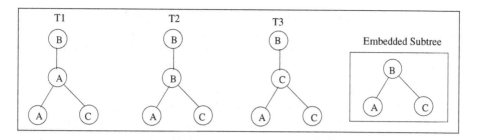

Fig. 1. Embedded subtree pattern illustration

This paper focuses on tree patterns, or more specifically, to mine frequent "embedded" subtrees in a database of "rooted", "labeled", and "ordered" trees. Here, "rooted" means that the tree root matters, "ordered" means that the order of children nodes matters, and "embedded" means that the tree edge in a subtree pattern only needs to capture the ancestor-descendant relationship (i.e., can skip nodes in the middle) rather than a direct parent-child edge (the latter is called "induced"). We illustrate the concept of an embedded subtree pattern using Fig. 1, which shows a database of three trees. The subtree shown in the box is considered frequent as it appears in all 3 the trees T_1, T_2 and T_3, obtained by skipping the "middle" node in each tree, even though the subtree is the induced subgraph of only T_2 alone.

This problem is useful in many applications. In bioinformatics, researchers have collected vast amounts of RNA structures, which are essentially trees. To get information about a newly sequenced RNA, they compare it with known RNA structures, looking for common topological patterns, which provide important clues to the function of the RNA [10]. In web usage mining [7], given a database of web access logs at a popular site, one can mine the tree-structured browsing history of users to find frequently accessed subtrees (where nodes are webpages) at the site for prioritized investment. In web applications, tree-structured XML/JSON documents are popular for data transmission and storage, and discovering the commonly occurring subtrees that appear in these documents can help locate frequent user queries and data responses to be cached for faster access.

Tree mining has been well studied in the serial algorithm domain by a number of algorithms such as TreeMiner [13], FREQT [4], CMTreeMiner [6], Chopper [11], Xspanner [11] and PrefixTreeSpan [14]. We select PrefixTreeSpan for parallelization since it was reported to beat all the other algorithms. However, [14] treats TreeMiner to be an Apriori-like algorithms that check patterns of size-i only when all patterns of size-$(i-1)$ are found, while TreeMiner is actually a PrefixSpan[9]-like similar to PrefixTreeSpan, therefore we also select TreeMiner for parallelization to compare with PrefixTreeSpan.

We parallelize PrefixTreeSpan and TreeMiner using the PrefixFPM framework [12], which is found to be able to fully utilize the available CPU cores in a multi-core machine as long as the implemented algorithm provides sufficient opportunity for concurrent execution. PrefixFPM is designed for writing a general frequent pattern mining algorithm following the prefix-projection paradigm pioneered by PrefixSpan [9], and PrefixTreeSpan and TreeMiner naturally fit in this paradigm. The main contributions and insights of this paper are as follows:

- We developed the parallel PrefixFPM algorithms for both PrefixTreeSpan and TreeMiner, and empirically compared them under different conditions.
- We find that TreeMiner is more effective in reducing the total mining workloads and thus faster when using up to only a moderate number of CPU cores. This is in contrary to the finding in PrefixTreeSpan's paper [14], which could be due to [14]'s treating TreeMiner as an Apriori-like algorithm.
- We find that, in contrast, PrefixTreeSpan is more amenable to parallel execution with a higher speedup ratio, and can beat TreeMiner when given enough CPU cores. This is a new finding since prior works have not considered parallel mining, and can shed light on the architecture-aware algorithm choice.

The rest of this paper is organized as follows. Section 2 reviews the related work including the idea of prefix projection illustrated with the pioneering PrefixSpan algorithm, and the PrefixFPM programming paradigm for parallelizing a PrefixSpan-like algorithm. Section 3 introduces the PrefixTreeSpan algorithm and its parallel implementation in PrefixFPM, and Sect. 4 describes the TreeMiner algorithm and its parallel implementation in PrefixFPM. Finally, Sect. 5 reports the results of our experimental comparison and Sect. 6 concludes this paper.

2 Preliminaries

A Tour of PrefixSpan. To understand the idea of prefix projection, let us first briefly review the pioneering PrefixSpan [9] algorithm for mining frequent sequential patterns from a sequence database.

We denote $\alpha\beta$ to be the sequence resulted from concatenating sequence α with sequence β. We also use $\alpha \sqsubseteq s$ to denote that sequence α occurs as a subsequence of sequence s in the database. Given a sequential pattern α and a sequence s, the α-projected sequence $s|_\alpha$ is defined to be the suffix γ of s such that $s = \beta\gamma$ with β being the minimal prefix of s satisfying $\alpha \sqsubseteq s$. To highlight the fact that γ is a suffix, we write it as $\_\gamma$. To illustrate, when $\alpha = BC$ and $s = ABCBC$, we have $\beta = ABC$ and $s|_\alpha = \_\gamma = \_BC$.

Given a sequential pattern α and a sequence database D, the α-projected database $D|_\alpha$ is defined to be the set $\{s|_\alpha \mid s \in D \wedge \alpha \sqsubseteq s\}$. Note that if $\alpha \not\sqsubseteq s$, then the minimal prefix β of s satisfying $\beta \sqsubseteq s$ does not exist, and therefore s is not considered in $D|_\alpha$.

Consider the sequence database D shown in Fig. 2(a). The projected databases $D|_A$, $D|_{AB}$ and $D|_{ABC}$ are shown in Fig. 2(b), (c) and (d), respectively. Let us define the support of a pattern α as the number of sequences in D that contain α as a subsequence, then the support of α is simply the size of $D|_\alpha$. PrefixSpan finds the frequent patterns (with support at least τ_{sup}) by

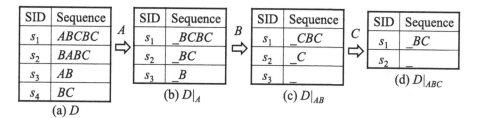

Fig. 2. Illustration of PrefixSpan

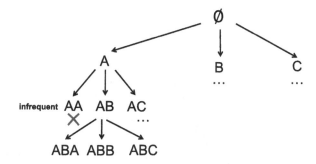

Fig. 3. Depth-first search space tree

recursively checking the frequentness of patterns with growing lengths. In each recursion, if the current pattern α is checked to be frequent, it will recurse on all the possible patterns α' constructed by appending α with one more element. PrefixSpan checks whether a pattern α is frequent using the projected database $D|_\alpha$, which is constructed from the projected database of the previous iteration. Figure 2 presents one recursion path when $\tau_{sup} = 2$, where, for example, $s_1|_{ABC}$ in $D|_{ABC}$ is obtained by removing the element C from $s_1|_{AB}$ in $D|_{AB}$.

We remark that the PrefixSpan algorithm presented here is a simplified version where each element in a sequence can be only one item. In general, each element can be an itemset (e.g., the purchase of multiple goods in one supermarket transaction), and we refer readers to [9] for more details.

Prefix Projection. We can summarize the PrefixSpan algorithm's pattern (which is also the prefix) search space by a tree as illustrated in Fig. 3. The idea actually generalizes to other patterns including the embedded subtrees that we consider. The key insight is that we can establish a one-to-one correspondence between each subtree pattern and its sequence encoding, so that we can examine the pattern encodings by a PrefixSpan-style algorithm.

For example, consider the 3 subtrees shown in Fig. 4. We can encode a tree T by adding vertex labels to the encoding in a depth-first preorder traversal of T, and by adding a unique label "$" whenever we backtrack from a child to its parent. For example, the encoding of T_1 in Fig. 4 is BAB$D$$BC, the encoding of T_2 is BAB$D$$CB, while the encoding of T_3 is BCBAB$D$$.

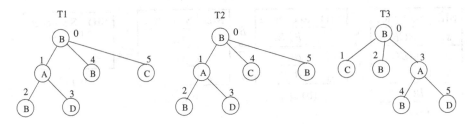

Fig. 4. Illustrative tree patterns

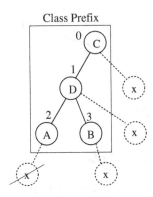

Fig. 5. Pattern extension along rightmost path

If we consider "$" as the smallest label, and combined with the other node labels in the alphabet where label ordering is defined, then we can check through the subtree patterns similarly as in Fig. 3, imagining that the sequence encoding at each node is obtained by the depth-first preorder traversal of its corresponding subtree pattern. Recall that there is a one-to-one correspondence between a subtree pattern and its sequence encoding. This is exactly the mining workflow adopted by PrefixTreeSpan and TreeMiner.

In this case, the root node ∅ in the search tree of Fig. 3 basically finds node labels that are frequent in the tree database (e.g., A, B and C). Then, at the next layer node A basically finds frequent edges where the source node is A (e.g., AA, AB and AC). In the next layer, node AB (whose pattern only contains one edge AB) is basically extending the pattern with one more edge, which can give child-patterns like ABA or ABA$$ that corresponds to different subtrees for frequentness checking (Fig. 3 is for PrefixSpan so only a sequence ABA is shown). In a nutshell, each pattern as a node α in the search tree is extended by one more edge to generate a child-pattern β.

It is not difficult to see that to avoid redundant pattern examination from different subtrees, we should only extend a pattern using an adjacent edge on its rightmost path. For example, in Fig. 5, we can only extend the subtree pattern in the box using an adjacent edge on its rightmost path CDB, since the extension from vertex A has an encoding CDAx⋯ which does not match the pattern prefix CDA$B and should have been covered in the other search space subtree rooted at node CDA (i.e., the child CDAx rather than CDA$B).

In frequent subtree mining, the difference from PrefixSpan lies in the maintenance of projected database, where each tree data after prefix projection can give rise to multiple instances (for example, pattern B-B can map to node pairs 0–2 and 0–4 in T_1 of Fig. 4) that lead to different future extension trajectories; also, special encodings need to be maintained to facilitate the checking of ancestor-descendant relationship between a matched node in a data tree T and another node in T to extend the current pattern.

PrefixFPM Review. PrefixFPM associates each pattern α (which corresponds to a node in the search tree of Fig. 3) with a task t_α that checks the frequentness of α using its projected database $D|_\alpha$, and which grows the pattern by one more element to generate the children patterns $\{\beta\}$ and their projected databases $\{D|_\beta\}$ (computed incrementally from $D|_\alpha$ rather from the entire D). These children patterns give rise to new tasks $\{t_\beta\}$ which are added to a shared task queue for concurrent processing. PrefixFPM runs a number of mining threads that fetch pattern-tasks from a shared task queue Q_{task} for concurrent processing. Since each task t_α needs to maintain $D|_\alpha$ to compute the projected databases of the child-patterns grown from α, a depth-first task fetching priority in the pattern search tree tends to minimize the memory footprint of patterns in processing. This is because we tend to grow those patterns that have been grown deeper, which are larger (and thus with smaller projected databases) and are closer to finishing their growth (due to the support becoming less than τ_{sup}).

Since fetching tasks from a shared task queue and adding new child-tasks to Q_{task} incur locking overheads, this is only worthwhile if each task contains sufficient computing workloads such that the locking overhead is negligible. We therefore only add child-pattern tasks to Q_{task} if the number of projected data instances in $D|_\alpha$ is above a size threshold τ_{split}, so that the workloads can be divided by other computing threads; otherwise, t_α is not expensive and the current computing thread simply processes its entire search space subtree in depth-first order directly.

PrefixFPM Programming Interface. PrefixFPM is written as a set of C++ header files defining some base classes and their virtual functions for users to inherit in their subclasses and to specify the application logic. We call these virtual functions as user-defined functions (UDFs). The base classes also contain C++ template arguments for users to specify with the proper data types (data structures) that fit the target FPM application. We refer readers to [12] for the complete API. Here, we briefly review the key UDFs that users need to specify in order to implement a parallel mining algorithm.

The most important base class is *Task*. A *Task* object t_α maintains 2 fields: a pattern α (along with its relevant data such as $D|_\alpha$), and a children table *children* that keeps $\{D|_\beta\}$: specifically, *children*$[e] = D|_\beta$ if β is grown from α with element e. *Task* has an internal function *run(fout)* which executes the processing logic of the task t_α. The behavior of *run(.)* is specified by *Task* UDFs defined by users which are called in *run(.)*, and Fig. 6 shows the details.

```
1    void run(ostream& fout){
2            if(!pre_check(fout)) return;
3            //generate new patterns
4            setChildren(children);
5            //run new child tasks
6            while(Task* t= get_next_child()){
7                    if(needSplit()){
8                            q_mtx.lock();
9                            queue().push(t);
10                           q_mtx.unlock();
11                   }
12                   else{
13                           t->run(fout);
14                           delete t;
15                   }
16           }
17   }
```

Fig. 6. The *run(fout)* function of base class *Task*

Specifically, in Line 2, t_α first runs UDF *pre_check(fout)* to see if α is frequent and if so, to output α to an output file stream *fout*. If α is frequent and thus not pruned by *pre_check(.)*, Line 4 then runs UDF *setChildren(children)* to scan $D|_\alpha$ and compute $\{D|_\beta\}$ into the table field *children*. In this step, every infrequent child pattern β should be removed from the table *children* as a postprocessing step after $\{D|_\beta\}$ are constructed.

Line 6 then wraps each child pattern β in table *children* as a task t_β, and calls the UDF *needSplit()* to predict if t_β is time-consuming (e.g., $D|_\beta$ is big). If so, we add t_β to the task queue Q_{task} (Lines 8–10) to be fetched by available task computing threads (Q_{task} is a global last-in-first-out task stack protected by a mutex to prioritize depth-first task processing order), which divides the computing workloads by multithreading. Otherwise, we recursively call t_β's *run(fout)* to process the entire checking and extension of β by the current thread, which avoids contention on Q_{task}. Since *needSplit()* just estimates if t_β is time-consuming and could have false negatives that become stragglers, we also count the time elapsed since t_α begins, and if it is larger than a timeout threshold, we also add t_β to Q_{task} for concurrent processing as in Lines 8–10.

The other important base class is *Worker*, which is the main thread that loads the database and creates the computing threads to process tasks. A *Worker* object is responsible for generating the initial tasks into Q_{task} from the database, the logic of which is specified by UDF *setRoot()*.

Implementing *Worker::setRoot(.)* is similar to implementing *Task::set Children(.)* (Line 4 of Fig. 6): instead of constructing $\{D|_\beta\}$ from $D|_\alpha$, we construct $\{D|_e\}$ from D: each seed task $t_e = \langle e, D|_e \rangle$ is added to Q_{task} to initiate the parallel task computation.

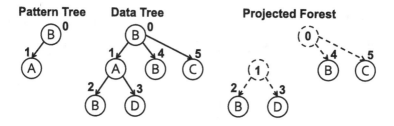

Fig. 7. Forests after pattern projection

At the beginning of *Worker::setRoot(.)*, we also need to get the element frequency statistics and eliminate infrequent elements (i.e., they are not considered when growing patterns), which is a common and effective pruning. In frequent subtree mining, one pass over the database is needed to filter out infrequent edges (determined by labels of its end-nodes), followed by another pass to (1) delete data edges that match those infrequent pattern-edges (in terms of end-node labels) and to (2) count the frequency of pattern-edges.

To summarize, to implement a parallel frequent pattern mining algorithm in PrefixFPM, we need to specify 2 key UDFs: *Worker::setRoot(.)* and *Task::setChild- ren(children)*.

3   PrefixTreeSpan in PrefixFPM

Recall from Sect. 2 that the data tree in Fig. 7 can be encoded as BAB$D$$BC following preorder traversal that finally returns back to root B. To facilitate prefix projection, PrefixTreeSpan encodes this tree instead as:

$$\text{B A B -1 D -1 -1 B -1 C -1 -1}$$

Here, backtracking is encoded with -1 which is basically the same as $. However, PrefixTreeSpan lets each node to be paired with a corresponding partner "-1" in the encoding so that the first B is now also paired with a -1 at last. The part between a node and its partner is called the node's scope.

The definition of scope allows a quick checking of ancestor-descendant relationships. For example, in Fig. 7, after prefix projection by the pattern tree, the data tree now gets split into a so-called "postfix-forest" with two trees, the node of which can be used to further extend the current pattern.

To see how this is achieved, PrefixTreeSpan requires the scanning of the data tree (i.e., its preorder encoding) to be from right after the position that matches the last node in the pattern subtree. For the example in Fig. 7, we should start from after "A" at the second position of the above encoding. Based on A's scope we can obtain the first tree in the projected forest as shown in Fig. 7, encoded as B-1D-1 which is hooked to Node 1 in the pattern tree (1 is encoded

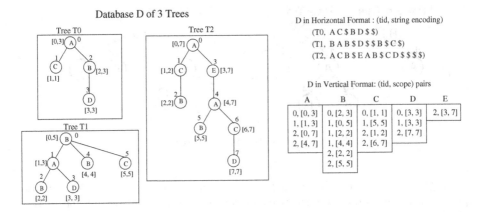

Fig. 8. Scope lists

by preorder traversal of the pattern). Continuing the scanning, we will obtain the second projected postfix-tree encoded as B-1C-1 which is hooked to Node 0 in the pattern tree.

We remark that by scanning the data tree encoding from the last matched position, we effectively extend a pattern along its rightmost path. For example, referring to Fig. 5 again, we will not consider extending Node 2 since the last pattern node matched to a data tree is Node 3.

The implementation of this algorithm in PrefixFPM is straightforward, where in *Task::setChildren*(.) each task t_α scans its projected postfix-forest database once to determine the frequent edges (called growth elements) to extend pattern α, and then scans the projected database for another pass to create the projected postfix-forest database in *children*[e] for each frequent edge e. Each child pattern β that extends α with e is then wrapped as a child task t_β for further processing.

Worker::setRoot(.) is slightly different, where after frequent nodes (in terms of labels) are identified to create singleton-node patterns, it is only matched to the so-called "independent-occurrences" of the node in each data tree, i.e., the node does not have an ancestor that is also matched. This is to avoid redundancy [14].

4   TreeMiner in PrefixFPM

TreeMiner Review. TreeMiner [13] captures the ancestor-descendant relationship among nodes by assigning each node v a so-called *scope* $[\ell, r]$, where ℓ is the rank of v in a preorder traversal of the tree, and r is the rank of the rightmost node in the subtree rooted at v (i.e., the largest node rank in the subtree). For example, for tree T_0 in Fig. 8, Node 0 has scope $[0, 3]$, Node 1 has $[1, 1]$, and Node 3 has $[3, 3]$. Then, the ancestor-descendant relationship can be judged by the scope containment relationship. For example, Nodes 1 and 3 are both the descendant of Node 0 since $[1, 1], [3, 3] \subset [0, 3]$, but Node 3 is not a child of Node 1 since $[1, 1] \cap [3, 3] = \emptyset$.

Since a pattern α can have multiple matches in a data tree, TreeMiner represents each projected transaction in $D|_\alpha$ as a pair $(tid, scope)$ where tid is the transaction ID of the data tree T_i whose subtree matches α, and $scope$ is the scope of last matched node in T_i that matches the last extended node in pattern α. For example, Fig. 8 shows the vertical representation of initial patterns $\alpha = $ A, B, C, D and E. The rectangle for pattern B, which is called its *scope list*, contains 3 matched instances in tree T_1, corresponding to Nodes 0, 2 and 4, respectively.

Recall from Sect. 2 that a tree T is encoded by listing vertex labels in a depth-first preorder traversal of T, and by adding a unique symbol "$" whenever we backtrack from a child to its parent. This sequence encoding of T is also called its horizontal format as shown in Fig. 8.

TreeMiner adopts prefix projection to enumerate patterns by their horizontal encodings. One way is to always extend a pattern by a frequent edge from its rightmost path to avoid redundant pattern checking, which is similar to Prefix-TreeSpan as we have reviewed in Sect. 3.

TreeMiner adopts a different approach called "equivalence class-based extension": instead of extending a pattern α with frequent edges, TreeMiner generates a size-$(k+1)$ pattern from two size-k patterns that share the same size-$(k-1)$ prefix encoding. Obviously, the latter is more selective and thus faster.

This is where the scope-list comes into play. Refer back to Fig. 5 in Sect. 2 again, we have a size-3 prefix encoding $P = CDA\$B$ (as there are 3 solid edges), from which we can grow size-4 patterns (i.e., using each of the 3 valid dashed edges long the rightmost path). Let each dashed edge be denoted by (i, x) where i is the hooked node ID in P, and x is a node label. Let us denote the new pattern extended with (i, x) by $\beta = P_x^i$, then all $\{P_x^i\}$ constitute an equivalence class where patterns share the prefix P, denoted by $[P]$.

To build the equivalence class $[P_x^i]$ where patterns share the prefix P_x^i, we can extend P_x^i using another edge $(j, y) \in [P]$. Sleuth keeps a projected database $D|_\beta$ for each $\beta = P_x^i$, which is represented as a scope list described before. To incrementally compute $D|_\gamma$ for the pattern γ obtained by extending P_x^i with (j, y), we can join the scope list of P_x^i with the scope list of every $P_y^j \in [P]$.

While we refer readers to [13] for the details of the join, the idea is simple: two scopes $(tid_1, scope_1)$ and $(tid_2, scope_2)$ can be joined only if $tid_1 = tid_2$ (i.e., the match is from the same transaction T), the matched prefix occurrences (i.e., their node IDs in T) are the same, and y's matched node in T is a descendant or cousin of x's matched node (need to check $scope_1$ and $scope_2$). Since we always order scope list items by tid, the joining of two scope lists requires only one pass over the two lists similar to the merge operation in merge sort.

Implementation on PrefixFPM. To adapt the serial TreeMiner algorithm to PrefixFPM, a task t_P now maintains a prefix encoding P along with a list of extending edges of the form $(i, x) \in [P]$, each associated with the scope list (i.e., projected database) for P_x^i. Note that task object here maintains a list of projected databases, which is different from the PrefixFPM algorithm for PrefixTreeSpan where each task object only maintains one project database.

```
1:  for each (i, x) ∈ [P]
2:      L₁ ← scope list of Pₓⁱ
3:      for each (j, y) ∈ [P]
4:          if i < j: continue
5:          L₂ ← scope list of Pᵧʲ
6:          Qᵧʲ ← join(L₁, L₂)   // note that Q = Pₓⁱ
7:          if Qᵧʲ is frequent:   children[Q].add(Qᵧʲ)
```

Fig. 9. Algorithm of *TreeMinerTask::setChildren*(.) in PrefixFPM

UDF *Task::setChildren*(.) computes every task object related to $Q = P_x^i$, including the extending edges $(j, y) \in [Q]$ and their scope lists, as detailed in the algorithm shown in Fig. 9. Note that each children table entry *children[Q]* to construct maintains the content a task object t_Q, including a list of Q_y^j each associated with its scope list.

In the UDF *Task::setChildren*(.) of task t_P, for each extending edge (i, x) in $[P]$ (Line 1), we build $[Q]$ $(Q = P_x^i)$ to be added to *children[Q]* (Line 7). Specifically, Lines 3–6 join the scope list of Q with the scope list of every $P_y^j \in [P]$ to generate the scope list of the new pattern Q_y^j, which are then added to *children[Q]* one by one (if Q_y^j is frequent which is judged using its scope list). This allows UDF *Task::get_next_child*(.) (recall Line 6 of Fig. 6) to then wrap each *children[Q]* into a task t_Q that processes $[Q]$ (containing $\{Q_y^j\}$) for further processing.

One tricky issue is to estimate the cost of task t_Q as needed by Line 7 of Fig. 6 to determine whether to add t_Q to Q_{task} for concurrent processing or to directly process it recursively. Unlike in PrefixTreeSpan where we simply check the size of a child-task's projected database, here, we need to sum the lengths of the scope lists of $[Q] = \{Q_y^j\}$ to reflect the total task workloads, and if the sum is above threshold τ_{split}, the child task t_Q is added to Q_{task} rather than processed by the current computing thread.

Worker::setRoot(.) first scans D to count label frequencies and remove infrequent node labels. Let the set of frequent labels be $\mathcal{F}_1$, the UDF then counts the frequencies of edges $e = (X, Y)$ with a counter array of size $|\mathcal{F}_1| \times |\mathcal{F}_1|$ by scanning D, and only considers frequent (labeled) edges (denoted by $\mathcal{F}_2$) for subsequent edge extension. The UDF then builds the pattern object $[X]$ for each $X \in \mathcal{F}_1$, constructs its scope list with all edge-patterns $(X, Y) \in \mathcal{F}_2$, and then wraps them as the set of initial tasks to be added to Q_{task}.

5   Experiments

Summary of Algorithm Differences. One difference is that TreeMiner joins the **rightmost node** (using scope list) of two size-k frequent patterns to generate a size-$(k+1)$ pattern, which tends to have a smaller candidate set size than if we extend size-k frequent patterns with one frequent edge, as is done by the encoding

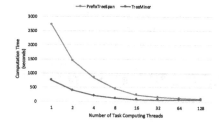

	PrefixTreeSpan		TreeMiner	
Thread#	Time (S)	Speedup	Time	Speedup
1	2706	1	746.1	1
2	1441	1.88	393.6	1.90
4	840.7	3.22	214.1	3.49
8	447.3	6.05	118.7	6.29
16	241.6	11.20	72.25	10.33
32	155.5	17.41	56.07	13.30
64	117.0	23.14	59.62	12.51
128	99.27	27.26	61.01	12.23

Fig. 10. Results on the synthetic data

scanning method of PrefixTreeSpan which basically extends the residual forest along the **rightmost matched path**. As a result, the total mining workload of TreeMiner tends to be smaller than that of PrefixTreeSpan.

However, each task t_P in TreeMiner is essentially an equivalent class $[P]$, or a cluster of prefix projections $\{P_x^i\}$ along with their projected databases. In contrast, each task t_P in PrefixTreeSpan is simply pattern P along with its projected postfix-forest database, so that task granularity is finer than that of a task in TreeMiner, making it more amenable to concurrent processing.

Experimental Setup. We evaluate the performance of PrefixTreeSpan and TreeMiner on top of PrefixFPM, and all our codes are open-sourced at

https://github.com/wenwen-Q/PrefixFPM

To thoroughly test the scale-up capability of both algorithms, we ran our programs on the BlueBlaze server donated by IBM to UAB CS Department, which has 160 CPU cores and 1 TB RAM. The CPU model is IBM POWER8 with 3491 MHz. The large number of CPU cores allows us to test the scalability with 1, 2, 4, 8, 16, 32, 64 and 128 cores, and the 1 TB RAM is more than enough and we actually only use a tiny fraction.

Results on a Synthetic Dataset. We follow [13] and generate a tree transaction database using a synthetic data generator [1] that creates a database of artificial website browsing behavior: a website browsing "master tree" is first created based on parameters supplied by the users; then, one can generate random subtrees of the master tree as the tree transactions for mining. The details of data generation can be found in [13].

We use the default parameters for master tree: depth = 5, fan-out factor = 5, number of labels = 10, and we set the number of nodes in the master tree as 50 to generate 10,000,000 subtree transactions. We call this dataset as *TreeGen*. We set $\tau_{sup} = 50$ and the timeout threshold as 0.01 s.

Figure 10 shows the scalability results where good speedup ratio is achieved all the way up to 16 threads, but TreeMiner does not show significant further improvement and even becomes slower beyond 32 threads. This is because TreeMiner operates on the big unit of equivalent class $[P]$ which can only keep less than 32 cores busy, and using more threads only incurs more lock contention and backfires. PrefixTreeSpan has a better scaleup ratio but due to its larger total workloads, it cannot beat TreeMiner in all settings in this experiment.

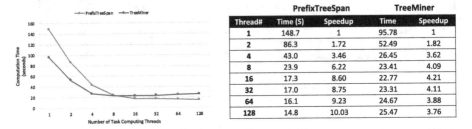

Thread#	PrefixTreeSpan		TreeMiner	
	Time (S)	Speedup	Time	Speedup
1	148.7	1	95.78	1
2	86.3	1.72	52.49	1.82
4	43.0	3.46	26.45	3.62
8	23.9	6.22	23.41	4.09
16	17.3	8.60	22.77	4.21
32	17.0	8.75	23.31	4.11
64	16.1	9.23	24.67	3.88
128	14.8	10.03	25.47	3.76

Fig. 11. Results on Treebank ($\tau_{sup} = 30,000$)

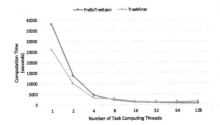

Thread#	PrefixTreeSpan		TreeMiner	
	Time (S)	Speedup	Time	Speedup
1	37778.8	1	25918.6	1
2	13502.5	1.99	9909.9	2.62
4	4472.0	6.02	3194.6	8.11
8	2032.5	13.24	2636.3	9.83
16	1089.7	24.70	1302.7	19.90
32	837.7	32.13	1157.5	22.39
64	607.5	44.31	1269.1	20.44
128	510.6	52.72	1285.0	20.12

Fig. 12. Results on Treebank ($\tau_{sup} = 10,000$)

Results on a Real Dataset. Treebank [2] is a parsed text corpus that annotates syntactic or semantic sentence structure. The XML file contains 52,851 trees. We first set $\tau_{sup} = 30,000$ and the timeout threshold as 0.1s. Since τ_{sup} is large, most patterns will be pruned early leading to limited workload for parallel mining. Figure 11 shows the scalability results where we can see that TreeMiner's performance saturates with merely 4 CPU cores. PrefixTreeSpan scales better but the speedup is still quite limited. Interestingly, despite more workload, PrefixTreeSpan breaks a tie with TreeMiner when there are 8 CPU cores, and PrefixTreeSpan beats TreeMiner when the number of CPU cores increases further, already significantly faster than TreeMiner even when 16 CPU cores are used. This is thanks to the finer task granularity of PrefixTreeSpan which allows more CPU cores to be utilized.

We then set $\tau_{sup} = 10,000$ so that most patterns will be valid allowing for more parallelism. Figure 12 shows the scalability results where we can see that TreeMiner's performance now saturates at up to 32 CPU cores thanks to the more parallelism provided by a lower τ_{sup}. PrefixTreeSpan scales even better and achieves an impressive 52.72× speedup with 128 cores, and ultimately beats TreeMiner by more than 2.5×.

To summarize, while the total mining workload of TreeMiner can be much smaller than that of PrefixTreeSpan due to the scope list join technique, it does limit TreeMiner's capability for massively parallel execution due to the larger task granularity. When there are enough CPU cores, PrefixTreeSpan can be a better choice that is worth trying out, and can ultimately beat TreeMiner by several times. We remark that these conclusions are made assuming that the underlying parallel execution engine is able to utilize as much parallelism as is available, which is ideally provided by PrefixPFM as explained in [12] which is recently proposed to overcome the IO-bound execution bottleneck of a few prior systems and solutions.

6   Conclusion

This paper implemented the parallel versions of two frequent embedded subtree mining algorithms, PrefixTreeSpan and TreeMiner, on top of the PrefixFPM system that follows a prefix-projection programming paradigm and that is able to fully carry out the parallelism potential of the algorithms on top.

A few new insights are obtained: (i) PrefixTreeSpan does not beat TreeMiner in the serial setting as what was claimed in PrefixTreeSpan's paper [14], likely because [14] implemented TreeMiner as an Apriori-like algorithm rather than a PrefixSpan-like one. However, TreeMiner's workload optimization requires a larger task granularity which limits its potential for parallel execution, and could be beaten by PrefixTreeSpan when enough CPU cores are available.

Acknowledgments. This work was partially supported by NSF OAC-1755464 and DGE-1723250.

References

1. Tree Generator. https://github.com/zakimjz/TreeGen
2. Treebank. http://aiweb.cs.washington.edu/research/projects/xmltk/xmldata/www/repository.html#treebank
3. Aggarwal, C.C., Han, J. (eds.): Frequent Pattern Mining. Springer, Heidelberg (2014). https://doi.org/10.1007/978-3-319-07821-2
4. Asai, T., Abe, K., Kawasoe, S., Arimura, H., Sakamoto, H., Arikawa, S.: Efficient substructure discovery from large semi-structured data. In: Grossman, R.L., Han, J., Kumar, V., Mannila, H., Motwani, R. (eds.) SDM, pp. 158–174. SIAM (2002)
5. Cheng, J., Ke, Y., Ng, W., Lu, A.: FG-index: towards verification-free query processing on graph databases. In: SIGMOD, pp. 857–872 (2007)
6. Chi, Y., Xia, Y., Yang, Y., Muntz, R.R.: Mining closed and maximal frequent subtrees from databases of labeled rooted trees. IEEE Trans. Knowl. Data Eng. **17**(2), 190–202 (2005)
7. Cooley, R., Mobasher, B., Srivastava, J.: Web mining: information and pattern discovery on the world wide web. In: ICTAI, pp. 558–567. IEEE Computer Society (1997)
8. Kudo, T., Maeda, E., Matsumoto, Y.: An application of boosting to graph classification. In: NIPS, pp. 729–736 (2004)

9. Pei, J., et al.: PrefixSpan: mining sequential patterns by prefix-projected growth. In: Proceedings of the 17th International Conference on Data Engineering, Heidelberg, Germany, 2–6 April 2001, pp. 215–224 (2001)
10. Shapiro, B.A., Zhang, K.: Comparing multiple RNA secondary structures using tree comparisons. Comput. Appl. Biosci. **6**(4), 309–318 (1990)
11. Wang, C., Hong, M., Pei, J., Zhou, H., Wang, W., Shi, B.: Efficient pattern-growth methods for frequent tree pattern mining. In: Dai, H., Srikant, R., Zhang, C. (eds.) PAKDD 2004. LNCS (LNAI), vol. 3056, pp. 441–451. Springer, Heidelberg (2004). https://doi.org/10.1007/978-3-540-24775-3_54
12. Yan, D., Qu, W., Guo, G., Wang, X.: PrefixFPM: a parallel framework for general-purpose frequent pattern mining. In: ICDE (2020)
13. Zaki, M.J.: Efficiently mining frequent trees in a forest. In: SIGKDD, pp. 71–80 (2002)
14. Zou, L., Lu, Y., Zhang, H., Hu, R.: PrefixTreeESpan: a pattern growth algorithm for mining embedded subtrees. In: Aberer, K., Peng, Z., Rundensteiner, E.A., Zhang, Y., Li, X. (eds.) WISE 2006. LNCS, vol. 4255, pp. 499–505. Springer, Heidelberg (2006). https://doi.org/10.1007/11912873_51

An Axiomatic Role Similarity Measure Based on Graph Topology

Weiren Yu[1](✉), Sima Iranmanesh[1], Aparajita Haldar[1], Maoyin Zhang[2], and Hakan Ferhatosmanoglu[1]

[1] University of Warwick, Coventry CV4 7AL, UK
{weiren.yu,sima.iranmanesh,aparajita.haldar,
h.ferhatosmanoglu}@warwick.ac.uk
[2] Nanjing University of Science and Technology, Jiangsu, China
maoyinzhang@hotmail.com

Abstract. RoleSim and SimRank are popular graph-theoretic similarity measures with many applications in, *e.g.,* web search, collaborative filtering, and sociometry. While RoleSim addresses the automorphic (role) equivalence of pairwise similarity which SimRank lacks, it ignores the neighboring similarity information out of the automorphically equivalent set. Consequently, two pairs of nodes, which are not automorphically equivalent by nature, cannot be well distinguished by RoleSim if the averages of their neighboring similarities over the automorphically equivalent set are the same.

To alleviate this problem: 1) We propose a novel similarity model, namely RoleSim*, which accurately evaluates pairwise role similarities in a more comprehensive manner. RoleSim* not only guarantees the automorphic equivalence that SimRank lacks, but also takes into account the neighboring similarity information outside the automorphically equivalent sets that are overlooked by RoleSim. 2) We prove the existence and uniqueness of the RoleSim* solution, and show its three axiomatic properties (*i.e.,* symmetry, boundedness, and non-increasing monotonicity). 3) We provide a concise bound for iteratively computing RoleSim* formula, and estimate the number of iterations required to attain a desired accuracy. 4) We induce a distance metric based on RoleSim* similarity, and show that the RoleSim* metric fulfills the triangular inequality, which implies the sum-transitivity of its similarity scores. Our experimental results on real and synthetic datasets demonstrate that RoleSim* achieves higher accuracy than its competitors while retaining comparable computational complexity bounds of RoleSim.

1 Introduction

RoleSim is a role-based similarity measure that quantifies the closeness between two objects based on graph topology, with a proliferation of real-life applications [9,10,23] in, *e.g.,* link prediction (social network), co-citation analysis (bibliometrics), motif discovery (bioinformatics), and collaborative filtering (information retrieval). It recursively follows a SimRank-like reasoning that "two nodes

© Springer Nature Switzerland AG 2020
L. Qin et al. (Eds.): SFDI 2020/LSGDA 2020, CCIS 1281, pp. 33–48, 2020.
https://doi.org/10.1007/978-3-030-61133-0_3

are assessed as role similar if they interact with automorphically equivalent sets of in-neighbors". Intuitively, automorphically equivalent nodes in a graph are objects having similar roles that can be exchanged with minimum effect on the graph structure. Similar to the well-known measure SimRank [7], the recursive nature of RoleSim allows to capture the multi-hop neighboring structures that are automorphically equivalent in a network. Unlike SimRank that measures the similarity of two nodes from the paths connecting them, RoleSim quantifies their similarities through the paths connecting their different roles. As a result, two nodes that are disconnected each other will not be considered as dissimilar by RoleSim if they have similar roles. For evaluating similarity score $s(a, b)$ between nodes a and b, as opposed to SimRank whose similarity $s(a, b)$ takes the average similarity of all the neighboring pairs of (a, b), RoleSim computes $s(a, b)$ by averaging only the similarities over the maximum bipartite matching of all the neighboring pairs of (a, b). This subtle difference enables RoleSim to guarantee the automorphic equivalence, which SimRank lacks, in final scoring results. Therefore, RoleSim has been demonstrated as an effective similarity measure in many real applications. We summarize two of these applications below.

Application 1 (Similarity Search on the Web). Discovering web pages similar to a query page is an important task in information retrieval. In a Web graph, each node represents a web page, and an edge denotes a hyperlink from one page to another. RoleSim can be applied to measure the similarity of two web pages, based on the intuition that "two web pages are role-similar if they are pointed to by the automorphically equivalent sets of their in-neighboring pages". This similarity measure produces more reliable similarity results than the SimRank model [10].

Application 2 (Social Network De-anonymisation). Social network de-anonymisation is a method to validate the strength of anonymisation algorithms that protect a user's privacy. RoleSim has been applied to de-anonymise node mappings based on the similarity information between a crawled network and an anonymised one. Based on the observation that "correct mappings tend to have higher similarity scores", RoleSim iteratively evaluates pairwise node similarities between two networks, and captures the reasoning that "a pair of nodes between two networks is more likely to be a correct mapping if their neighbors are correct mappings". RoleSim has demonstrated superior performance as compared with other existing de-anonymization algorithms [23].

Despite its popularity in real-world applications, RoleSim has a major limitation: with the aim to achieve automorphic equivalence, its similarity score $s(a, b)$ only considers the limited information of the average similarity scores over the automorphically equivalent set (*i.e.,* the maximum bipartite matching) of a's and b's in-neighboring pairs, but neglects the rest of the pairwise in-neighboring similarity information that is out of the automorphically equivalent set. Consequently, RoleSim does not always produce comprehensive similarity results because two pairs of nodes, which are not automorphically equivalent by nature, should be distinguished from each other even though the average values of their

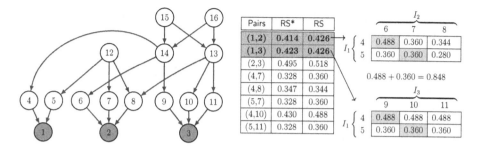

Fig. 1. Limitation of RoleSim (RS) on a tiny web graph, where node-pairs $(1,2)$ and $(1,3)$ have the same RoleSim score (0.426) since RS aggregates only the in-neighboring pairs that are automorphically equivalent (colored in green) whose sums are the same $(0.488 + 0.360 = 0.848)$, while ignoring the remaining pairs. (Color figure online)

in-neighboring similarities over the set of the maximum bipartite matching are the same, as illustrated in Example 1.

Example 1 (Limitation of RoleSim). Consider the web graph G in Fig. 1, where each node denotes a web page, and each edge depicts a hyperlink from one page to another. Using RoleSim, we evaluate pairs of similarities between nodes, as partially illustrated in the 'RS' column of the right table. It is discerned that node-pairs $(1,2)$ and $(1,3)$ have the same RoleSim similarity values, which is not reasonable. Because node 2 and node 3 are not strictly automorphically equivalent by nature, their similarities with respect to the same query node 1, *i.e.,* $s(1,2)$ and $s(1,3)$, should not be the same.

We notice that the main reason why $s(1,2)$ and $s(1,3)$ are assessed to be the same by the RoleSim model is that its similarity $s(a,b)$ considers only the average similarity scores over the maximum bipartite matching, denoted as $M_{a,b}$, of (a,b)'s in-neighboring pairs $I_a \times I_b$, where I_a denotes the in-neighbor set of node a, and $\times$ is the Cartesian product of two sets. Thus, the similarity information in the remaining in-neighboring pairs of (a,b), *i.e.,* $I_a \times I_b - M_{a,b}$, are totally ignored. For example, if unfolding the in-neighboring pairs of $(1,2)$ and $(1,3)$ respectively, we see that, in the gray cells, $M_{1,2} = \{(4,6),(5,7)\}$ (*resp.* $M_{1,3} = \{(4,9),(5,10)\}$) is the maximum bipartite matching of $(1,2)$'s (*resp.* $(1,3)$'s) in-neighboring pairs $I_1 \times I_2$ (*resp.* $I_1 \times I_3$). The sum of the similarity values over $M_{1,2}$ is $0.488 + 0.360 = 0.848$, which is the same as that over $M_{1,3}$. Thus, RoleSim cannot distinguish $s(1,2)$ from $s(1,3)$. □

Example 1 illustrates that, to effectively evaluate $s(a,b)$, relying only on the in-neighboring-pairs similarities in the maximum bipartite matching $M_{a,b}$ (*e.g.,* RoleSim) is not enough. Although RoleSim has the advantage of finding the most influential pairs $M_{a,b}$ among all the in-neighboring pairs $I_a \times I_b$ for achieving automorphic equivalence, it *completely* ignores the similarity information outside $M_{a,b}$. For instance in Example 1, there are opportunities to take good advantage of the similarity values in the regions $I_1 \times I_2 - M_{1,2}$ and $I_1 \times I_3 - M_{1,3}$

which would be helpful to distinguish $s(1, 2)$ from $s(1, 3)$ further when the average similarities over $M_{1,2}$ and $M_{1,3}$ are the same.

Contributions. Motivated by this, our main contributions are as follows:

1) We first propose a novel similarity model, RoleSim*, which accurately evaluates pairwise role similarities in a more comprehensive fashion. Compared with the existing well-known similarity models (*e.g.*, SimRank and RoleSim), RoleSim* not only guarantees the automorphic equivalence that SimRank lacks, but also takes into consideration the pairwise similarities outside the automorphically equivalent sets that are overlooked by RoleSim. (Sect. 3.1)

2) We prove the existence and uniqueness of the RoleSim* solution, and show three key axiomatic properties of RoleSim*, *i.e.*, symmetry, boundedness, and non-increasing monotonicity of its iterative similarity scores. (Sect. 3.2)

3) We derive an iterative formula for computing RoleSim* similarities, and a concise upper bound is obtained, which can estimate the total number of iterations required for attaining a desired accuracy. (Sects. 3.3 and 3.4)

4) We induce a distance metric based on our RoleSim* measure, and rigorously show that the RoleSim* distance metric fulfills the triangular inequality which other measures (*e.g.*, cosine distance) lack. This implies the sum-transitivity of the RoleSim* measure. (Sect. 3.5)

5) We conduct an experimental study to validate the effectiveness of our RoleSim* model. Our empirical results show that RoleSim* achieves higher accuracy than the existing competitors (*e.g.*, RoleSim and SimRank) while entailing comparable computational complexity bounds of RoleSim. (Sect. 4)

2   Related Work

Graph-based similarity models have been popular since SimRank measure was proposed by Jeh and Windom [7]. SimRank is a node-pair similarity measure, which follows the recursive idea that "two nodes are considered as similar if they are pointed to by similar nodes". Since then, there have been surges of studies focusing on optimization problems to accelerate SimRank computation as the naive SimRank computing method entails quadratic time in the number of nodes. According to assumptions on data updates, recent results can be divided into static algorithms [1,4,5,11,15,20,24,27,29,32,37], and dynamic algorithms on evolving graphs [8,12,18,22,25,31,35]. According to types of queries, these results are classified into single-source SimRank [8,11,18,24,35], single-pair Sim-Rank [6,14], all-pairs SimRank [1,19,29,30], and partial-pairs SimRank [20,34].

There are many studies on semantic problems of pairwise similarity measures. Various SimRank-like measures have come into play, including C-Rank [26], Sim-Fusion [33], P-Rank [36], RoleSim [9], MatchSim [17], ASCOS [2], SimRank* [32], CoSimRank [21], SemSim [27]. Among them, RoleSim has stood out as a promising role-based similarity model, due to its elegant intuition that "if two nodes are automorphically equivalent, they should share the same role and their role similarity should be maximal". To speed up the RoleSim computation, an approximate heuristic, named Iceberg RoleSim, was devised to prune small similarity values below a threshold.

Unlike SimRank that takes the average similarity of all the neighboring pairs of (a, b), RoleSim computes $s(a, b)$ by averaging only the similarities over the maximum bipartite matching $M_{a,b}$. However, all the similarity information not included in the matching $M_{a,b}$ is completely ignored by RoleSim. In contrast, our RoleSim* model can effectively capture these information while guaranteeing automorphic equivalence.

There have also been a host of studies on variations of RoleSim [3, 13, 17, 23]. Lin et al. [17] introduced MatchSim whose similarity is defined to be the average similarity of (a, b)'s maximum matched neighbors. It differs from RoleSim in that MatchSim initialises $s_0(a, b) = 1$ if $a = b$, and 0 otherwise, whereas RoleSim initialises all $s_0(*, *) = 1$. As a result, MatchSim scores do not guarantee automorphic equivalence. Li et al. [13] proposed CentSim, a centrality based role similarity measure, which compares the centrality values of two nodes to evaluate their similarity. This measure employs several types of centralities including PageRank, Degree and Closeness for each node, and considers the weighted average of them for evaluating CentSim scores. Recently, Shao et al. [23] introduced RoleSim++, an extension of RoleSim, which considers both incoming and outgoing neighbors in a digraph for social network de-anonymisation. It employs a novel matching algorithm, called NeighborMatch, to find matching for inner and outer neighbors, respectively. Furthermore, a threshold based version, α-RoleSim++, is proposed to eliminate tiny scores for speedup further. Most recently, Chen et al. [3] suggest a scalable model, StructSim, with an efficient BinCount matching algorithm and present a hierarchical scheme, which achieves a more efficient role similarity computation.

3   RoleSim*

3.1   RoleSim* Formulation

The central intuition underpinning RoleSim* follows a recursive concept that "two distinct nodes are assessed to be similar if they

1. *mainly interact with the automorphically equivalent sets of in-neighbors, and*
2. *are in-linked by similar nodes that are out of automorphically equivalent sets.*

The starting point for this recursion is to assign each pair of nodes a similarity score 1, meaning that initially no pairs of nodes are thought of to be more (or less) similar than others.

Notations. Before illustrating the mathematical definition to reify the RoleSim* intuition, we introduce the following notations.

Let $G = (V, E)$ be a directed graph with a set of nodes V and a set of edges E. Let I_a be all in-neighbors of node a, and $|I_a|$ the cardinality of the set I_a. For a pair of nodes (a, b) in G, we denote by $I_a \times I_b = \{(x, y) \mid \forall x \in I_a \text{ and } \forall y \in I_b\}$ all in-neighboring pairs of (a, b), and $s(a, b)$ the RoleSim* similarity score between

Table 1. Description of main symbols

Symbol	Description
G	Directed graph $G = (V, E)$ with a set nodes V and a set of edges E
I_a	All in-neighbors of node a in G
$|I_a|$	Cardinality of the set I_a (*i.e.*, the number of nodes in I_a)
$M_{a,b}$	Maximum weighted matching in bipartite graph $K_{|I_a|,|I_b|} = (I_a \cup I_b, I_a \times I_b)$
$s(a, b)$	RoleSim* similarity score between nodes a and b
β	Damping factor $(0 < \beta < 1)$
λ	Relative weight that balances similarities inside and outside $M_{a,b}$ $(0 < \lambda < 1)$
K	Total number of iterations

nodes a and b. Using $I_a \times I_b$ and $s(a, b)$, we define a weighted complete bipartite graph, denoted by $K_{|I_a|,|I_b|} = (I_a \cup I_b, I_a \times I_b)$, with each edge $(x, y) \in I_a \times I_b$ carrying the weight $s(a, b)$. We denoted by $M_{a,b}$ ($\subseteq I_a \times I_b$) the maximum weighted matching in bipartite graph $K_{|I_a|,|I_b|}$.

Example 2. Recall digraph G in Fig. 1. For nodes 1 and 2, their in-neighbors sets are $I_1 = \{4, 5\}$ and $I_2 = \{6, 7, 8\}$, respectively. The set of all in-neighboring pairs of $(1, 2)$ is $I_1 \times I_2 = \{(4, 6), (4, 7), (4, 8), (5, 6), (5, 7), (5, 8)\}$. The maximum matching of bipartite graph $(I_1 \cup I_2, I_1 \times I_2)$ is $M_{1,2} = \{(4, 6), (5, 7)\}$ (bold). $\square$

Other notations frequently used throughout this paper are listed in Table 1.

RoleSim* Formula. Based on our aforementioned intuition, we formally formulate the RoleSim* model as follows:

$$
s(a, b) = \beta \times \left(\lambda \times \overbrace{\frac{1}{|I_a| + |I_b| - |M_{a,b}|} \sum_{(x,y) \in M_{a,b}} s(x, y)}^{\text{Part 1: average similarity over maximum matching } M_{a,b}} \right.
$$

$$
\left. + (1 - \lambda) \times \underbrace{\frac{1}{|I_a| \times |I_b| - |M_{a,b}|} \sum_{(x,y) \in (I_a \times I_b) - M_{a,b}} s(x, y)}_{\text{Part 2: average similarity over } (I_a \times I_b) - M_{a,b}} \right) + (1 - \beta) \tag{1}
$$

In Eq. (1), for every pair of nodes (a, b), the set of their in-neighboring pairs, $I_a \times I_b$, is split into two subsets: $I_a \times I_b = M_{a,b} \cup (I_a \times I_b - M_{a,b})$. As a result, the definition of RoleSim* consists of two parts: Part 1 is the average similarity over maximum matching $M_{a,b}$, indicating the contribution from (a, b) interacting with the automorphically equivalent set, $M_{a,b}$, of (a, b)'s in-neighbors pairs. Part 2 is the average similarity over $(I_a \times I_b) - M_{a,b}$, corresponding to the contribution from (a, b) being pointed to by the rest of (a, b)'s in-neighbors pairs out of automorphically equivalent set $M_{a,b}$. The relative weight of Part 1 and 2 is balanced by a user-controlled parameter $\lambda \in [0,1]$. β is a damping factor between 0 and 1, which is often set to 0.6 or 0.8, implying that similarity propagation made with distant in-neighbors is penalised by an attenuation factor β across edges. When I_a (or I_b) $= \emptyset$, which implies the maximum matching $M_{a,b} = \emptyset$, we define Part 1 and Part 2 $= 0$ in order to avoid the denominators of the fraction in Part 1 and 2 being zeros.

Fixed-Point Iteration. To solve RoleSim* similarity $s(a,b)$ in Eq. (1), we adopt the following fixed-point iterative scheme:

$$s_0(a,b) \quad = 1 \quad (\forall a, b) \tag{2}$$

$$s_{k+1}(a,b) \quad = \beta \times \left(\frac{\lambda}{|I_a| + |I_b| - |M_{a,b}|} \sum_{(x,y) \in M_{a,b}} s_k(x,y) \right.$$

$$\left. + \frac{1-\lambda}{|I_a| \times |I_b| - |M_{a,b}|} \sum_{(x,y) \in (I_a \times I_b) - M_{a,b}} s_k(x,y) \right) + (1 - \beta) \tag{3}$$

where $s_k(a,b)$ denotes the RoleSim* score between nodes a and b at iteration k. Based on Eqs. (2) and (3), we can iteratively compute all pairs of similarity scores $s_{k+1}(*, *)$ from those at the last iteration $s_k(*, *)$. The fixed-point scheme in Eqs. (2) and (3) implies an iterative algorithm for RoleSim* computation, which requires $O(K|E|^2)$ time to compute $|V|^2$ node-pairs for K iterations.

Threshold-Based RoleSim*. To accelerate RoleSim* computation, we notice that there are a significant number of node pairs whose iterative similarity values $s_k(*, *)$ are very close to their convergent scores $s(*, *)$ and thus will not change much in subsequent iterations. Hence, we propose the following threshold-based RoleSim* model, where δ is a user-controlled threshold, which is a speed-accuracy trade-off.

$$s_0^\delta(a,b) \quad = 1$$

$$s_{k+1}^\delta(a,b) = \begin{cases} s_k^\delta(a,b) & \text{if } s_{k-1}^\delta(a,b) - s_k^\delta(a,b) < \delta \\ 1-\beta & \text{if } s_k^\delta(a,b) < (1-\beta) + \delta \\ \beta \times \left(\frac{\lambda}{|I_a|+|I_b|-|M_{a,b}|} \sum_{(x,y) \in M_{a,b}} s_k^\delta(x,y) \right. & \text{otherwise} \\ \left. + \frac{1-\lambda}{|I_a| \times |I_b|-|M_{a,b}|} \sum_{(x,y) \in (I_a \times I_b) - M_{a,b}} s_k^\delta(x,y) \right) + (1-\beta) \end{cases}$$

3.2 Axiomatic Properties for RoleSim* Iterative Similarity

Based on the definition of iterative similarity $s_k(a,b)$ in Eqs. (2) and (3), we next show three axiomatic properties of RoleSim*, *i.e.*, symmetry, boundedness, and non-increasing monotonicity, based on the following theorem.

Theorem 1. *The iterative RoleSim* $\{s_k(a,b)\}$ *in Eqs. (2) and (3) have the following key properties: for any node pair (a,b) and each iteration $k = 0, 1, \cdots$,*

1. **(Symmetry)** $s_k(a, b) = s_k(b, a)$
2. **(Boundedness)** $1 - \beta \leq s_k(a, b) \leq 1$
3. **(Monotonicity)** $s_{k+1}(a, b) \leq s_k(a, b)$

Proof. Please refer to [28] for a detailed proof of all theorems and lemmas.

Theorem 1 indicates that, for every iteration $k = 0, 1, 2, \cdots$, $\{s_k(a, b)\}$ is a bounded symmetric scoring function. Moreover, as $k \to \infty$, it can be readily verified that the exact solution $s(a, b)$ also is a bounded symmetric measure, which is similar to SimRank and RoleSim. In comparison, other measures (*e.g.*, Hitting Time and Random Walk with Restart) are asymmetric ones.

3.3   Existence and Uniqueness

It is worth mentioning that, as opposed to SimRank whose iterative similarity is non-decreasing between 0 and 1 *w.r.t.* k, RoleSim* similarity is non-increasing between $1 - \beta$ and 1. The bounded non-increasing property of RoleSim* guarantees the existence and uniqueness of its exact solution $s(a, b)$, as shown below:

Theorem 2 (Existence and Uniqueness).   *There always exists a unique solution $s(a, b)$ (i.e., the exact RoleSim score) to Eqs. (2) and (3) such that the iterative RoleSim similarity $\{s_k(a, b)\}$ converges to it, i.e., $\lim_{k \to \infty} s_k(a, b) = s(a, b)$.*

3.4   Accuracy Estimation

Having proved the existence and uniqueness of the exact RoleSim* solution, we are now ready to investigate the error bound of the difference between the k-th iterative similarity $s_k(a, b)$ and exact one $s(a, b)$. In virtue of the non-increasing monotonicity of $\{s_k(a, b)\}$, one can readily show that the exact $s(a, b)$ is the lower bound of all the iterative similarities $\{s_k(a, b)\}$, i.e., $s_k(a, b) \geq s(a, b)$ $(\forall k)$. The following theorem further provides a concise upper bound to measure the closeness between $s_k(a, b)$ and $s(a, b)$.

Theorem 3 (Iterative Error Bound).   *For every iteration number $k = 0, 1, 2, \cdots$, the difference between $s_k(a, b)$ and $s(a, b)$ is bounded by*

$$s_k(a, b) - s(a, b) \leq \beta^{k+1} \qquad (\forall a, b) \qquad (4)$$

Theorem 3 derives a concise exponential upper bound for the difference between the k-th iterative similarity $s_k(a, b)$ and exact $s(a, b)$. Combining this bound with the non-increasing monotonicity $s_k(a, b) \geq s(a, b)$, we can obtain that the k-th iterative error $s_k(a, b) - s(a, b)$ is between 0 and β^{k+1}. Moreover, Theorem 3 also implies that, given desired accuracy $\epsilon > 0$, the total number of iterations required for computing RoleSim* similarity is $K = \lceil \log_\beta \epsilon \rceil$.

3.5 "Sum-Transitivity" of RoleSim* Similarity

In this section, we investigate the transitive property of the proposed RoleSim* similarity measure. Intuitively, when a similarity measure $s(*, *)$ fulfills the transitive property, it means that, for any three nodes a, b, c in the graph, if a is similar to b and b is similar to c, it implies that a is likely to be similar to c. The transitivity feature is useful in many real applications, e.g., for predicting and recommending links in a graph.

To study the transitive property of RoleSim*, let us induce a distance $d(a, b) := 1 - s(a, b)$ from the RoleSim* measure. Due to $s(*, *) \in [1 - \beta, 1]$, the distance $d(*, *)$ is between 0 and β. In what follows, we will show that $d(*, *)$ satisfies the triangular inequality, which is an indication of $s(*, *)$ transitivity.

We first show the following lemma, which is needed for further proof of RoleSim* triangular inequality.

Lemma 1. *Let $s_k(*, *)$ be the k-th iterative RoleSim* similarity to Eqs. (2) and (3). For any three nodes a, b, c in a graph, if $s_k(a, b) + s_k(b, c) - s_k(a, c) \leq 1$ holds at iteration k, the following inequalities holds:*

$$P_1 := \frac{\sum\limits_{(x,y) \in M_{a,b}} s_k(x,y)}{|I_a| + |I_b| - |M_{a,b}|} + \frac{\sum\limits_{(y,z) \in M_{b,c}} s_k(y,z)}{|I_b| + |I_c| - |M_{b,c}|} - \frac{\sum\limits_{(x,z) \in M_{a,c}} s_k(x,z)}{|I_a| + |I_c| - |M_{a,c}|} \leq 1 \quad (5)$$

$$P_2 := \frac{\sum\limits_{(x,y) \in (I_a \times I_b) - M_{a,b}} s_k(x,y)}{|I_a| \times |I_b| - |M_{a,b}|} + \frac{\sum\limits_{(y,z) \in (I_b \times I_c) - M_{b,c}} s_k(y,z)}{|I_b| \times |I_c| - |M_{b,c}|} - \frac{\sum\limits_{(x,z) \in (I_a \times I_c) - M_{a,c}} s_k(x,z)}{|I_a| \times |I_c| - |M_{a,c}|} \leq 1 \quad (6)$$

Leveraging Lemma 1, we are now ready to show the sum-transitivity of the RoleSim* similarity distance, which is the main result in this subsection:

Theorem 4. *The RoleSim* similarity $s(a, b)$ defined by Eq. (1) satisfies the following "sum-transitive" property: Let $d(a, b) := 1 - s(a, b)$ be the closeness between nodes a and b. Then, for any three nodes a, b, c in a graph, the following triangular inequality holds, i.e.,*

$$d(a, b) + d(b, c) \geq d(a, c) \quad (7)$$

4 Experimental Evaluation

4.1 Experimental Settings

Datasets. We use both real and synthetic datasets, as illustrated below:

Datasets	Abbr.	#Node-Pairs	#Nodes	#Edges	Type
Amazon	(AMZ)	$25,867,396$	$5,086$	$8,970$	Directed
DBLP	(DBLP)	$5,626,384$	$2,372$	$7,106$	Undirected
Synthetic	(SYN)	$4,000,000$	$2,000$	$5,481$	Undirected

- <u>Amazon</u>. A co-purchasing digraph crawled from *Customers Who Bought This Item Also Bought* feature of Amazon[1]. Each node is a product, and edge $i \to j$ means that product j appears in the frequent co-purchasing list of i.
- <u>DBLP</u>. A collaboration (undirected) graph taken from DBLP bibliography.[2] We extract a co-authorship subgraph from six top conferences in computer science (SIGMOD, VLDB, PODS, KDD, SIGIR, ICDE) during 2018–2020. If two authors (nodes) co-authored a paper, there is an edge between them.
- <u>Synthetic</u>. A random scale-free graph with a power-law degree distribution, generated by GenRndPowerLaw function in C++ SNAP Library.[3]

All experiments are conducted on a PC with Intel Core i7-10510U 2.30GHz CPU and 16 GB RAM, using Windows 8 Professional 64-bit. Each experiment is repeated 5 times and the average is reported.

Compared Algorithms. We implemented all the following algorithms in VC++:

Models	Abbr.	Description
RoleSim*	(RS*)	Our proposed RoleSim* model in Section 3.1
SimRank	(SR)	A pairwise similarity model proposed by Jeh and Widom [7]
MatchSim	(MS)	A similarity model relying on the matched neighbors of node pairs [16]
RoleSim	(RS)	A model that guarantees the automorphically equivalence of nodes [9]
RoleSim++	(RS++)	An enhanced RoleSim that considers both in- and out-neighbors [23]
CentSim	(CS)	A similarity model that compares the centrality values of node pairs [13]

Parameters. We use the following parameters as default: (a) damping factor $\beta = 0.8$, (b) relative weight $\lambda = 0.7$, (c) total number of iterations $K = 4$.

Semantic Evaluation. We design an unsupervised evaluation setting to quantify the effectiveness of the similarity measures in preserving self-similarity under different conditions. In particular, we study the effect of sampling the immediate neighborhood of a query point on similarity scores in RoleSim* compared with SimRank and RoleSim. Consider a single query node q. In our experiment, we create a node q' and add it to the graph. We connect q' to some proportion (η) of the total number of neighbors of q, and hereby refer to q' as the "sampled

---

[1] www.amazon.co.uk.
[2] www.informatik.uni-trier.de/~ley/db/.
[3] https://snap.stanford.edu/data/index.html.

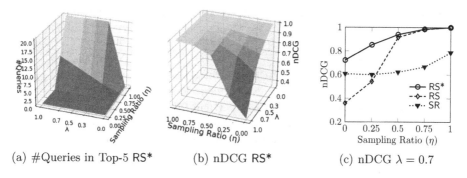

(a) #Queries in Top-5 RS*   (b) nDCG RS*   (c) nDCG $\lambda = 0.7$

Fig. 2. Effect of Sampling Ratio (η) and Weight (λ) on Ranking Quality (DBLP)

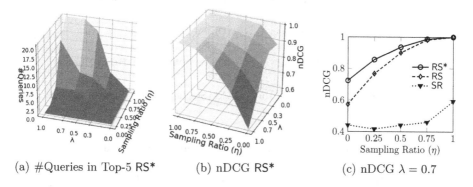

(a) #Queries in Top-5 RS*   (b) nDCG RS*   (c) nDCG $\lambda = 0.7$

Fig. 3. Effect of Sampling Ratio (η) and Weight (λ) on Ranking Quality (AMZ)

clone". The similarity scores of q to all other points in the graph are computed using SimRank, RoleSim, and RoleSim*. We evaluate how much the relative similarities are preserved when different measures are used. We vary η in q' with step size 0.25 (and ensuring no orphaned nodes), and additionally consider $\lambda = 0.0, 0.3, 0.5, 0.7, 1.0$ for RoleSim*. Our results are aggregated over 20 queries on DBLP and AMZ graphs respectively, where query nodes are chosen as having high degree of neighbors.

4.2   Experimental Results

Semantic Accuracy. We first count the number of queries where the sampled clone q' appears in the top-k ($k = 1, 5, 10$) similar nodes to query q for RoleSim*. Intuitively, this studies how much structural information is gleaned about a query node. Figure 2(a) presents the number of such queries out of 20 on the undirected DBLP graph, considering top-5 similarity scores. Other top-k plots are omitted, but show that with increasing k for a given sampling proportion there are more such queries even at lower λ.

Table 2. Similarity rankings for "Philip S. Yu" on DBLP co-authorships data

#	RS*($\lambda = 0.6$)	RS*($\lambda = 0.8$)	RS	SR
1	Nitesh V. Chawla	Xia Hu	Xia Hu	Yuan Fang
2	Danai Koutra	Nitesh V. Chawla	Nitesh V. Chawla	Chenwei Zhang
3	Yanjie Fu	Yanjie Fu	Yanjie Fu	Nan Du
4	**Jure Leskovec**	**Jure Leskovec**	**Huan Liu**	Wei Fan
5	Haifeng Chen	Danai Koutra	**Jure Leskovec**	Lichao Sun
6	Xia Hu	Haifeng Chen	Haifeng Chen	Weiran Huang
7	Xing Xie	Xing Xie	Danai Koutra	Jianxin Ma
8	Xiangnan He	Xiangnan He	Xing Xie	Xinyue Liu
9	Di Niu	Di Niu	Xiangnan He	Binbin Hu
10	Jennifer G. Dy	**Huan Liu**	Fenglong Ma	Daixin Wang
...	...	...	...	...
28	**Huan Liu**	Dawei Yin	Di Wu	Ning Wu
...	...	...	...	...
89	Xiang Li	Han Zhu	Qinyong Wang	**Huan Liu**
...	...	...	...	...
350	Mao Yang	Houdong Hu	Xi (Stephen) Chen	**Jure Leskovec**

Next, we test the impact of sampling η and λ on ranking quality in RoleSim*. We plot the average ranking quality (normalized discounted cumulative gain (nDCG)), considering top-100 similar nodes of the sampled clone and comparing this to the baseline original query. We observe that the trend (with respect to η) seen in Fig. 2(b) and Fig. 3(b) for $\lambda = 1$ resembles that for RoleSim, and the trend for $\lambda = 0.5$ is close to that for SimRank.

Finally, we consider a fixed value of $\lambda = 0.7$ and confirm that the RoleSim* has higher ranking quality compared to SimRank and RoleSim, with respect to the average nDCG. Figure 2(c) with undirected DBLP graph shows that RoleSim* produces a more consistent nDCG even with small η. For the directed AMZ graph in Fig. 3(c) too, RoleSim shows significant improvement at lower sampling, and the performance of SimRank is negatively affected throughout, while RoleSim* remains stable.

Qualitative Case Study. Table 2 compares the similarity ranking results from three algorithms (SR, RS and RS*) for retrieving top-10 most similar authors *w.r.t.* query "Philip S. Yu" on DBLP. From the results, we see that the top rankings of RS* are similar to RS, highlighting its capability to effectively capture automorphic equivalent neighboring information. For instance, "Jure Leskovec" is top-ranked in RS* list. This is reasonable because he and "Philip S. Yu" have similar roles - they are both Professors in Computer Science with close research expertise (*e.g.*, knowledge discovery, recommender systems, commonsense reasoning). However, the rankings of RS* are different from those of RS. For example, "Jure Leskovec" is ranked 350th by SR, but 4th by RS* and RS. This is because SimRank can only capture connected paths between two authors

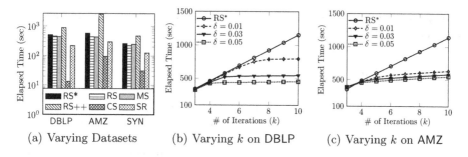

(a) Varying Datasets (b) Varying k on DBLP (c) Varying k on AMZ

Fig. 4. Elapsed time comparison for different threshold-based RS*

while ignoring their automorphic equivalent structure. "Jure Leskovec" has rare collaborations with "Philip S. Yu", both direct and indirect, thus leading to a low SimRank score.

To evaluate RS* further, we choose two different values for $\lambda \in \{0.6, 0.8\}$ to show how RS* ranking results are perturbed $w.r.t.$ λ. From the results, we notice that, when λ is varied from 0.6 to 0.8, nodes with small SR scores (e.g., "Jure Leskovec") exhibit a stable position in RS* ranking, whereas nodes having higher SR scores (e.g., "Huan Liu") have a substantial change. This conforms with our intuition because "Huan Liu"'s collaboration with "Philip S. Yu" is closer than "Jure Leskovec"'s, and RS* is able to capture both connectivity and automorphic equivalence of two authors using a balanced weight λ.

Computational Time. Figure 4(a) compares the computational time of six algorithms (RS*, RS, MS, RS++, CS, SR) on various datasets (AMZ, DBLP, SYN), respectively. We notice that, on each dataset, RS* has comparable computational time to RS and MS. This implies that RS* achieves high accuracy without sacrificing running speed. In addition, RS*, RS, and MS are 2–4 times faster than RS++. This is because RS* need to find two maximum bipartite matchings for both in- and out-neighboring pairs, as opposed to RS* that involves the computation of only one matching. SR is slightly slower than RS*. This is consistent with our analysis as SR simply takes the average of all similarities of the in-neighboring pairs without the need to find the maximum bipartite matching. CS achieves the fastest speed since it simply assesses a node-pair similarity by aggregating their centrality values, thereby leading to low accuracy.

Figures 4(b) and (c) show the effect of iteration number k and threshold δ on the running time of RS* on DBLP and AMZ, respectively. For each dataset, we vary δ from 0 to 0.05. When $\delta = 0$, it reduces to RS* algorithm. From the results on both datasets, we discern that, for each fixed δ, the running time of threshold-based RS* increases as k grows. When δ becomes larger, the growth rate of RS* time tends to be sublinear. For example, when $\delta = 0.05$ on DBLP, only after $k = 5$ iterations, the increasing time of threshold-based RS* has leveled off. In contrast, when $\delta = 0.01$, the time becomes steady after $k = 8$ iterations. The reason is that a higher setting of threshold δ implies a larger number of pairs to be pruned per iteration, thus leading to the growth rate of the running time decreasing in an earlier stage during iterations.

5 Conclusion

We propose RoleSim*, a novel similarity model that guarantees automorphic equivalence and also considers neighboring similarity information beyond automorphically equivalent sets, thereby achieving better performance than both SimRank and RoleSim. We prove the existence and uniqueness of the RoleSim* solution, show that iteratively computing RoleSim* is bounded, and induce a RoleSim* distance obeying sum-transitivity of similarity scores. We also evaluate our model on DBLP, AMZ, and SYN datasets to demonstrate its superior ranking quality and comparable complexity to competitors.

Acknowledgments. This work was supported by the National Natural Science Foundation of China (61972203), and Natural Science Foundation of Jiangsu Province (BK20190442).

References

1. Antonellis, I., Garcia-Molina, H., Chang, C.-C.: SimRank++: query rewriting through link analysis of the click graph. In: PVLDB, vol. 1, no. 1 (2008)
2. Chen, H., Giles, C.L.: ASCOS++: an asymmetric similarity measure for weighted networks to address the problem of SimRank. ACM Trans. Knowl. Discov. Data **10**(2), 15:1–15:26 (2015)
3. Chen, X., Lai, L., Qin, L., Lin, X.: StructSim: querying structural node similarity at billion scale. In: ICDE, pp. 1950–1953 (2020)
4. Fujiwara, Y., Nakatsuji, M., Shiokawa, H., Onizuka, M.: Efficient search algorithm for SimRank. In: ICDE, pp. 589–600 (2013)
5. He, G., Feng, H., Li, C., Chen, H.: Parallel SimRank computation on large graphs with iterative aggregation. In: KDD (2010)
6. He, J., Liu, H., Yu, J.X., Li, P., He, W., Du, X.: Assessing single-pair similarity over graphs by aggregating first-meeting probabilities. Inf. Syst. **42**, 107–122 (2014)
7. Jeh, G., Widom, J.: SimRank: a measure of structural-context similarity. In: KDD, pp. 538–543 (2002)
8. Jiang, M., Fu, A.W., Wong, R.C., Wang, K.: READS: a random walk approach for efficient and accurate dynamic SimRank. PVLDB **10**(9), 937–948 (2017)
9. Jin, R., Lee, V.E., Hong, H.: Axiomatic ranking of network role similarity. In: Apté, C., Ghosh, J., Smyth, P. (eds.) Proceedings of the 17th ACM SIGKDD International Conference on Knowledge Discovery and Data Mining, San Diego, CA, USA, 21–24 August 2011, pp. 922–930. ACM (2011)
10. Jin, R., Lee, V.E., Li, L.: Scalable and axiomatic ranking of network role similarity. TKDD **8**(1), 3:1–3:37 (2014)
11. Kusumoto, M., Maehara, T., Kawarabayashi, K.: Scalable similarity search for SimRank. In: SIGMOD, pp. 325–336 (2014)
12. Li, C., et al.: Fast computation of SimRank for static and dynamic information networks. In: EDBT (2010)

13. Li, L., Qian, L., Lee, V.E., Leng, M., Chen, M., Chen, X.: Fast and accurate computation of role similarity via vertex centrality. In: Dong, X.L., Yu, X., Li, J., Sun, Y. (eds.) WAIM 2015. LNCS, vol. 9098, pp. 123–134. Springer, Cham (2015). https://doi.org/10.1007/978-3-319-21042-1_10

14. Li, P., Liu, H., Yu, J.X., He, J., Du, X.: Fast single-pair simrank computation. In: Proceedings of the SIAM International Conference on Data Mining, SDM 2010, Columbus, Ohio, USA, 29 April–1 May, pp. 571–582. SIAM (2010)

15. Li, Z., Fang, Y., Liu, Q., Cheng, J., Cheng, R., Lui, J.C.S.: Walking in the cloud: parallel SimRank at scale. PVLDB **9**(1), 24–35 (2015)

16. Lin, Y., Sundaram, H., Chi, Y., Tatemura, J., Tseng, B.L.: Detecting splogs via temporal dynamics using self-similarity analysis. TWEB **2**(1), 4:1–4:35 (2008)

17. Lin, Z., Lyu, M.R., King, I.: MatchSim: a novel similarity measure based on maximum neighborhood matching. Knowl. Inf. Syst. **32**(1), 141–166 (2012). https://doi.org/10.1007/s10115-011-0427-z

18. Liu, Y., et al.: ProbeSim: scalable single-source and top-k SimRank computations on dynamic graphs. PVLDB **11**(1), 14–26 (2017)

19. Lizorkin, D., Velikhov, P., Grinev, M.N., Turdakov, D.: Accuracy estimate and optimization techniques for SimRank computation. VLDB J. **19**(1), 45–66 (2010). https://doi.org/10.1007/s00778-009-0168-8

20. Maehara, T., Kusumoto, M., Kawarabayashi, K.: Scalable simrank join algorithm. In: ICDE, pp. 603–614 (2015)

21. Rothe, S., Schütze, H.: CoSimRank: a flexible & efficient graph-theoretic similarity measure. In: ACL, pp. 1392–1402. The Association for Computer Linguistics (2014)

22. Shao, Y., Cui, B., Chen, L., Liu, M., Xie, X.: An efficient similarity search framework for SimRank over large dynamic graphs. PVLDB **8**(8), 838–849 (2015)

23. Shao, Y., Liu, J., Shi, S., Zhang, Y., Cui, B.: Fast de-anonymization of social networks with structural information. Data Sci. Eng. **4**(1), 76–92 (2019). https://doi.org/10.1007/s41019-019-0086-8

24. Tian, B., Xiao, X.: SLING: a near-optimal index structure for SimRank. In: SIGMOD, pp. 1859–1874 (2016)

25. Wang, Y., Lian, X., Chen, L.: Efficient simrank tracking in dynamic graphs. In: ICDE pp. 545–556 (2018)

26. Yoon, S., Kim, S., Park, S.: C-Rank: a link-based similarity measure for scientific literature databases. Inf. Sci. **326**, 25–40 (2016)

27. Youngmann, B., Milo, T., Somech, A.: Boosting SimRank with semantics. In: EDBT, pp. 37–48 (2019)

28. Yu, W., Iranmanesh, S., Haldar, A., Ferhatosmanoglu, M.Z.H.: An axiomatic role similarity measure based on graph topology, Technical report (2020). https://warwick.ac.uk/fac/sci/dcs/people/weiren_yu/rolesim_star.pdf

29. Yu, W., Lin, X., Zhang, W.: Towards efficient SimRank computation on large networks. In: ICDE, pp. 601–612 (2013)

30. Yu, W., Lin, X., Zhang, W., McCann, J.A.: Fast all-pairs SimRank assessment on large graphs and bipartite domains. IEEE Trans. Knowl. Data Eng. **27**(7), 1810–1823 (2015)

31. Yu, W., Lin, X., Zhang, W., McCann, J.A.: Dynamical SimRank search on time-varying networks. VLDB J. **27**(1), 79–104 (2017). https://doi.org/10.1007/s00778-017-0488-z

32. Yu, W., Lin, X., Zhang, W., Pei, J., McCann, J.A.: SimRank*: effective and scalable pairwise similarity search based on graph topology. VLDB J. **28**(3), 401–426 (2019). https://doi.org/10.1007/s00778-018-0536-3

33. Yu, W., Lin, X., Zhang, W., Zhang, Y., Le, J.: SimFusion+: extending simfusion towards efficient estimation on large and dynamic networks. In: SIGIR, pp. 365–374 (2012)

34. Yu, W., McCann, J.A.: Efficient partial-pairs SimRank search for large networks. PVLDB 8(5), 569–580 (2015)

35. Yu, W., Wang, F.: Fast exact CoSimRank search on evolving and static graphs. In: WWW, pp. 599–608 (2018)

36. Zhao, P., Han, J., Sun, Y.: P-Rank: a comprehensive structural similarity measure over information networks. In: CIKM (2009)

37. Zhu, R., Zou, Z., Li, J.: SimRank computation on uncertain graphs. In: ICDE, pp. 565–576 (2016)

Scalable In-Memory Graph Pattern Matching on Symmetric Multiprocessor Systems

Alexander Krause$^{(\boxtimes)}$ [iD], Dirk Habich [iD], and Wolfgang Lehner [iD]

Technische Universität Dresden, Nöthnitzer Straße 46, 01187 Dresden, Germany
{alexander.krause,dirk.habich,wolfgang.lehner}@tu-dresden.de
http://wwwdb.tu-dresden.de

Abstract. Graph-structured data can be found in nearly every aspect of today's world which contributes to an increasing importance of this data structure for storing and processing data. From a processing perspective, finding comprehensive patterns in graph-structured data is a processing primitive in a variety of applications, such as fraud detection, biological engineering or social graph analytics. On the hardware side, multiprocessor systems—consisting of multiple processors in a single scale-up server—are the next important wave on top of multi-core systems. In particular, symmetric multiprocessor systems (SMP) are characterized by the fact, that each processor has the same architecture, e.g., every processor is a multi-core and all multiprocessors share a common and huge main memory space. Moreover, large SMPs will feature a non-uniform memory access (NUMA), whose impact on the design of efficient data processing concepts is considerable. In this paper, we give an overview of NeMeSys, our system for scalable near-memory graph pattern matching (GPM) on SMPs. NeMeSys is built on a synthesis of well-known concepts of database systems including a set of graph-tailored and hardware-oriented optimization techniques for scalable GPM on SMPs.

1 Introduction

A resurgence of interest in graph structured data has become evident during the last decades [1,6,24]. Among others, a major driver behind that is a shift in the interest of analytics from merely reporting towards data-intensive science and discovery [7]. In 2017, Sahu, et al. [25] conducted a survey and showed, that the size of real world graphs ranges from less than 10 k to more than 10 B edges. Furthermore, they indicated that graphs are used by larger companies, that are not Google, Facebook or Twitter. This implies that the graph data format is a valid form of representation, widely used and accepted among industrial companies and research facilities. In our work, we focus on *edge-labeled multigraphs* as a general and widely employed graph data model [20,21,23]. An edge-labeled multigraph is defined as $G = \langle V, E, \rho, \Sigma, \lambda \rangle$, which consists of a set of vertices V, a set of edges E, an incidence function $\rho : E \to V \times V$, and a labeling function $\lambda : E \to \Sigma$ assigning labels to each edge.

© Springer Nature Switzerland AG 2020
L. Qin et al. (Eds.): SFDI 2020/LSGDA 2020, CCIS 1281, pp. 49–62, 2020.
https://doi.org/10.1007/978-3-030-61133-0_4

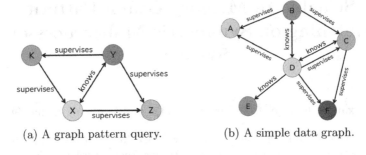

(a) A graph pattern query.   (b) A simple data graph.

Fig. 1. A graph pattern matching example.

In many application use cases, users are interested in identifying logical connections between vertices of their data graph. Thus, recognizing comprehensive patterns on large graph-structured data is a common use case and a prerequisite for a variety of application domains such as fraud detection [23], biomolecular engineering [20], scientific computing [27], or social network analytics [21], only to name a few. That means, graph pattern matching (GPM) can be considered as a crucial processing primitive. GPM queries are usually given as a subgraph of the queried data graph. Figure 1(a) shows an example, whereby the query requests all two-sets of entities, that know each other and that both supervise two distinct other entities. Considering the data graph from Fig. 1(b), the query would get only one distinct result, namely $\langle$A, B, D, C$\rangle$ which match to the query vertices $\langle$K, Y, X, Z$\rangle$ respectively. Obviously, the mappings for X and Y as well as K and Z could be permuted to get additional matches, with the same data vertices.

Fundamentally, GPM can require a high amount of compute resources, depending on the size of the underlying data graph as well as the number of issued queries. To satisfy this demand, symmetric multiprocessor systems (SMP) are an interesting hardware foundation. SMPs are composed by multiple processors (also called nodes or sockets) each with the same architecture, e.g, a multi-core processor and all multiprocessors share a common and huge main memory space. Unfortunately, large SMPs will feature a non-uniform memory access (NUMA), whose impact on the design of efficient data processing concepts is considerable as shown in [11,16,31]. Therefore, we developed NeMeSys, a novel scalable in-memory graph pattern matching engine specifically designed for large NUMA-SMPs. In this paper, we give a comprehensive overview about NeMeSys, which was demonstrated in our previous work [13]. In particular, we will summarize a set of graph-tailored and hardware-oriented optimization techniques.

2   NeMeSys System Design

In our work, we target the previously described *symmetric multiprocessor systems* as hardware foundation for a scalable GPM execution. Modern systems

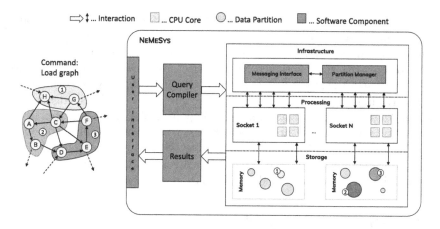

Fig. 2. Architectural overview of NeMeSys.

distinguish between *Uniform Memory Access* (UMA) and *Non-Uniform Memory Access* (NUMA). UMA defines, that the access of any memory address in the whole address space is performed with equal latencies. In contrast, NUMA means, that the memory access latency can vary significantly between different addresses. Considering a mesh-connected four-socket system, we can face up to two NUMA hops, before the actual memory access can happen. With every hop, the memory access latency increases, but also the effective memory bandwidth decreases [10]. Several previous works prove, that considering the NUMA effect is crucial for competitive performance [11,16,22,31]. This underlines our hardware focus, since handling a single box NUMA-SMP well will also result in higher performance, when a compute cluster consists of multiple of such machines.

We built our research prototype called NeMeSys to fully exploit the provided hardware capacities of SMPs for graph pattern matching. NeMeSys is based on ERIS, a relational data processing engine [11], from which we borrow architectural design principles for superior scalability on SMP systems. In this paper, we explore possibilities to transport the positive effects of this architecture from relational to graph processing. The overall NeMeSys architecture is depicted in Fig. 2. Our engine features multiple layers, such as a *storage layer*, a *processing layer* and a *communication layer*, which we call infrastructure, and components related to user I/O. Its internal architecture is a synthesis of four well-known architecture design principles: *Shared Everything (SE)*, *Partition Serial Execution (PSE)*, *Delegation* and the *Data-Oriented Architecture (DORA)* as described by [2]. NeMeSys combines the shared memory for metadata from SE, the physical data partitioning from PSE, the message passing from Delegation and the thread-to-data mapping from DORA to create a highly scalable architecture for NUMA-SMPs. In detail, every logical core is assigned with one worker, which runs its own event loop. Among other tasks like processing local partitions, this loop contains a role swap to a socket-local coordinator that sends and collects the messages from local workers and remote coordinators. Being an in-memory engine, NeMeSys allows for online data ingestion as well as online query generation and processing through a terminal based user interface. Storing a graph on a NUMA system inherently requires data partitioning to cope with the mentioned NUMA effect, as illustrated in Fig. 2. Hence, we need to dissect the graph into a disjunct set of partitions, which can then be stored on the individual memory domains. Because of our employed edge-labeled graph model, we can express a graph's topology in triples. Thus, a vertex is represented by a set of [source,target,label] triples, which define its outgoing edges. Naturally, we store these edges in a triple-table, with an indexed source column to allow for direct lookup of all edges of a given vertex. After assigning a vertex to any partition, we store its locality information in the *partition manager*.

3   NeMeSys Processing Model

In NeMeSys, we pin a dedicated worker thread to all logical cores of every processor in the SMP system and limit their access to data partitions of their local processor. Furthermore, according to the previously mentioned thread-to-data mapping, there is always only one worker allowed to process a distinct partition at the same time. Every worker periodically processes incoming messages from other workers. Each message contains the code of a to-be-executed operator and some corresponding intermediate results according to the delegation concept.

NeMeSys is designed to process GPM queries given in the form of conjunctive queries (CQs) [29], i.e., a sequence of logically *AND* connected edge predicates, with every edge predicate being a triple, which consists of a source vertex, a target vertex and an edge label, where labels could also be expressed as a wildcard using the * character. Reading a query string in triples from front to back yields an initial binding order and thus known and unknown variable bindings at a given processing step. We identified that, based on the order of variables in a query, we can have 0, 1 or 2 bound variables for any given edge predicate and thus the following three operators are considered to be sufficient for GPM processing on our target hardware:

Scan Operator. The Scan operator performs a parallel vertex scan over all partitions only when the source as well as the target vertex of a CQ triple are unknown. By specifying a certain edge label predicate, the operator returns only bindings for vertices, where the connecting edge is labeled accordingly. The Scan operator is always the first operator in the pattern matching process. As a straightforward optimization step, this operator can be fused with the following operators VB and EB to create a processing pipeline.

Vertex-Bound (VB) Operator. The VB operator takes an intermediate pattern matching result from either the Scan or the EB operator as input and tries to match new vertices in the query pattern according to the following CQ triple. The operator has to be only applied when either the source vertex or target vertex is known in the current processing step and thus bound.

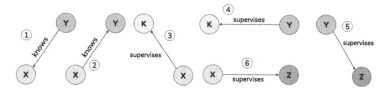

Fig. 3. Edge predicates for the query from Fig. 1(a).

Edge-Bound (EB) Operator. The EB operator ensures the existence of additional edge label predicates between known vertex matching candidates for certain vertices of the CQ. It performs a data lookup with a given source and target vertex as well as a given edge label. If the lookup fails, both vertices are eliminated from the matching candidates. Otherwise the matching state is passed to the next operator or is returned as final result. In this case, both vertex variables are bound.

Parsing the query pattern from Fig. 1(a) leads to the six edge predicates from Fig. 3 and thus creates the operator chain $Scan \rightarrow EB \rightarrow VB \rightarrow EB \rightarrow VB \rightarrow EB \rightarrow Result$. Operators can be individually instanced by every worker and consequently executed on their isolated data partitions. During its execution, an operator matches intermediate results from previous operators according to the edge predicate, which is assigned to it, and sends out new intermediate states to the succeeding operator in the chain, until final matching states are formed to a result. Depending on the available locality information, an operator produces either a unicast, i.e., a message targeting exactly one partition, or a broadcast, which is transferred to all partitions in the system. Broadcasts can occur, if the incoming edge of a vertex is requested, since we only store outgoing edges for all vertices. If a query requests an incoming edge for a known target vertex, but the source vertex is a yet unbound variable, then we can only scan the target column in all partitions of the edge table, which is triggered by the broadcast. After processing all messages for a given operator chain of a graph pattern, the collected results are pruned of duplicates.

4   Optimization Techniques

NUMA systems usually provide a sufficient amount of main memory to accommodate bigger graphs completely and enable a high degree of parallelism through many logical processors. In this section, we discuss our measures to optimize GPM processing on NUMA SMPs. The discussed optimization techniques can be applied both offline and online, i.e., before or during query execution. We generated our benchmark graphs using gMark [3], which represent a bibliographical and a protein network with approx. 6 M edges each and a social network with 36 M edges. The experiments were run on a four socket system with Intel Xeon Gold 6130 processors and 384 GB of main memory, if not stated otherwise.

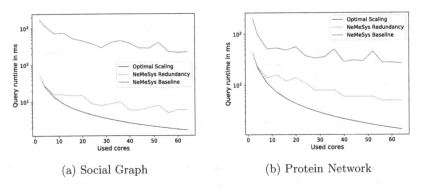

(a) Social Graph   (b) Protein Network

Fig. 4. Runtime scalings with increasing worker count on different graphs.

4.1 Eliminating Broadcasts Through Redundancy

Efficient messaging is a key component for *Delegation*-based systems like
NEMESYS. According to [18], asynchronous computation can usually outperform synchronous approaches on CPU-bound problems, whereas the opposite is
true for memory-bound problems. However, the authors state, that due to the
asynchronous execution, the inherent messaging is unable to exploit optimization
techniques like batching. This becomes especially true, if a GPM query contains
several edges that generate broadcasts during evaluation. Therefore, the superior
scalability of the naturally relational architecture of NEMESYS – c.f. [11] – does
not easily carry over to GPM. Despite having large amounts of main memory,
the limiting resource is the size of cpu cache. For efficient processing on a single
SMP box, we want the locality information to be cache resident, which is why we
do not straight up consider state-of-the-art sextuple indexing of traditional RDF
stores like Hexastore [28]. Thus, we investigated the effect of explicit redundancy
in the graph data in [15].

As outlined in Sect. 2, storing the outgoing edges of all vertices mirrors the
graph's topology. However, adding incoming edges allows for bidirectional graph
traversal. Thus, we allocate a second triple table, which contains all reversed
edges. That is, for every outgoing edge [source,target,label], we create an inverted
edge [target,source,label], which is stored in the incoming edge table. This seem-
ingly trivial adjustment has hidden implications, which we want to highlight.
First, we need to build more index structures, to allow for a direct lookup of all
incoming edges of a given vertex in this second table. Second, we also need a second set of locality information in the *partition manager*, since the incoming edge
table also has to be partitioned and distributed among the sockets. This leads
to the observation, that explicitly adding incoming edges completely eliminates
broadcasts, since we can always lookup either source or target vertices of any
given edge predicate. On the other hand, this leads to doubled infrastructure
cost, since also locality information is doubled. In the worst case, parts of the
locality information could not be hold in the processor cache anymore, which in
turn narrows the positive impact of a redundant graph storage. Figure 4 shows

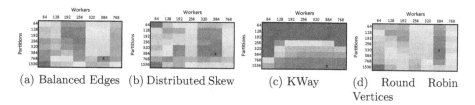

(a) Balanced Edges   (b) Distributed Skew   (c) KWay   (d) Round Robin
Vertices

Fig. 5. Relative system configuration performance of an SGI UV 3000 for different partitioning strategies of a social graph.

the runtime of a dummy query, where half of its edge predicates produce broadcasts, if no redundancy is available. The experiment was performed on a four socket NUMA machine with 64 logical cores in total. We observe that intuitively, GPM with broadcasts does not scale. When we enable redundancy, the system is not only generally more performant, but exhibits an overall better scalability behavior.

4.2   Partitioning Strategy Selection

Graphs can come in many types, e.g., social, road or bibliographical networks. Based on its type, a given graph exhibits certain data characteristics. These can range between sparse and dense graphs, evenly distributed vertex degrees or general edge distributions like we see them in scale free networks, where the degrees of the vertices follow a power law distribution. In our previous work [14], we investigated the influence of different partitioning strategies in combination with varying system configurations on an SGI UV 3000 server with 768 logical cores on 64 NUMA nodes.

Partitioning a graph can be done manifoldly, however the graph partitioning problem is known to be NP-complete [8] and thus we carefully designed heuristic approaches. *Balanced Edges (BE)* and *Distributed Skew (DS)* both try to balance the total amount of edges stored in a partition by sorting vertices descending by their degrees, iterating over them and assigning the next vertex to the partition with the currently lowest amount of edges. In addition, DS distributes all edges of a vertex v among all partitions, if the degree of v is larger than a given threshold, to avoid overloading partitions with a high-degree vertex. *Round Robin Vertices (RRV)* simply assigns all vertices to their partitions in the eponymous manner and mutlilevel k-Way (KWay) partitioning was taken from [9]. We define a system configuration (SC) as a combination of active workers and employed partition count and present the results in Fig. 5. The heat maps show the relative performance of an SC compared to the local optimum, which is marked with an X. On this machine, the individually highest performance could always be achieved, when the worker count equaled the physical core count of 384, since core siblings usually do not provide the same amount of processing power. However, depending on the partitioning strategy, the optimal number of partitions varied. Additionally, we can identify the greenish *performance islands*,

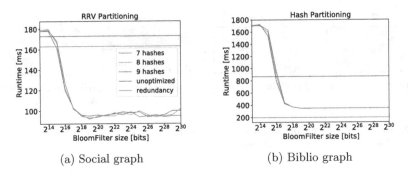

(a) Social graph   (b) Biblio graph

Fig. 6. Influence of Bloom filters vs. redundancy.

which allow us to adapt both worker and partition count, if any constraints on memory or worker count arise.

4.3   Reducing Messages Through Filtering

Having targeted messaging and the correct partitioning SC in place already helps with scalable processing. However, the memory footprint of redundancy is not negligible and thus, we elaborate measures to maintain locality information for both outgoing *and* incoming edges, but reducing the memory footprint to a minimum in [12]. The main challenge can be reduced to a *set containment problem*, where the *set* is a partition and the *elements* are edges or vertices, which are a set of edges. Usually, a hashset is used for fast lookups, however, this would still use a high amount of memory. We therefore concluded, that a probabilistic data structure like a Bloom filter [5] could be employed. Bloom filters allow us to adjust their size, based on a given memory constraint and therefore enable adaptivity between ranges of assumed false positive rates. As hash functions, we developed a fast residual class ring based prime number hashing called Prime-Hash: $H_i(x) = y = (a_i \cdot x) \wedge (M - 1)$, with a_i being the prime number for the ith hash function and M being the size of the Bloom filter in bits. We instantiate one Bloom filter per partition with its size $M \approx -1.44N \log_2(p)$ [5], with N being the vertex count per partition and p being the desired false positive rate.

Figure 6 shows the runtime benefits for different Bloom filter sizes, compared to the standard baseline in red and the runtime with full redundancy in blue on a bibliographical and a social network. A lower false positive rate (i.e., bigger Bloom filter) can lead to speedups even beyond the benefit of full redundancy in Fig. 6(a), due to the prevented additional memory usage. However, we usually observe the effect of Fig. 6(b), where the resulting performance suffers at first, due to the general overhead of handling the Bloom filter, but eventually resides somewhere between the baseline and full redundancy performance.

4.4   Workload-Driven Partition Placement

As a general rule of thumb, a workload should be as distributed as necessary, but as local as possible. Thus, reducing messages is not the only way to optimize the GPM performance on a NUMA system. We can also manipulate the partition placement to enforce utmost local computation, while preserving maximum parallelism. However, optimizing the data placement can only be solved heuristically and not fully enumeratively. Calculating all partition placement combinations is prohibitively expensive. The amount of possible, equally distributed combinations ζ for placing n partitions on an s socket system, assuming n is integer divisible by s, can be calculated with the binomial coefficient: $\zeta = \prod_{i=0}^{s-1} \binom{n-\tau \cdot i}{\tau}$, with $\tau = \frac{n}{s}$. For 64 partitions on a 4 socket system, this yields $\zeta \approx 6.6 \times 10^{35}$ possible combinations. Thus, to reduce the search space, we leverage the well known gradient descent optimization technqiue (GDO) [4]. The GDO is an iterative algorithm, which requires us to assess all trivial neighborhoods of a given allocation scheme and use the *best scoring* allocation schema as baseline for the next iteration, until no better scoring solution can be found. Within this paper, *best scoring* refers to the lowest communication cost.

In NEMESYS, we can represent an allocation schema using a binary $s \times n$ matrix A, where a 1 denotes that the partition with id i at column $n_i, 0 \leq i < n$ is located on socket $s_j, 0 \leq j < s$. By default, partitions are allocated to iteratively fill the available sockets and match the worker count on this socket. A neighbor is called trivial, if it is created through an *atomar* change in the original matrix. For our partition allocation scenario, *atomar* means to move exactly one partition to another socket. However, to avoid all partions being eventually moved to a single socket, we define a trivial change to be swapping one partition of $socket_x$ with one partition of $socket_y$. The communication matrix K is an $n \times n$ matrix and created through message tracing during the query execution. Every row vector k_i of K represents the respective traffic, originating from the ith partition towards all other partitions, including itself. This model only covers sending messages, since receiving them is already contained in the cost of the originating sockets. To calculate the communication cost, we need to estimate the actual cost for exchanging messages between sockets. In this paper, we leverage the ratio of the memory bandwidths between the individual sockets and use them as values for our $s \times s$ cost matrix C, with examples given in (1).

$$A = \begin{pmatrix} 1 & 1 & 0 & 0 & 0 & 0 & 0 & 0 \\ 0 & 0 & 1 & 1 & 0 & 0 & 0 & 0 \\ 0 & 0 & 0 & 0 & 1 & 1 & 0 & 0 \\ 0 & 0 & 0 & 0 & 0 & 0 & 1 & 1 \end{pmatrix} \quad K = \begin{pmatrix} 0 & 3 & 9 & 6 & 5 & 7 & 0 & 0 \\ 0 & 0 & 2 & 1 & 9 & 4 & 6 & 9 \\ 9 & 5 & 0 & 7 & 0 & 2 & 6 & 0 \\ 1 & 6 & 0 & 0 & 1 & 8 & 4 & 4 \\ 5 & 9 & 3 & 3 & 0 & 0 & 5 & 1 \\ 3 & 9 & 0 & 0 & 2 & 0 & 3 & 2 \\ 9 & 5 & 4 & 8 & 0 & 5 & 0 & 0 \\ 1 & 8 & 0 & 9 & 7 & 2 & 6 & 0 \end{pmatrix} \quad C = \begin{pmatrix} 1.00 & 6.29 & 6.29 & 6.29 \\ 6.25 & 1.00 & 6.29 & 6.25 \\ 6.31 & 6.31 & 1.00 & 6.31 \\ 6.31 & 6.31 & 6.31 & 1.00 \end{pmatrix} \quad (1)$$

With the three matrices A, K and C, we can now calculate the communication cost per socket i. First, we calculate the communication, that originates from socket c_i with the ith row vector a_i of A using $a_i K$. This resets to cost of all partitions, which are not located on c_i, to 0. Then we weight the communication of all partitions, with the cost vector of socket c_i by calculating $c_i A$. Multiplying

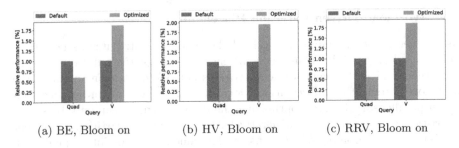

(a) BE, Bloom on   (b) HV, Bloom on   (c) RRV, Bloom on

Fig. 7. Relative query runtimes for *Quad* and *V* query, varying partitionings. Biblio graph, 64 partitions, Bloom filter active, Redundancy off.

the communication originating from socket c_i with the transposed result of the actual communication of socket c_i yields the total communication cost of socket $c_i = (a_i K)(c_i A)^T$. Thus, the total communication cost γ can be expressed as the sum of the individual socket cost scores: $\gamma = \sum_{i=0}^{|sockets|-1} (a_i K)(c_i A)^T$. The previously created A' with the cheapest cost is selected as new baseline and further optimized, until no cheaper matrix can be found. To avoid local optima, we perform three targeted restarts with heuristically selected A'' matrices. Feeding the example matrices from (1) into our optimizer yields $\gamma_A = 1308.7$. As a final result, the optimized allocation matrix has $\gamma_{optimized} = 1101.68$, i.e., a 16% cost reduction, for the optimized allocation.

Figure 7 shows the results for two test queries, *Quad* and *V*, ran against the Biblio graph with active Bloom filters. The relative performances of the optimized executions are only to be considered against the respective baseline, i.e., the *Quad* default execution has another query runtime than the *V* query. Clearly, colocating partitions does improve the query runtime for the *Quad* query in all three cases. The general slowdown for the *V* query might be an artifact of the results of our optimizer. Since all partitions are potentially communicating with each other, we built a 64 × 64 communication matrix, to represent all possible communication paths. However, not all partitions hold data, which is relevant for every query and thus do not produce or receive any messages. This leads to the effect, where we see half of the sockets being filled with all communicating and the other half with silent partitions. Despite locally minimized communication scores, this effect can introduce more overhead. The system is unable to perform messaging optimizations like batching, when only one partition on a remote socket is touched. On the machine level, sending a message is a `memcpy` operation. Performing many `memcpy` operations on small chunks of data is always slower than using `memcpy` on one large chunk of data. Thus, if only very few messages are sent to a remote socket, we can face runtime slowdowns.

Figure 8 shows the potential speedups for co-locating partitions with higher message traffic in a workload scenario. We executed a workload of 100 GPM queries, for which we performed the message tracing both individually per query and in workload batches of 10. The optimal placement for single queries can achieve considerable higher performance gains of up to 80%. However, such fine

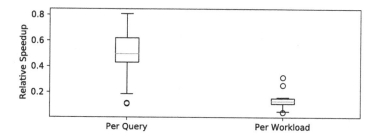

Fig. 8. Speedup variances for scenario dependent partition movement.

granular movement is rarely efficient, because moving the partitions within a NUMA system can impose a significant cost, depending on how much partitions have to be moved and if the NUMA system is fully connected or not. The workload-based optimization still yields performance gains ranging from 5% to 40%, which amortizes the partition movement cost.

During our experiments, we observed partly strong variations of the query runtimes for all queries and workloads. To isolate the root cause, we repeated the experiments from Fig. 8 with the same queries and workload configurations using all combinations of active and inactive Bloom filters and redundancy. The results are shown in Fig. 9. We also investigated the effect of *hot* and *cold* adaption, where *cold* means, we restart NEMESYS for every measurement and *hot* experiments mean, we load the graph once, move the partitions and measure the query performance for all queries and workloads subsequently. All measurements were repeated 20 times and we used the average runtime as value per query and workload to create the individual *hot* and *cold* bars. Most surprising are the individually huge slowdowns of almost $-3\,\mathrm{x}$ for a single query in Fig. 9(a). We found, that mainly short running queries, i.e., around 50 ms, are affected by larger slowdowns. The same observations hold true for Figs. 9(b) to 9(d). Figure 9(c) has the same configuration as Fig. 8, yet it also exhibits individual slowdowns for some queries. We see the inherent asynchronous processing as potential issue, since it can result in unpredictable runtime behavior. For example, the workers monitor themselves, if any work has been performed. If not, a worker will put itself to sleep for a grace period, to avoid infinite polling. If a message arrives just after starting the sleep cycle, its processing is delayed. We tested the influence of the sleep cycles with varying sleep times, ranging from 0 ms to 100 ms. Completely disabling sleeps leads to permanent polling, which in turn produces more pressure on the local message buffers. The permanent checks for messages will then lead to further decreased performance, since enqueuing messages can only be done if the buffers are not locked. Thus, on the one hand, sleep cycles can help to increase the system's throughput. On the other hand, ill-timed sleep cycles have varying impacts on the performance of a single query.

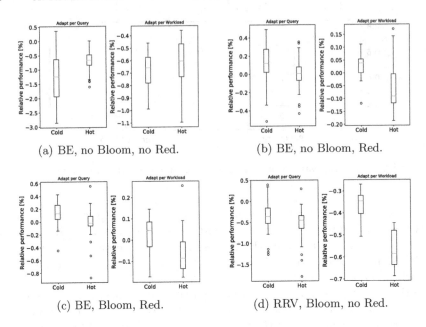

(a) BE, no Bloom, no Red.

(b) BE, no Bloom, Red.

(c) BE, Bloom, Red.

(d) RRV, Bloom, no Red.

Fig. 9. Speedup variances for different configurations with 64 partitions.

5   Related Work

Graph partitioning is state-of-the-art among many systems, e.g., Ligra [26] or Galois [19]. However, the reasoning behind the selected partitioning algorithms is rarely stated. We have shown that using one specific partitioning scheme for all graphs or workloads is not the optimal solution and may result in huge slowdown factors, compared to the possibly best system configuration.

Another NUMA-aware graph analytics system was produced by [31] with the name Polymer. In order to cope with the NUMA effect, they leverage a novel page allocation method. That is, to alleviate the inherent random memory access from graph algorithms. Another hardware-conscious optimization is their hierarchical scheduling, which helps with expensive thread level synchronization among NUMA-nodes. Like the other authors, we found random memory accesses and synchronization to be problematic. However, this is already addressed by the synthesis of the architectural principles, as stated in Sect. 2. Since NEMESYS works completely asynchronous, we do not need a concrete scheduler. Operators are always executed, whenever a message arrives and because of the data isolation, no further synchronization is necessary.

A system with vertex centric graph processing is Pregel+ [30]. This system was considered as the fastest graph engine [17]. They use MPI to realize the inter-worker communication and replicating a subset of vertices among partitions as an optimization method for message reduction. However, we showed in Sect. 4.3 that redundancy can be outperformed by an intelligent Bloom filter.

6   Conclusions

In this paper, we presented NEMESYS, our research prototype for in-memory graph pattern matching on symmetric multiprocessor systems. We showed that a scalable graph pattern matching on such servers is possible by leveraging modern architecture principles. Furthermore, we demonstrated a set of hand-crafted optimization techniques, which benefit from each other to allow for scalable performance.

We envision to continue our research on more sophisticated optimization methods, such as an adaptive graph storage or continuous online adaption. Furthermore, we want to develop a more robust asynchronous processing model to allow for runtime guarantees and more predictable performance.

Acknowledgment. This work was partly funded by the German Research Foundation (DFG) within the CRC 912 (HAEC).

References

1. Angles, R.: A comparison of current graph database models. In: ICDE Workshop, pp. 171–177 (2012)
2. Appuswamy, R., Anadiotis, A., Porobic, D., Iman, M., Ailamaki, A.: Analyzing the impact of system architecture on the scalability of OLTP engines for high-contention workloads. PVLDB **11**(2), 121–134 (2017)
3. Bagan, G., Bonifati, A., Ciucanu, R., Fletcher, G.H.L., Lemay, A., Advokaat, N.: gmark: schema-driven generation of graphs and queries. IEEE Trans. Knowl. Data Eng. **29**(4), 856–869 (2017)
4. Bishop, C.M.: Pattern Recognition and Machine Learning. Springer, New York (2006)
5. Bloom, B.H.: Space/time trade-offs in hash coding with allowable errors. Commun. ACM **13**(7), 422–426 (1970)
6. Färber, F., Cha, S.K., Primsch, J., Bornhövd, C., Sigg, S., Lehner, W.: SAP HANA database: data management for modern business applications. SIGMOD Rec. **40**(4), 45–51 (2011)
7. Hey, T., Tansley, S., Tolle, K.M. (eds.): The Fourth Paradigm: Data-Intensive Scientific Discovery. Microsoft Research (2009)
8. Hyafil, L., Rivest, R.L.: Graph partitioning and constructing optimal decision trees are polynomial complete problems. IRIA, Laboratoire de Recherche en Informatique et Automatique (1973)
9. Karypis, G., Kumar, V.: MeTis: unstructured graph partitioning and sparse matrix ordering system, Version 5.1 (2013). http://www.cs.umn.edu/~metis
10. Kiefer, T., Schlegel, B., Lehner, W.: Experimental evaluation of NUMA effects on database management systems. In: BTW, pp. 185–204 (2013)
11. Kissinger, T., Kiefer, T., Schlegel, B., Habich, D., Molka, D., Lehner, W.: ERIS: A numa-aware in-memory storage engine for analytical workload. In: ADMS@VLDB, pp. 74–85 (2014)
12. Krause, A., Ebner, F., Habich, D., Lehner, W.: Trading memory versus workload overhead in graph pattern matching on multiprocessor systems. In: DATA, pp. 400–407 (2019)

13. Krause, A., Kissinger, T., Habich, D., Lehner, W.: Nemesys - A showcase of data oriented near memory graph processing. In: Proceedings of the 2019 International Conference on Management of Data, SIGMOD Conference 2019, Amsterdam, The Netherlands, June 30–July 5, pp. 1945–1948 (2019)
14. Krause, A., Kissinger, T., Habich, D., Voigt, H., Lehner, W.: Partitioning strategy selection for in-memory graph pattern matching on multiprocessor systems. In: Rivera, F.F., Pena, T.F., Cabaleiro, J.C. (eds.) Euro-Par 2017. LNCS, vol. 10417, pp. 149–163. Springer, Cham (2017). https://doi.org/10.1007/978-3-319-64203-1_11
15. Krause, A., Ungethüm, A., Kissinger, T., Habich, D., Lehner, W.: Asynchronous graph pattern matching on multiprocessor systems. In: Kirikova, M., Nørvåg, K., Papadopoulos, G.A., Gamper, J., Wrembel, R., Darmont, J., Rizzi, S. (eds.) ADBIS 2017. CCIS, vol. 767, pp. 45–53. Springer, Cham (2017). https://doi.org/10.1007/978-3-319-67162-8_6
16. Leis, V., Boncz, P.A., Kemper, A., Neumann, T.: Morsel-driven parallelism: a numa-aware query evaluation framework for the many-core age. In: SIGMOD, pp. 743–754 (2014)
17. Lu, Y., Cheng, J., Yan, D., Wu, H.: Large-scale distributed graph computing systems: an experimental evaluation. PVLDB 8(3), 281–292 (2014)
18. McCune, R.R., Weninger, T., Madey, G.: Thinking like a vertex: a survey of vertex-centric frameworks for large-scale distributed graph processing. ACM Comput. Surv. 48(2), 25:1–25:39 (2015)
19. Nguyen, D., Lenharth, A., Pingali, K.: A lightweight infrastructure for graph analytics. In: SOSP, pp. 456–471 (2013)
20. Ogata, H., Fujibuchi, W., Goto, S., Kanehisa, M.: A heuristic graph comparison algorithm and its application to detect functionally related enzyme clusters. Nucleic Acids Res. 28(20), 4021–4028 (2000)
21. Otte, E., Rousseau, R.: Social network analysis: a powerful strategy, also for the information sciences. J. Inf. Sci. 28(6), 441–453 (2002)
22. Pandis, I., Johnson, R., Hardavellas, N., Ailamaki, A.: Data-oriented transaction execution. PVLDB 3(1), 928–939 (2010)
23. Pandit, S., Chau, D.H., Wang, S., Faloutsos, C.: NetProbe: a fast and scalable system for fraud detection in online auction networks. In: WWW, pp. 201–210 (2007)
24. Rother, C., Kolmogorov, V., Blake, A.: "grabcut": interactive foreground extraction using iterated graph cuts. ACM Trans. Graph. 23(3), 309–314 (2004)
25. Sahu, S., Mhedhbi, A., Salihoglu, S., Lin, J., Özsu, M.T.: The ubiquity of large graphs and surprising challenges of graph processing. PVLDB 11(4), 420–431 (2017)
26. Shun, J., Blelloch, G.E.: Ligra: a lightweight graph processing framework for shared memory. In: PPoPP, pp. 135–146 (2013)
27. Tas, M.K., Kaya, K., Saule, E.: Greed is good: optimistic algorithms for bipartite-graph partial coloring on multicore architectures. CoRR abs/1701.02628 (2017)
28. Weiss, C., Karras, P., Bernstein, A.: Hexastore: sextuple indexing for semantic web data management. PVLDB 1(1), 1008–1019 (2008)
29. Wood, P.T.: Query languages for graph databases. SIGMOD Rec. 41(1), 50–60 (2012)
30. Yan, D., Cheng, J., Lu, Y., Ng, W.: Effective techniques for message reduction and load balancing in distributed graph computation. In: WWW, pp. 1307–1317 (2015)
31. Zhang, K., Chen, R., Chen, H.: NUMA-aware graph-structured analytics. In: PPoPP, pp. 183–193 (2015)

A Graph-Based Approach Towards Risk Alerting for COVID-19 Spread

Aibo Guo, QianZhen Zhang, and Xiang Zhao[✉]

Science and Technology on Information System Engineering Laboratory,
National University of Defense Technology, Changsha, Hunan, China
{aiboguo,zhangqianzhen18,xiangzhao}@nudt.edu.cn

Abstract. With the spiraling pandemic of the Coronavirus Disease 2019 (COVID-19), it has becoming inherently important to disseminate accurate and timely information about the disease. Due to the ubiquity of Internet connectivity and smart devices, social sensing is emerging as a dynamic sensing paradigm to collect real-time contacts between both people and places. For example, we can rely on the Bluetooth signals that smartphones can both send out and receive to collect the real-time user contacts data. Based on the contacts data, in this paper, we investigate to propose an efficient approach to calculate the risk level of each person to have COVID-19. It can help pinpoint the people who need to be isolated. (1) We model the real-time contact data between people as a straming graph, which is a constantly growing sequence of edges. (2) We provide a risk alerting model to find the people who came in contact with someone having COVID-19. (3) In addition, we design efficient algorithms to calculate the risk level of each person and update the levels in real time. (4) Extensive experiments verify the effectiveness and efficiency of our approach.

1 Introduction

Public health experts say tracing who people infected with the coronavirus have been in contact with is a critical step in easing social distancing restrictions. Thanks to the pervasion of smart devices, some softwares, i.e., TWS[1] and Trace-Together[2], have been designed for collecting the real-time contact data between people. The technologies used in them rely on the Bluetooth signals that smartphones can both send out and receive. Using Bluetooth signals can capture the contact records between users and each contact record is used to answer the question "was user A in contact with user B at time T?" Time is important since there maybe multi-times contacts between two users. Based on the collected data, we design efficient algorithms to find the potential users who may have COVID-19.

---

[1] http://easytws.com/.

[2] https://www.tracetogether.gov.sg/.

© Springer Nature Switzerland AG 2020
L. Qin et al. (Eds.): SFDI 2020/LSGDA 2020, CCIS 1281, pp. 63–69, 2020.
https://doi.org/10.1007/978-3-030-61133-0_5

From the perspective of data management, there may exist two types of solutions—relational and graph-based—to the user-contact data. Using relational databases does not always offer an elegant solution towards efficiently searching, and still lacks best practices currently. In this paper, we design a graph-based solution, attributed to the fact that the user-contact data is a universal graph model of data. As a result, we model the use-contact data as a streaming graph $\mathbb{G}$, which is a constantly growing of edges $\{\sigma_1, \sigma_2, \ldots, \sigma_x\}$ where each σ_i arrives a particular time t_i. Note that, σ_i may have multi-timestamps since σ_i will appear multi-times in $\mathbb{G}$. Specially, we only collect each user's contact data in the prior 14 days. This is because the incubation period of COVID-19 is 1~14 days.

In order to find the users who came in contact with someone having COVID-19, we propose a risk alerting model to assign each user a risk-level, denoted as RL. That is, when a user tests positive for COVID-19, we assign RL–1, RL–2 and RL–3 to the users who are one-hop, two-hops and three-hops neighbors, respectively. Furthermore, if a user does not have COVID-19 after 14 days or all the neighbors of the user have no risk-level, we can remove the user's risk-level directly. Note that, the time constraints are important in this model, more details will described in Sect. 3.

To achieve real-time responsiveness is the foremost problem we need to face when updating the risk-levels over the streaming graph $\mathbb{G}$; if not, we cannot get efficient updating results over a time span. A naïve method to solve this problem is to recompute risk-levels for the users who have COVID-19. However, it can be prohibitively costly, and we will redo the work. Instead, we design an incremental updating algorithm to calculate the risk-level for each new user-contact record and update the risk-levels for corresponding users only from the newly user who tests positive.

Contributions. In short, we make the following contributions:

- We model the user-contact records collected from the Bluetooth signals of corresponding users' smartphones as a streaming graph.
- Based on the streaming graph, we design a risk alerting model which help to trace the people have been in contact with someone infected with the coronavirus.
- We propose an incremental updating algorithm to update the risk-levels for corresponding users.

Experiment results demonstrate the effectiveness and efficiency of our techniques.

2 Preliminaries

A typical data schema for the *topology of user-contact records* consists of a number of vertices representing users, and links between the nodes representing contacts between them. This schema naturally translates to a vertex-labeled undirected graph $g = (V, E, L)$.

Definition 1 (Streaming graph). *A* Streaming graph $\mathbb{G}$ *is a constantly grow-ing sequence of undirected edges* $\{\sigma_1, \sigma_2, \ldots, \sigma_x\}$ *where each* σ_i *arrives at a par-ticular time* t_i *(*$t_i < t_j$ *when* $i < j$*).* t_i *is also referred to as the timestamp of* σ_i*. Each edge* σ_i *has two labelled vertices and two edges are connected if and only if they share one common endpoint.*

Since two users may have multiple contacts with each other, there may be multi-edges between two vertices in $\mathbb{G}$ representing contact records between them in different timestamps. For each user's contact records, we use the *time-based sliding window model*, where a sliding window W defines a timespan with fixed duration $|W|$. Here, we set $|W| = 14$ since the incubation period of COVID-19 is $1 \sim 14$ days. An example of a streaming graph $\mathbb{G}$ is shown in Fig. 1(a). For each vertex, i.e., v_1 or v_2, we record the corresponding edges within 14 days.

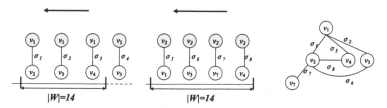

(a) Graph stream under time window of size 14 for each vertex   (b) A snapshot of the streaming graph

Fig. 1. An example of the streaming graph

Definition 2 (A Snapshot of a Streaming Graph). *Given a streaming graph* $\mathbb{G}$ *at current time point* t*, the current snapshot of* $\mathbb{G}$ *is a graph* $\mathbb{G}_t = (\mathbb{V}_t, \mathbb{E}_t)$ *where* $\mathbb{E}_t$ *is the set of edges that occurs on each vertex at time* t*.*

Figure 1(b) shows the snapshot of Fig. 1(a) at time point σ_1.

3   Risk Alerting Model

In this section, we design a risk alerting model for COVID-19 spread, namely, RAMC, to trace the people who have been in contact with someone infected with the coronavirus. The model consists of two steps: (1) assign each user in the streaming graph a risk-level according to the users who have COVID-19; (2) eliminate the risk-level of a user whose status becomes safe.

3.1   Risk-Level Assignment

We rely on the BFS search algorithm to assign each user who has been in contact with someone infected with the coronavirus directly or indirectly a risk-level.

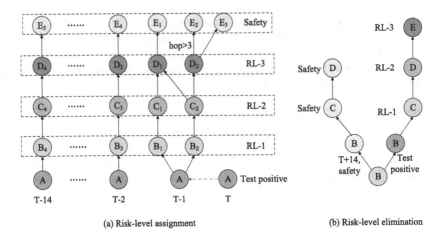

Fig. 2. Risk alerting model

Given a vertex $\mathcal{V}$ in $\mathbb{G}$ that represents a user who tests positive for COVID-19 at timepoint T, we can obtain corresponding contact records of $\mathcal{V}$ from T-1 to T-14. Here, we only assign the risk-levels for 1-hop to 3-hops neighbors of $\mathcal{V}$. In detail, for each neighbor $\mathcal{V}'$ of $\mathcal{V}$, we first set $\mathsf{RL}(\mathcal{V}') = 1$ where $\mathsf{RL}(\mathcal{V}')$ represents the risk-level of $\mathcal{V}'$. Note that, there may be multi-edges between $\mathcal{V}$ and $\mathcal{V}'$ with different timepoints. The earliest timestamp, denoted as $\mathsf{ET}(\mathcal{V}')$, will be used in the BFS process to calculate the risk-levels for other vertices. Then for each unvisited neighbor $\mathcal{V}''$ of $\mathcal{V}'$, we check whether there is an edge $\langle \mathcal{V}', \mathcal{V}'' \rangle$ with timestamp $t_{v''}$ such that $t_{v''} \geq \mathsf{ET}(\mathcal{V}')$; if so, we set $\mathsf{RL}(\mathcal{V}'') = 2$. What's more, we set $\mathsf{ET}(\mathcal{V}'') = t_{v''}$ if $t_{v''}$ is the earliest timestamp that can confirm above condition. Specially, there may be another neighbor $\mathcal{V}^*$ of $\mathcal{V}''$ and $\mathsf{RL}(\mathcal{V}^*) = 1$. As a result, we need also calculate another value for $\mathsf{ET}(\mathcal{V}'')$ based on the edges between $\mathcal{V}''$ and $\mathcal{V}^*$. In this case, we set $\mathsf{ET}(\mathcal{V}'')$ as the smallest value between all the values. Finally, we calculate the risk-levels for the 3-hops neighbors of $\mathcal{V}$ in a similar manner. Omitted in the interest of space, we do not describe here.

Figure 3(a) gives the example to calculate corresponding users' risk-levels when the user A tests positive for COVID-19 at time T.

3.2 Risk-Level Elimination

In our model, a user's risk-level will be eliminated if we can make sure the status of the user is safe.

For each vertex $\mathcal{V}$ in $\mathbb{G}$ with its $\mathsf{RL}(\mathcal{V}) = 1$ at timestamp T, if (1) the user represented by the vertex $\mathcal{V}$ has no symptoms of COVID-19 at timestamp T+14; and (2) there is no user represented by the neighbor of $\mathcal{V}$ who tests positive for COVID-19 between time T and T+14, we can eliminate the risk-level of $\mathcal{V}$. As for other vertices $\{\mathcal{V}'\}$, we check whether (1) there exists a neighbor $\mathcal{V}''$ with its $\mathsf{RL}(\mathcal{V}'') > \mathsf{RL}(\mathcal{V}')$; and (2) there is an edge $\langle \mathcal{V}', \mathcal{V}'' \rangle$ with its timestamp later than $\mathsf{ET}(\mathcal{V}'')$. If not, we can eliminate the risk-level of $\mathcal{V}'$. Figure 3(b) shows the elimination process when the status of becomes safe.

4   Incremental Algorithms

In this section, we propose an effective algorithm, namely, updateRL, to update the risk-levels of corresponding users when a new contact record is added into the streaming graph $\mathbb{G}$.

Now we explain updateRL, which is invoked for each edge insertion $\langle v, v' \rangle$ with timestamp t_1. Firstly, updateRL checks the risk-levels of v and v', respectively. Note that, each user who tests positive for COVID-19 will not have new contact record. As a result, we have the following two cases that may cause the update of the risk-levels.

① **From RL -3 to RL -2.** Suppose that $\mathsf{RL}(v') = 3$ and $\mathsf{RL}(v) = 1$. If $t_1 > \mathsf{ET}(v)$, updateRL transits $\mathsf{RL}(v')$ from 3 to 2 and sets $\mathsf{ET}(v') = t_1$.

② **From safety to RL -2 (or RL -3).** Suppose that the status of v' is safety and $\mathsf{RL}(v) = 1$ (or $\mathsf{RL}(v) = 2$). If $t_1 > \mathsf{ET}(v)$, updateRL sets $\mathsf{RL}(v') = 2$ (or $\mathsf{RL}(v') = 3$) and sets $\mathsf{ET}(v') = t_1$.

5   Experiments

In this section, we report experiment results and analyses.

5.1   Experiment Setup

The proposed algorithms were implemented using C++, running on a Linux machine with two Core Intel Xeon CPU 2.2 Ghz and 32 GB main memory. Particularly, three algorithms were implemented: (1) RAMC, our algorithm to assign and eliminate corresponding users' risk levels; (2) updateRL, our update algorithm for newly added contact record; (3) updateRL-R, our algorithm that recomputes the users' risk-levels from the uses who have COVID-19.

Fig. 3. The mainly process of RAMC

Since we do not have the real-life user-contact records, we use two human contact temporal networks, i.e., HS [1] and PS [1] to simulate the user-contact records. HS contains 2,367,984 triples while the edge insertions consist of 225,124 triples. PS contains 1,254,132 triples while the edge insertions consists of 112,607 triples. We also use a synthetic streaming social graph data LSBench which contains 23,549,621 triples.

5.2 Evaluating the Effectiveness of RAMC

In this subsection, we evaluate the effectiveness of our proposed risk alerting model. We ran experiments on HS and PS and randomly set 1000 vertices as the users who test positive for COVID-19 on both datasets. According to the experiment results, we find that the risk-levels of corresponding users can be efficient calculated within 600ms on both datasets. Figure 3 shows the partial visualization results in our experiment by using HS dataset. In detail, the first picture shows the partial initial graph; the second picture shows some users who have COVID-19 are emerged in the graph; the third graph shows the risk-level assignment process and the last picture shows the risk-level elimination process.

5.3 Varying the Edge Insertion Size

In this subsection, we evaluate the impact of edge insertions on the performance of updateRL and updateRL-R. We vary the number newly-inserted triples from $25K (= 25 \times 10^3)$ 100K in 25K increments on both datasets. Figure 4(1) and Fig. 4(2) shows the processing time for each algorithm. We see that updateRL has consistently better performance than updateRL-R. What's more, the figure reads a non-exponential increase as edge insertion size grows. Specially, updateRL outperforms updateRL-R by up to 42.78 times.

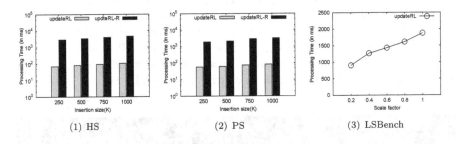

(1) HS   (2) PS   (3) LSBench

Fig. 4. Experiment results

5.4 Varying Data Sizes

We evaluate the scalability of updateRL on LSBench dataset. We randomly sampled about 20% to 100% from the LSBench dataset so that the data and result distribution remain approximately the same with the whole dataset. Figure 4(3) reads a non-exponential increase as data size grows. In generally, the processing time grows at no more than twice the speed of growth in the size of the dataset. The scalability suggests that updateRL can handle reasonably large real-life graphs as those existing algorithms for deterministic graphs.

6   Related Work

Representative algorithms for pattern matching/search from the streaming graph include TurFlux [2] and TreeMat [3], etc. However, these work are about continuous subgraph matching and cannot be used in our model. To the best of our knowledge, this is among the first attempts to design a risk alerting for COVID-19 spread based on a graph search algorithm. We believe that this work will benefit for fighting COVID-19.

7   Conclusion

In this paper, we have investigated a systematic graph-based approach to risk alerting for COVID-19 spread. We design a risk alerting model to help trace the people who have been in contact with someone infected with the coronavirus and propose an incremental updating algorithm to update the risk-levels.

References

1. Fournet, J., Barrat, A.: Contact patterns among high school students. CoRR, vol. abs/1409.5318 (2014)
2. Kim, K., et al.: TurboFlux: a fast continuous subgraph matching system for streaming graph data. In: Proceedings of the 2018 International Conference on Management of Data, SIGMOD Conference 2018, Houston, TX, USA, 10–15 June 2018, pp. 411–426 (2018)
3. Zhang, Q., Guo, D., Zhao, X., Guo, A.: On continuously matching of evolving graph patterns. In: Proceedings of the 28th ACM International Conference on Information and Knowledge Management, CIKM 2019, Beijing, China, 3–7 November 2019, pp. 2237–2240 (2019)

Distributed Graph Analytics
with Datalog Queries in Flink

Muhammad Imran$^{(\boxtimes)}$, Gábor E. Gévay, and Volker Markl

Technische Universität Berlin, Berlin, Germany
`muhammad.imran@campus.tu-berlin.de`

Abstract. Large-scale, parallel graph processing has been in demand over the past decade. Succinct program structure and efficient execution are among the essential requirements of graph processing frameworks. In this paper, we present *Cog*, which executes Datalog programs on the Apache Flink distributed dataflow system. We chose Datalog for its compact program structure and Flink for its efficiency. We implemented a parallel *semi-naive evaluation* algorithm exploiting Flink's *delta iteration* to propagate only the tuples that need to be further processed to the subsequent iterations. Flink's delta iteration feature reduces the overhead present in acyclic dataflow systems, such as Spark, when evaluating recursive queries, hence making it more efficient. We demonstrated in our experiments that Cog outperformed BigDatalog, the state-of-the-art distributed Datalog evaluation system, in most of the tests.

Keywords: Datalog · Recursive queries · Graph processing · Cyclic dataflows

1 Introduction

Graphs can represent numerous real-world problems. With the advancement of the web and the vast number of its users, *efficiently* processing massive graphs is becoming essential. Efficiency can be achieved by scaling out computations to a cluster and thereby reducing computation times. Existing state-of-the-art systems that choose Datalog as their language, such as BigDatalog [18] and Myria [20], suffer either from significant scheduling overhead or shuffling overhead to perform each iteration of a graph computation.

From the users' perspective, having concise programming constructs that are easy to learn is also an essential factor to consider. Existing large-scale graph processing systems, such as Gelly [25] of Flink [6], or GraphX [11] of Spark [21], do not provide *conciseness* and require significant effort to perform even simple analytics. These systems are complex and verbose due to their APIs being embedded in general-purpose languages, such as Java or Scala. In contrast, Datalog offers more conciseness [13], i.e., shorter programs, and therefore makes it easier to implement graph-analytics or artificial intelligence algorithms.

© Springer Nature Switzerland AG 2020
L. Qin et al. (Eds.): SFDI 2020/LSGDA 2020, CCIS 1281, pp. 70–83, 2020.
https://doi.org/10.1007/978-3-030-61133-0_6

This paper presents *Cog*, which is a Flink-based evaluation system of positive Datalog programs that do not contain aggregates. The core feature of Cog is the efficient evaluation of Datalog's linear recursive queries by exploiting Flink's native delta iterations [8]. Flink is particularly suitable to evaluate Datalog programs because of its ability to evaluate iterative algorithms efficiently by cyclic dataflows. From relational queries (i.e., join, union, recursive queries) to graph processing algorithms (e.g., transitive closure) can conveniently be implemented in Cog, and executed on a cluster in a scalable way.

Contributions. We made the following contributions:

- We created logical plans for Datalog programs to be executed on a distributed dataflow engine. The logical plan also includes an explicit representation of recursive queries.
- We implemented a Datalog query execution engine that exploits Flink's *delta iteration* feature, which we found to be particularly well-suited for the classic *semi-naive* Datalog evaluation algorithm.
- We experimentally confirmed that evaluating recursive queries of Datalog using Flink's delta iteration performs better than the Spark-based BigDatalog [18] system, which is the state of the art in scalable Datalog execution.

2 Preliminaries

We will now briefly review Datalog and Apache Flink. We will also show why Flink's delta iteration is suitable to evaluate Datalog programs efficiently.

2.1 Datalog

Datalog [7] is a rule-based query language. Each rule is expressed as a *function-free* horn clause, such as h :- $b_1, ..., b_n$, where h is the *head* predicate of the rule, and each b_i is a *body* predicate separated by a comma "," which represents the logical AND ($\land$). A predicate is also known as a *relation*. A *fact* is a tuple in a relation. A Datalog rule is *recursive* if the head predicate of a rule also appears in the body of the rule. After evaluating all body predicates, the produced facts are assigned to the head predicate of the rule. A relation that comes into existence as a result of a rule execution is called an *intensional database (IDB)*. A stored relation is called an *extensional database (EDB)*. The transitive closure (TC) program in Datalog is given in Listing 1 as an example. In the example, the predicate `arc` is an EDB, whereas the predicate `tc` is an IDB. The rule r_2 is a recursive rule as it has the predicate `tc` in its head and body. A *join* is created between `tc` and `arc` predicates in rule r_2, and the resulting facts are assigned to the head predicate `tc`.

```
r₁: tc(X, Y) :- arc(X,Y).
r₂: tc(X, Y) :- tc(X,Z),arc(Z,Y).
```

Listing 1. Transitive Closure (TC) program in Datalog.

2.2   Apache Flink

Apache Flink [6] is a distributed dataflow system. While nowadays Flink is mostly known for efficient stream processing, it initially focused on iterative dataflows in batch computations [8]. In this paper, we rely only on its batch-processing capabilities for translating Datalog programs to iterative dataflows.

Flink's batch API is centered around the DataSet class, which represents a scalable collection of tuples. DataSets offer numerous data processing operators (such as map, filter, join), which create new DataSets. From a Flink program written using DataSet operators, Flink creates a *dataflow job*, a directed graph where nodes represent data processing operators and edges represent data transfers. Flink executes these dataflow jobs in a scalable way, by parallelizing the execution of each dataflow node on the available worker machines in a cluster. Flink executes all operators *lazily*, i.e., the operator is first only added to the dataflow job as a node, and then later executed as part of the dataflow job execution. The dataflow job is executed when Flink encounters an *action* operator (such as counting the elements in a DataSet, or printing its elements), or when the user explicitly triggers the execution of the dataflow job that was built up so far. Flink provides libraries and APIs to perform relational querying, graph processing [25], and machine learning.

Iteration APIs. Flink supports two types of iterations: *bulk* and *delta*. Bulk iterations are general-purpose iterations, where the result of each iteration is a completely new *solution set* computed from the previous iteration's solution set [8]. On the other hand, delta iterations are a form of incremental iterations, which is suitable for iterative algorithms with sparse computational dependencies, i.e., where each iteration's result differs only partially from the previous iteration. In the context of Datalog evaluation, the semantics of delta iteration matches well with the principles of the classic *semi-naive* evaluation algorithm [3], thus making it suitable for recursive Datalog program executions: applying a recursive Datalog rule once often adds only a small number of tuples compared to the total result size.

Iteration Execution in Cyclic Dataflow Jobs. Flink executes iterative programs written using the above iteration APIs in a single, *cyclic* dataflow job, i.e., where an iteration's result is fed back as the next iteration's input through a backwards dataflow edge. This is in contrast to many other dataflow systems, such as Apache Spark [21], which execute iterative programs as a series of acyclic dataflow jobs. Flink's cyclic dataflows are more efficient for several reasons:

- Having a single dataflow job for all iterations avoids the inherent overhead of launching a dataflow job on a cluster of machines. The main overhead of launching a job is the (centralized) scheduling of the constituent tasks of the job to a large number of machines.
- Operator lifespans can be extended to all iterations. (Whereas in Spark, new operators are launched for each iteration.) This enables Flink to naturally perform two optimizations:

- In the case of a delta iteration, Flink can keep the solution set in the state of an operator that spans all iterations. Thereby, the solution set does not need to be newly rebuilt for each iteration, and instead small changes can be efficiently accommodated by just modifying the existing operator state.
- Loop-invariant datasets, i.e., datasets that are reused without changes in each iteration (e.g., `arc` in Listing 1), can be more efficiently handled. For example, when one input of an equi-join is a loop-invariant dataset, the join operator can build a hash table of the loop-invariant input only once, and just probe that same hash table at every iteration.

3 Cog

In this section, we discuss Cog, our system that executes Datalog programs on Flink. We implemented positive Datalog without aggregation. Cog parses a Datalog program, converts the parsed program to an intermediate representation, creates and optimizes a logical plan, and finally creates a Flink plan for execution. Listing 2 shows an example for writing Datalog programs in Cog.

```
1   DatalogEnvironment datalogEnv = DatalogEnvironment.create(flinkEnv);
2   String transitiveClos =
3           "tc(X,Y) :- graph(X,Y).\n" +
4           "tc(X,Y) :- tc(X,Z),graph(Z,Y).\n";
5   String query = "tc(X,Y)?";
6   // Read input data using standard Flink operators:
7   DataSet<Tuple2<Integer, Integer>> inputGraph = ...;
8   // Register it for use in Datalog queries:
9   datalogEnv.registerDataSet("graph", inputGraph);
10  // Execute the query:
11  DataSet<Tuple2<Integer, Integer>> result =
12    datalogEnv.executeQuery(transitiveClos, query);
13  // The result is a standard Flink DataSet, which we can further process:
14  System.out.println(result.count());
```

Listing 2. An implementation of Transitive Closure (TC) program in Cog.

3.1 Query Representation and Planning

Query Representation. A parsed Datalog program is represented in the form of a *predicate connection graph (PCG)* [2]. Figure 1 shows the PCG for the TC query as an example. A PCG is an annotated AND/OR tree, i.e., it has alternating levels of AND and OR nodes. The AND nodes represent head predicates of rules, and the OR nodes represent body predicates of rules. The root and the leaves are always OR nodes. The root of the tree represents the query predicate.

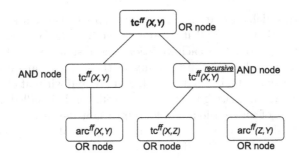

Fig. 1. Predicate Connection Graph (PCG) for Transitive Closure (TC) query.

Logical Plan. We used the algebra module of Apache Calcite [5] to represent logical plans. Calcite provides numerous operators (such as join, project, union) to represent a query algebra. To evaluate recursive Datalog queries, the *repeat union* operator is an important one. The repeat union operator has two child nodes: *seed* and *iterative*. The seed node represents facts generated by non-recursive rule(s), whereas the iterative node represents facts generated by the recursive rule(s). The semantics of the repeat union operator are as follows: it first evaluates the seed node, whose result will be the input to the first iteration; then, it repeatedly evaluates the iterative node, using the previous iteration's result as input. The evaluation terminates when the result does not change between two iterations. Figure 2 shows the logical plan created for the TC program given in Listing 1. The Calcite-based logical plans are then transformed into Flink's own logical plans and then to Flink's `DataSet`-based plan. During these transformations, standard relational optimizations are also performed.

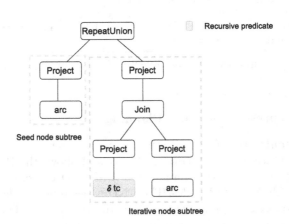

Fig. 2. Cog logical plan for Transitive Closure (TC) query.

Flink Plan. The optimized logical plans are translated into Flink's `DataSet`-based plans. We utilized existing Flink `DataSet` operators for scans, joins, unions, filters, and projections. However, we implemented a translation from the *repeat union* and *transient table scan* operators to Flink `DataSet` operators to enable the execution of recursive queries, which we discuss in the next subsection.

3.2 Semi-Naive Evaluation in the Flink DataSet API

Semi-naive evaluation [3] is an efficient way to evaluate Datalog programs. With this technique, each iteration processes only the tuples that were produced by the previous iteration, and thus redundant work is eliminated. The final result is obtained by the union of the results produced by each iteration. Algorithm 1 shows the pseudocode of semi-naive evaluation. In the algorithm, *seed* represents the non-recursive rule(s) (e.g., r_1 in TC), whereas *recursive* represents one execution of the recursive rule(s) (e.g., r_2 in TC). W represents the *differential* that is calculated in each iteration, and S stores the final result at the end.

Algorithm 1	Algorithm 2
1: **function** SEMI-NAIVE(*seed, recursive*)	1: **function** FLINK-DELTA(S, W, u, δ, key)
2: $S \leftarrow seed$	2:
3: $W \leftarrow seed$	3:
4: **while** $W \neq \emptyset$ **do**	4: **while** $W \neq \emptyset$ **do**
5: $D \leftarrow recursive(W) - S$	5: $D \leftarrow u(S, W)$
6: $W \leftarrow D$	6: $W \leftarrow \delta(D, S, W)$
7: $S \leftarrow S \cup D$	7: $S = S \cup D$

Compare Algorithm 1 with Algorithm 2, which shows the general template of a Flink Delta Iteration. There is an initial solution set (S), and an initial workset (W), and then each iteration first computes a differential (D), which is to be merged into the solution set (Line 7), and also computes the workset for the next iteration. Note that the merging into the solution set is denoted by $\dot\cup$, which means that elements that not yet appear in the solution set should be added, and elements which have the same key as an element already in the solution set should override the old element: $S \dot\cup D = D \cup \{s \in S : \neg\exists d \in D | key(d) = key(s)\}$. We can see that with the following mapping, a Flink Delta Iteration performs exactly the semi-naive evaluation of a Datalog query:
$S = seed$; $W = seed$; $u(S, W) = recursive(W) - S$; $\delta(D, S, W) = D$; $key(x) = x$. Note that by choosing the key to be the entire tuple, we make the $\dot\cup$ behave as a standard union.

When translating from Cog logical plans, the semi-naive evaluation is implemented to translate the *repeat union* operator to `DataSet` operators. Listing 3 presents this translation. We use a CoGroup operation to compute which of the tuples created in this iteration are not already in the solution set. We also use this CoGroup operation to eliminate duplicates. The work set propagates the differential to the next iteration. The solution set accumulates the output of all iterations. The work set and the solution set are always kept in memory for efficiency. Note that all the created Flink operators are evaluated *lazily* upon the call of a sink operator. Figure 3 shows the Flink plan for the TC query as an example. The sync task is a special operator inserted by Flink, which waits for all operators in the iteration body to perform one iteration, and then signals to the Flink runtime that the next iteration can start.

```scala
1   // Evaluate seed node (non-recursive rules).
2   val seedDs = seed.translateToDatasetPlan(tableEnv, queryConfig)
3   val workSet: DataSet[Row] = seedDs
4   val solutionSet: DataSet[Row] = seedDs
5   // Define delta iteration.
6   val iteration = solutionSet.iterateDelta(
7                   workSet, // initial workset
8                   Int.MaxValue, // max number of iterations
9                   seedDs.allFields) // the key is composed of all the fields
10  // Register the work set as a temporary table to the Flink catalog
11  // so that it can be used by the iterative node.
12  updateCatalog(tableEnv, iteration.getWorkset, "workset-temp-table")
13  // Translate the subtree of the iterative node (recursive rules).
14  // The subtree contains a Transient Table Scan operator, which is the
15  // representation of the recursive reference (shown in yellow in Fig. 2.).
16  // We added a rule (not shown here) to translate this as a reference to the
17  // "workset-temp-table", i.e., the DataSet representing the workset.
18  val iterativeDs =
19      iterativeSubplan.translateToDatasetPlan(tableEnv, queryConfig)
20  // Compute the difference between the newly produced tuples
21  // and the solution set by a CoGroup operation. Flink will probe
22  // the hash table that it stores for the solution set throughout
23  // the job execution.
24  val delta = iterativeDs
25      .coGroup(iteration.getSolutionSet)
26      .where("*").equalTo("*") // all fields are included in the key
27      .with(new DeduplicatingMinusCoGroupFunction[Row]())
28  // At the end of each iteration, the delta is used both as
29  // the set of tuples to be added to the solution set (1st argument),
30  // and the next workset (2nd argument).
31  val result = iteration.closeWith(delta, delta)
```

Listing 3. An implementation of the classic semi-naive Datalog evaluation algorithm in Flink. We mapped the algorithm to just a few standard Flink API calls.

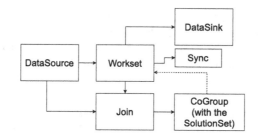

Fig. 3. The Flink plan for Transitive Closure (TC) query. Some operators are omitted/combined for clarity. Note that across all the iterations the Join operator keeps the hash table that it built for the **arc** dataset.

4 Experiments

4.1 Experimental Setup

Hardware and Software Environment. We performed our experiments on a cluster of 8 nodes, connected with Gigabit Ethernet. Each worker node has an IBM PowerPC 48-core CPU. We allocated 48 GB memory to the Flink and Spark worker processes. We implemented Cog on the current snapshot version of Flink (on the top of commit 8f8e358).

Benchmark Programs. Thus far, Cog supports positive Datalog with recursion, but without aggregation. We chose the following benchmark queries:

- **Transitive Closure (TC):** Finds all pairs of vertices in a graph that are connected by some path. Listing 1 shows TC in Datalog.
- **Same Generation (SG):** Two nodes are in the Same Generation (SG) if and only if they are at the same distance from another node in the graph. Listing 4 shows SG program in Datalog. The program finds all pairs that are in the same generation.

```
r₁: sg(X, Y):- arc(P, X), arc(P,Y), X!=Y.
r₂: sg(X, Y):- arc(A, X), sg(A, B), arc(B, Y).
```
Listing 4. Same Generation (SG) program in Datalog.

- **Single-Source Reachability:** Finds all vertices connected by some path to a given source vertex. Listing 5 shows the **Reachability** program in Datalog.

```
r₁: reach(X,Y):- arc(X,Y), X=source.
r₂: reach(X,Y):- reach(X,Z), arc(Z,Y).
```
Listing 5. **Reachability** program in Datalog.

Datasets. We used synthetic graph datasets to evaluate and benchmark our system. These datasets are `Tree11`, `Grid150`, and `g10K`. The same datasets are also used by Shkapsky et al. [18] for benchmark comparison of BigDatalog with Myria [20] and Distributed SociaLite [17] systems. Table 1 shows the properties of the datasets. These graphs have specific structural properties: `Tree11` has 11 levels, `Grid150` is a grid of 151 by 151, and the `G10K` graphs are 10k-vertex random graphs in which each randomly-chosen pair of vertices is connected with probability 0.001. The last three columns of Table 1 show the output size produced with these datasets by the benchmark queries. For the `Reachability` program, we used graph datasets generated with R-MAT [26] synthetic graph generator with probabilities $a = 0.45, b = 0.25, c = 0.15, d = 0.15$. For all the datasets, we calculated `Reachability` from vertex 977.

Table 1. Input- and output sizes, and the number of iterations (in parenthesis)

Name	Vertices	Edges	TC	SG	Reachability
Tree11	71,391	71,390	805,001 (11)	2,086,271,974 (11)	-
Grid150	22,801	45,300	131,675,775 (299)	2,295,050 (149)	-
G10K	10,000	100,185	100,000,000 (6)	100,000,000 (3)	-
R-MAT-1M	1 mill	10 mill	-	-	523,967 (4)
R-MAT-2M	2 mill	20 mill	-	-	1,047,937 (4)
R-MAT-4M	4 mill	40 mill	-	-	2,095,865 (4)
R-MAT-8M	8 mill	80 mill	-	-	4,191,735 (4)
R-MAT-16M	16 mill	160 mill	-	-	8,383,418 (5)
R-MAT-32M	32 mill	320 mill	-	-	16,767,026 (5)

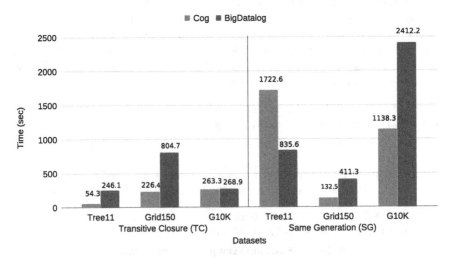

Fig. 4. Evaluation result comparison using TC and SG queries.

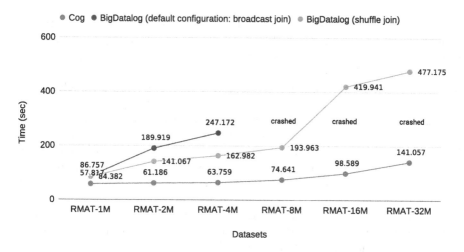

Fig. 5. Evaluation result comparison using `Reachability` query.

4.2 Results

We ran TC, SG, and `Reachability` in our system and another state-of-the-art distributed Datalog system, namely BigDatalog [18]. As BigDatalog demonstrated its efficiency compared to other distributed Datalog systems (such as Myria [20] and Distributed SociaLite [17]), our purpose here is to show how Cog performs w.r.t. BigDatalog. Figure 4 and Fig. 5 show the benchmark comparison of Cog and BigDatalog. We report the *median* values in Fig. 4 and Fig. 5.

TC. We used the query shown in Listing 1 for calculating TC. Cog outperformed BigDatalog for all the graphs. Notably, Cog showed 3x better performance than BigDatalog for `Tree11` and `Grid150` graphs. BigDatalog suffers from the overhead of scheduling caused by the large number of iterations, whereas no such overhead is present in Cog as it performs iterative programs in a cyclic dataflow job [10]. However, this overhead is negligible when there is only a small number of iterations (see Table 1). Cog can suffer performance loss due to data spilling during the CoGroup operation with the solution set, which is visible in the case of `G10K`. With default settings, BigDatalog always crashed due to running out of memory as it was caching resilient distributed datasets (RDDs) in memory and clearing lineage in order to avoid stack overflow from long lineages. For TC queries, we disabled such caching of RDDs to avoid crashes.

SG. We used Listing 4 for calculating SG. We found that Cog is 2x faster than BigDatalog for `Grid150` and `G10K` graphs, despite RDD caching to memory was enabled for BigDatalog. Though SG program produces a small number of output rows when `Grid150` is used as input, however, it is clear from the result of `G10K` that the scheduling overhead is not the only factor for slow execution speed. Cog suffered performance loss when executing SG on `Tree11` dataset. The reason for the inefficiency was the fact that the CoGroup operation with the solution set gets slower when the number of records stored in the solution set increases.

Single-Source Reachability. We used Listing 5 for calculating `Reachability` from a single vertex. Listing 5 shows that Cog outpaced BigDatalog in all the graph instances we used to evaluate `Reachability`. The difference in performance between Cog and BigDatalog gets more prominent with the increase in the size of the datasets. When running `Reachability` on BigDatalog with default configuration (e.g., broadcast join), we saw an increase of approximately 1.5x on each 2x increase in the size of the graphs. Though the overhead of scheduling did not increase (i.e., the number of iterations for 1M, 2M, 4M datasets was 4). With default settings, BigDatalog crashed for all the datasets of sizes greater than 4M. We discovered that BigDatalog uses a broadcast join by default, which broadcasts the entire graph to all the worker nodes. We believe that this was the reason for the crash, since a broadcast join works only if one of the inputs is small enough. Therefore, we changed the configuration to use a repartition join instead, which performed slightly faster and was able to process all of our datasets. The running time growth for Cog on all the datasets was small and steady. Cog was 3.4x faster for the largest dataset we tested.

5   Related Work

There is a large body of work discussing efficient Datalog evaluation [4,9,19]. In the following discussion we focus on distributed systems.

Distributed Dataflow Systems. Flink [1,6] is a modern dataflow system for general-purpose data processing, that employs the incremental iteration model (specifically, delta iterations) [8]. Spark [21] is a scalable, fault-tolerant, distributed in-memory dataflow engine. In contrast to Flink, it has a considerable scheduling overhead when used for iterative jobs, as each iteration is scheduled as a new job. Naiad [15] is a system based on the timely dataflow computational model that supports structured loops for streaming. The iteration mechanism in Naiad is similar to that in Flink. Therefore, it would be possible to implement semi-naive Datalog execution also on Naiad, similarly to how we implemented it for Cog. The Differential Datalog [16] system goes in this direction, but it supports only single-machine execution.

Pregel-Like Graph Processing Systems. The think-like-a-vertex paradigm for graph processing was introduced by Pregel [14], and is used in many large-scale graph processing systems, such as GraphX [11], Giraph [23], and Gelly [25]. Contrary to Datalog, the think-like-a-vertex paradigm provides a stateful computation model, whereas Datalog queries are more declarative. Note that Pregel-like systems usually support deactivating vertices, and thereby support a kind of incrementalization, akin to the incremental nature of semi-naive evaluation.

Datalog Evaluation in Distributed Systems. Several systems implemented Datalog to be executed on a cluster of machines. BigDatalog [18] implemented positive Datalog with recursion, non-monotonic aggregations, and aggregation in recursion with monotonic aggregates on Spark. BigDatalog uses a number of clever tricks to overcome some of the limitations of Spark in the area of iterative computations. It added scheduler-aware recursion by adding a specialized Spark stage (*FixPointStage*) for recursive queries to avoid the job launching overhead. Furthermore, reusing Spark tasks within a *FixPointStage* eliminates the cost of task scheduling and task creation; however, task reuse can only happen on so-called *decomposable* Datalog programs, and only if the joins can be implemented by broadcasting instead of repartitioning, which is not the case for large graphs. BigDatalog added specialized *SetRDD* and *AggregateRDD* to enable efficient evaluation of recursive queries. BigDatalog also pays special attention to joins with loop-invariant inputs. It avoids repartitioning the static input of the join, as well as rebuilding the join's hash table at every iteration. However, it does not ensure co-location of the join tasks with the corresponding cached build-side blocks, and thus cannot always avoid a network transfer of the build-side. (RaSQL [12] uses the same techniques plus operator code generation and operator fusion to implement recursive SQL with aggregations on Spark.)

When implementing Cog, we did not need to perform any of the above optimizations, as Flink has built-in support for efficient iterations with cyclic dataflow jobs. Having cyclic dataflow jobs means that all of the issues that Big-Datalog's optimizations are solving either do not even come up (per-iteration job-launching overhead and task-scheduling overhead), or already have simple solutions by keeping operator states across iterations (loop-invariant join inputs, incremental updates to the solution set). Thus, our view is that relying on Flink's native iterations being implemented as a single, cyclic dataflow job is a more natural way to evaluate Datalog (or recursive SQL) efficiently.

Distributed SociaLite [17], is a system developed for social network analysis that implemented Datalog with recursive monotone aggregate functions using a delta stepping method and gives the ability to programmers to specify data distribution. It uses message passing mechanism for communication among workers. It shows weaknesses in loading datasets (base relations) and poor shuffling performance on large datasets [18]. Myria [20] is a distributed execution engine that implemented Datalog with recursive monotonic aggregation function in a share-nothing engine and supports synchronous and asynchronous iterative models. Myria, however, suffers from shuffling overhead when running large datasets and becomes unstable (it often runs out of memory) [18].

GraphRex [22] is a recent distributed graph processing system with a Datalog-like interface. It focuses on making full use of the characteristics of modern data center networks, and thus achieves very high performance in such an environment. In contrast to Cog or BigDatalog, it is a standalone system, not built on an existing dataflow engine, such as Flink or Spark. Note that building on an existing dataflow engine has the advantage that declarative Datalog queries can be seamlessly integrated into larger programs written using the (typically more general) native API of the dataflow engine.

6   Conclusion and Future Work

In this paper, we presented Cog, which is a Datalog language implementation for batch processing tasks on Apache Flink. The main advantages of Cog over other systems from a user perspective are its efficiency and conciseness. Cog executes recursive queries of Datalog as a single, cyclic dataflow job, thus avoiding scheduling overhead that is present in acyclic dataflows. In our experiments, Cog outperformed BigDatalog, a state-of-the-art large-scale Datalog system, in most of the test cases. The code and the latest updates of Cog are available at [24].

Future Work. An implementation of negation, non-monotonic aggregations, and aggregation in recursion for Datalog can be added to the system. Datalog for Flink stream processing tasks can also be implemented to facilitate analytics on real-time datasets. We believe that Datalog's implementation for Flink stream processing API could surpass Cog's efficiency because a Flink streaming job would not need a synchronization barrier after each iteration. Another future direction is to add support to Flink for recursive SQL queries, which are similar to recursive Datalog queries. Cog already laid the groundwork for this by translating the recursive logical plans to the Flink `DataSet` API.

Acknowledgments. This work was funded by the German Ministry for Education and Research as BIFOLD (01IS18025A and 01IS18037A). We would like to thank Jorge-Arnulfo Quiané-Ruiz for helpful comments on a draft of this paper.

References

1. Alexandrov, A., et al.: The stratosphere platform for big data analytics. VLDB J. **23**(6), 939–964 (2014)
2. Arni, F., Ong, K., Tsur, S., Wang, H., Zaniolo, C.: The deductive database system LDL++. Theory Pract. Log. Program. **3**(1), 61–94 (2003)
3. Bancilhon, F.: Naive evaluation of recursively defined relations. In: Brodie, M.L., Mylopoulos, J. (eds.) On Knowledge Base Management Systems, pp. 165–178. Springer, New York (1986). https://doi.org/10.1007/978-1-4612-4980-1_17
4. Bancilhon, F., Ramakrishnan, R.: An amateur's introduction to recursive query processing strategies. In: Readings in Artificial Intelligence and Databases, pp. 376–430. Elsevier (1989)
5. Begoli, E., Camacho-Rodríguez, J., Hyde, J., Mior, M.J., Lemire, D.: Apache calcite: a foundational framework for optimized query processing over heterogeneous data sources. In: Proceedings of the 2018 International Conference on Management of Data, pp. 221–230 (2018)
6. Carbone, P., Katsifodimos, A., Ewen, S., Markl, V., Haridi, S., Tzoumas, K.: Apache flink: stream and batch processing in a single engine. Bull. IEEE Comput. Soc. Tech. Comm. Data Eng. **36**(4), 28–38 (2015)

7. Ceri, S., Gottlob, G., Tanca, L.: What you always wanted to know about datalog (and never dared to ask). IEEE Trans. Knowl. Data Eng. **1**(1), 146–166 (1989)
8. Ewen, S., Tzoumas, K., Kaufmann, M., Markl, V.: Spinning fast iterative data flows. Proc. VLDB Endow. **5**(11), 1268–1279 (2012)
9. Fan, Z., Zhu, J., Zhang, Z., Albarghouthi, A., Koutris, P., Patel, J.: Scaling-up in-memory Datalog processing: observations and techniques. arXiv preprint arXiv:1812.03975 (2018)
10. Gévay, G.E., Rabl, T., Breß, S., Madai-Tahy, L., Markl, V.: Labyrinth: compiling imperative control flow to parallel dataflows. arXiv preprint arXiv:1809.06845 (2018)
11. Gonzalez, J.E., Xin, R.S., Dave, A., Crankshaw, D., Franklin, M.J., Stoica, I.: GraphX: graph processing in a distributed dataflow framework. In: 11th USENIX Symposium on Operating Systems Design and Implementation OSDI 14). pp. 599–613 (2014)
12. Gu, J., et al.: RaSQL: greater power and performance for big data analytics with recursive-aggregate-SQL on Spark. In: Proceedings of the 2019 International Conference on Management of Data, pp. 467–484 (2019)
13. Hajiyev, E., Verbaere, M., de Moor, O.: *codeQuest*: scalable source code queries with datalog. In: Thomas, D. (ed.) ECOOP 2006. LNCS, vol. 4067, pp. 2–27. Springer, Heidelberg (2006). https://doi.org/10.1007/11785477_2
14. Malewicz, G., et al.: Pregel: a system for large-scale graph processing. In: Proceedings of the 2010 ACM SIGMOD International Conference on Management of data, pp. 135–146 (2010)
15. Murray, D.G., McSherry, F., Isaacs, R., Isard, M., Barham, P., Abadi, M.: Naiad: a timely dataflow system. In: Proceedings of the Twenty-Fourth ACM Symposium on Operating Systems Principles, pp. 439–455 (2013)
16. Ryzhyk, L., Budiu, M.: Differential datalog. In: Datalog 2.0 - 3rd International Workshop on the Resurgence of Datalog in Academia and Industry, CEUR-WS (2019)
17. Seo, J., Park, J., Shin, J., Lam, M.S.: Distributed sociaLite: a datalog-based language for large-scale graph analysis. Proc. VLDB Endow. **6**(14), 1906–1917 (2013)
18. Shkapsky, A., Yang, M., Interlandi, M., Chiu, H., Condie, T., Zaniolo, C.: Big data analytics with datalog queries on spark. In: SIGMOD, pp. 1135–1149 (2016)
19. Subotić, P., Jordan, H., Chang, L., Fekete, A., Scholz, B.: Automatic index selection for large-scale datalog computation. Proc. VLDB Endow. **12**(2), 141–153 (2018)
20. Wang, J., Balazinska, M., Halperin, D.: Asynchronous and fault-tolerant recursive datalog evaluation in shared-nothing engines. Proc. VLDB Endow. **8**(12), 1542–1553 (2015)
21. Zaharia, M., Chowdhury, M., Franklin, M.J., Shenker, S., Stoica, I., et al.: Spark: cluster computing with working sets. HotCloud **10**(10–10), 95 (2010)
22. Zhang, Q., et al.: Optimizing declarative graph queries at large scale. In: Proceedings of the 2019 International Conference on Management of Data, pp. 1411–1428 (2019)
23. Apache Giraph. http://giraph.apache.org/. Accessed 12 Apr 2020
24. Cog. https://github.com/imran-4/cog. Accessed 12 Apr 2020
25. Gelly: Flink Graph API. https://ci.apache.org/projects/flink/flink-docs-stable/dev/libs/gelly/. Accessed 12 Apr 2020
26. GTGraph. http://www.cse.psu.edu/~kxm85/software/GTgraph/. Accessed 12 Apr 2020

Explaining Results of Path Queries on Graphs
Single-Path Results for Context-Free Path Queries

Jelle Hellings[(✉)]

Department of Computer Science, University of California, Davis,
Davis, CA 95616-8562, USA
jhellings@ucdavis.edu

Abstract. Many graph query languages use, at their core, path queries that yield node pairs that are connected by a path of interest. For the end-user, such node pairs only give limited insight as to *why* this query result is obtained, as the pair does not directly identify the underlying path of interest. To address this limitation of path queries, we propose the *single-path semantics*, which evaluates path queries to, for each node pair (m, n), a single path from m to n satisfying the conditions of the query. To put our proposal in practice, we provide an efficient algorithm for evaluating *context-free path queries*, a particular powerful type of path queries, using the single-path semantics. Additionally, we perform a short evaluation of our techniques that shows that the single-path semantics is practically feasible, even when query results grow large.

Keywords: Graph queries · Path results · Context-free path queries

1 Introduction

The graph data model is one of the most versatile and natural data models in use: graph-structured data is everywhere and examples can be found in family trees, social networks, process models, gene networks, XML data, and RDF data [1,2,9,12,30]. As an example, consider the small social network visualized in Fig. 1 in which nodes represent peoples and edges represent the relationships between peoples.

A central step in the analysis of such graph data is the ability to *query* the data for relationships of interest. For this purpose, many different query languages have been developed, including XPATH for querying XML data [8, 9,11], SPARQL for querying RDF data [19,30], the graph query languages GXPATH [24], CYPHER [28], and GREMLIN [29], and formal verification languages such as PDL, KAT, CTL, and LTL [12,22,23]. At their core, these graph query languages depend on *path queries* that can be used to express *indirect relationships* that can be derived from the data [2]. Examples of such path queries are the well-known regular path queries [5] and the context-free path queries [18,20,23,31]. Unfortunately, path queries are typically evaluated to only

© Springer Nature Switzerland AG 2020
L. Qin et al. (Eds.): SFDI 2020/LSGDA 2020, CCIS 1281, pp. 84–98, 2020.
https://doi.org/10.1007/978-3-030-61133-0_7

a set of node pairs (m, n) that are connected by a path of interest, which gives little insight in the way pairs (m, n) are obtained, limiting their capabilities for graph analytics.

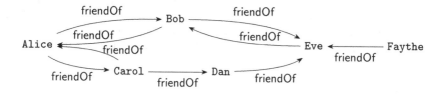

Fig. 1. A typical example of graph data: a social network relating peoples.

Example 1. Let $\mathfrak{G}$ be the social network visualized in Fig. 1. The path query indirectFriendOf = friendOf$^+$, expressed by a regular expression, will return the derived relationship between pairs (m, n) such that m is a friend of n, or a friend-of-a-friend of n, or a friend-of-a-friend-of-a-friend of n, and so on. The pair (Alice, Eve) is in the result of evaluating indirectFriendOf on graph $\mathfrak{G}$. Unfortunately, Alice cannot use this result to determine whom of her friends can help her to get in contact with Eve, and Alice will have to further analyze the underlying graph data.

Example 1 illustrates the need to answer path queries with the underlying paths of interest inspected by these queries. To address this need, we propose the *single-path semantics* for evaluating path queries: using the single-path semantics, a path query will evaluate to a shortest path connecting node pair (m, n) (for each node pair in the query result).

Example 2. Consider the setting of Example 1. Evaluation of indirectFriendOf using the single path semantics can result in the path "Alice friendOf Bob friendOf Eve", from which Alice can derive a way to contact Eve. As the single path semantics requires a single and shortest path between node pairs, the path "Alice friendOf Carol friendOf Dan friendOf Eve" cannot be in the output.

The need for the single-path semantics extends beyond the above toy example. Not only can single-path semantics provide more relevant information to end-users, the single-path semantics can also aid in graph analytics and data exploration, and can be used to provide *data provenance* for traditional path queries [10], this by providing paths that show why a path query includes a certain node pair in its output. Furthermore, in the large-scale graph data setting in which many complex path queries are evaluated, there is a need for tools to support query debugging [21], for which the single-path semantics can also be of use.

In this paper, we deal with the issues outlined by proposing the single-path semantics. We focus our study on the context-free path queries, as these are a particular powerful type of path queries that cannot only express all typical path queries (e.g. [5,20]), but also have applications in model checking [23], bioinformatics [31], and parser construction [17]. In specific, we formalize the *single-path semantics*, introduce the algorithm MINIMIZESETGG that provides efficient evaluation of context-free path queries on graphs using the single-path semantics, and evaluate the performance of MINIMIZESETGG in practice. Our results show promise, as MINIMIZESETGG can easily answer queries whose results contains tens-of-millions of paths, even if these paths have considerable lengths.

2   Preliminaries

First, we introduce the terminology and notation used throughout this paper.

Let Σ be a set of symbols. We call a sequence $s = \sigma_1 \ldots \sigma_n$ of symbols, $\sigma_1, \ldots, \sigma_n \in \Sigma$, a string over Σ. We write $|s| = n$ to denote the length of s. The empty string is denoted by ϵ and we usually treat individual symbols as strings of length one. The concatenation of two strings s_1 and s_2 is denoted by $s_1 \circ s_2$. We denote the set of all strings over Σ by Σ^*. A *language* over Σ is a (possibly infinite) set of strings over Σ.

A *graph* is a triple $\mathfrak{G} = (\mathcal{V}, \Sigma, \delta)$, in which $\mathcal{V}$ is a finite set of nodes, Σ is a finite set of alphabet symbols used as edge labels, and $\delta \subseteq \mathcal{V} \times \Sigma \times \mathcal{V}$ is a finite set of labeled edges. To simplify presentation, we assume that $\mathcal{V}$ and Σ do not overlap ($\mathcal{V} \cap \Sigma = \emptyset$). A *path* in $\mathfrak{G}$ is a sequence $\pi = m_1 \sigma_1 m_2 \ldots m_{n-1} \sigma_{n-1} m_n$ such that, for every $m_i \sigma_i m_{i+1}$ in the sequence, $1 \le i < n$, we have $(m_i, \sigma_i, m_{i+1}) \in \delta$. We write $m_1 \pi m_n$ to indicate that π is a path starting at node m_1 and ending at node m_n. We write $|\pi| = n - 1$ to denote the length of π and we write $\text{trace}(\pi) = \sigma_1 \ldots \sigma_{n-1}$ to denote the trace of π, the string represented by the sequence of edge labels in π.

A *path query* q is specified by a language $\mathcal{L}$ that contains all traces of paths of interest, e.g., via a regular expression (RPQs) or via a context-free grammar (CFPQs). The evaluation of q on graph $\mathfrak{G}$ using the standard *relational semantics* simply consists of all node pairs that are connected by paths whose trace is in $\mathcal{L}$. To denote the evaluation of q on $\mathfrak{G}$, we write $[\![q]\!]_{\mathfrak{G}}$, and we have $[\![q]\!]_{\mathfrak{G}} = \{(m, n) \mid \exists \text{ path } m\pi n \text{ in } \mathfrak{G} \text{ with } \text{trace}(\pi) \in \mathcal{L}\}$.

Example 3. In Example 1, the query indirectFriendOf was expressed by the regular expression friendOf$^+$. This regular expression represents the language

$$\mathcal{L} = \{\text{friendOf}, \text{friendOf} \circ \text{friendOf}, \text{friendOf} \circ \text{friendOf} \circ \text{friendOf}, \ldots\}.$$

We have (Alice, Eve) $\in$ [[indirectFriendOf]]$_{\mathfrak{G}}$, with $\mathfrak{G}$ the graph in Fig. 1, as there exists a path $\pi = $ "Alice friendOf Bob friendOf Eve" with $\text{trace}(\pi) \in \mathcal{L}$.

A *grammar* is a triple $\mathscr{C} = (\mathcal{N}, \Sigma, \mathcal{P})$, in which $\mathcal{N}$ is a set of non-terminals, Σ is a finite set of alphabet symbols, and $\mathcal{P}$ is a set of production rules. We require that $\mathcal{N}$ and Σ do not overlap ($\mathcal{N} \cap \Sigma = \emptyset$). The set of production rules, $\mathcal{P}$, consists of production rules of the form $A \mapsto B\ C$ or $A \mapsto \sigma$, in which $A, B, C \in \mathcal{N}$ and $\sigma \in \Sigma$.

Each non-terminal in $\mathcal{N}$ represents a language over Σ: the production rules in $\mathcal{P}$ describe how to produce strings out of non-terminals via rewrite steps. To illustrate this, consider a string $s = s_1 \circ A \circ s_2$ in which $s_1, s_2 \in (\mathcal{N} \cup \Sigma)^*$ and $A \in \mathcal{N}$. If there exists a production rule $(A \mapsto s') \in \mathcal{P}$, then we can rewrite s into $s_1 \circ s' \circ s_2$ by applying the rewrite $A \mapsto s'$. We write $s \rightarrow_{\mathcal{P}}^* s'$ if s can be rewritten into s' using production rules in $\mathcal{P}$, and we write $s \rightarrow_{\mathcal{P}}^+ s'$ if $s \rightarrow_{\mathcal{P}}^* s'$ and at least one rewrite step is necessary to rewrite s into s'.

The *language* of non-terminal $A \in \mathcal{N}$ is defined by $\mathcal{L}(\mathscr{C}; A) = \{s \in \Sigma^* \mid A \rightarrow_{\mathcal{P}}^* s\}$. Given a grammar with non-terminal A, we simply write A to denote the path query based on the language $\mathcal{L}(\mathscr{C}; A)$.

Example 4. Consider the grammar $\mathscr{C} = (\mathcal{N}, \Sigma, \mathcal{P})$ in which $\mathcal{N} = \{A\}$, $\Sigma = \{\mathsf{friendOf}\}$, and $\mathcal{P} = \{A \rightarrow \mathsf{friendOf}, A \rightarrow A\ A\}$. The language $\mathcal{L}(\mathscr{C}; A)$ is equivalent to the language $\mathcal{L}$ of Example 3. Hence, we have $(\mathtt{Alice}, \mathtt{Eve}) \in [\![A]\!]_{\mathfrak{G}}$, in which $\mathfrak{G}$ is the graph visualized in Fig. 1.

3   The Single-Path Semantics

In Sect. 2, we already introduced the typical *relational semantics* of path queries. Unfortunately, the step toward *path-based semantics*—in which a path query yields paths $m\pi n$ instead of node pairs (m, n)—is not straightforward. Even in basic situations, the resulting set of paths can already be unbounded in size, making it impossible to simply evaluate to such a set:

Example 5. Consider Example 1 and the graph $\mathfrak{G}$ visualized in Fig. 1. This graph is cyclic, as there is a path "$\mathtt{Alice}$ friendOf $\mathtt{Carol}$ friendOf $\mathtt{Dan}$ friendOf $\mathtt{Eve}$ friendOf $\mathtt{Bob}$ friendOf $\mathtt{Alice}$". Hence, we can make paths of arbitrary lengths that match the query $\mathsf{indirectFriendOf}$, and the set of all paths matching the query is unbounded in size.

Restricting the paths considered in the evaluation, e.g., to simple paths, assures that the set of paths considered is finite. Unfortunately, changing the paths considered during evaluation defeats the purpose of path-based semantics as a data provenance and debugging tool for normal path queries. Moreover, it is well-known that such restrictions make query evaluation prohibitive expensive [2, 3, 7, 25]. Restricting the number of paths in the result, e.g., to a single path per node pair, will also assure a finite result. Unfortunately, as Example 5 already shows, individual paths in such a finite result set can still have a practically unbounded length. To address these issues, we choose to return a single as-short-as-possible path for each node-pair (m, n):

Definition 1. *Let q be a path query specified by language $\mathcal{L}$ and let $\mathfrak{G}$ be a graph. The evaluation of q on $\mathfrak{G}$ using the* single-path semantics, *denoted by* $\mathsf{single}(q|_{\mathfrak{G}})$, *yields, for every $(m, n) \in [\![q]\!]_{\mathfrak{G}}$, a single shortest path $m\pi n$ in $\mathfrak{G}$ such that* $\mathsf{trace}(\pi) \in \mathcal{L}$. *(Hence, for every other path $m\pi' n$ in $\mathfrak{G}$ with $\mathsf{trace}(\pi') \in \mathcal{L}$, we have $|\pi| \leq |\pi'|$.)*

Toward evaluating context-free path queries using the single-path semantics, we proceed in three steps. First, in Sect. 3.1, we show that all paths of interest of a context-free path query can be represented by a grammar. Then, in Sect. 3.2, we propose MINIMIZESET, an algorithm for computing a shortest string in a context-free language. Finally, in Sect. 3.3, we combine these results and show how to evaluating context-free path queries using the single-path semantics.

3.1   Representing the Paths of Interest of a Path Query

Let $\mathfrak{G} = (\mathcal{V}, \Sigma, \delta)$ be a graph and $(m, n) \in \mathcal{V}$ a pair of nodes. There is a close correspondence between labeled graphs and finite automata and we can easily interpret $(\mathfrak{G}, m, n)$ as a finite automata with initial state m and final state n. The language of this finite automata is $\mathcal{L}(\mathfrak{G}; m, n) = \{\text{trace}(\pi) \mid m\pi n \text{ is a path in } \mathfrak{G}\}$. It is well-known that the intersection of a finite automaton and a grammar can be represented by another context-free grammar:

Lemma 1 (Bar-Hillel et al. [4]). *Let $\mathscr{C} = (\mathcal{N}, \Sigma, \mathcal{P})$ be a grammar, let $\mathfrak{G} = (\mathcal{V}, \Sigma, \delta)$ be a graph, let $A \in \mathcal{N}$, and let $m, n \in \mathcal{V}$. The language $\mathcal{L}(\mathscr{C}; A) \cap \mathcal{L}(\mathfrak{G}; m, n)$ can be represented by a grammar.*

Lemma 1 guarantees that there is a finite representation of the set of all strings in $\mathcal{L}(\mathscr{C}; A) \cap \mathcal{L}(\mathfrak{G}; m, n)$, each such string representing the trace of a path $m\pi n$ in $\mathfrak{G}$ with $\text{trace}(\pi) \in \mathcal{L}(\mathscr{C}; A)$. Unfortunately, there can be several paths with the same trace, complicating the derivation of the underlying paths. To improve on this, we show the existence of *graph-annotated grammars* that directly represent the set of paths instead of their traces:

Definition 2. *Let $\mathscr{C} = (\mathcal{N}, \Sigma, \mathcal{P})$ be a grammar and let $\mathfrak{G} = (\mathcal{V}, \Sigma, \delta)$ be a graph. We denote triples $(A, m, n) \in \mathcal{N} \times \mathcal{V}^2$ by $A|_{mn}$. An annotated grammar over $(\mathscr{C}, \mathfrak{G})$ is a grammar $\mathscr{C}|_{\mathfrak{G}} = (\mathcal{N}|_{\mathfrak{G}}, \Sigma, \mathcal{P}|_{\mathfrak{G}})$ in which*

1. $\mathcal{N}|_{\mathfrak{G}} = \{A|_{mn} \in \mathcal{N} \times \mathcal{V}^2 \mid \mathcal{L}(\mathscr{C}; A) \cap \mathcal{L}(\mathfrak{G}; m, n) \neq \emptyset\};$
2. $\mathcal{P}|_{\mathfrak{G}} = P_\Sigma \cup P_\mathcal{N}$ *with* $P_\Sigma = \{A|_{mn} \mapsto \sigma \mid (m, \sigma, n) \in \delta \wedge (A \mapsto \sigma) \in \mathcal{P}\}$ *and* $P_\mathcal{N} = \{A|_{mn} \mapsto B|_{mo} C|_{on} \mid (A \mapsto B\ C) \in \mathcal{P}\}.$

The notation $A|_{mn}$ denotes a node-annotated non-terminal: any string produced from rewriting this non-terminal is a trace of a path $m\pi n$. As rewriting $A|_{mn}$ eventually leads to rewrite steps using production rules in P_Σ, which represent single edges in $\mathfrak{G}$, the path π can be derived by keeping track of these node-annotations. Notice that $|\mathcal{N}|_{\mathfrak{G}}| \leq |\mathcal{N}||\mathcal{V}|^2$, $|P_\Sigma| \leq |\mathcal{P}||\delta|$, and $|P_\mathcal{N}| \leq |\mathcal{P}||\mathcal{V}|^3$. We illustrate these annotated grammars with an example:

Example 6. Let $\mathfrak{G}$ be the graph visualized in Fig. 1 and $\mathscr{C}$ the grammar of Example 4. We construct the annotated grammar $\mathscr{C}|_{\mathfrak{G}} = (\mathcal{N}|_{\mathfrak{G}}, \Sigma, \mathcal{P}|_{\mathfrak{G}})$. For brevity, we refer to each person by the first letter of their name. We have

$$\mathcal{N}|_{\mathfrak{G}} = \{Q|_{mn} \mid m, n \in \{A, B, C, D, E\}\} \cup \{Q|_{Fn} \mid n \in \{A, B, C, D, E\}\}.$$

We have $\mathcal{P}|_{\mathfrak{G}} = P_{\Sigma} \cup P_{\mathcal{N}}$, in which P_{Σ} represents all edges in $\mathfrak{G}$ and $P_{\mathcal{N}}$ represents all ways in which paths in $\mathfrak{G}$ can be combined. E.g., $Q|_{AB} \in P_{\Sigma}$, as $(\texttt{Alice}, \texttt{friendOf}, \texttt{Bob})$ is and edge in $\mathfrak{G}$, and $(Q|_{AB} \mapsto Q|_{AD}\, Q|_{DB}) \in P_{\mathcal{N}}$, as there is a friendOf-labeled path from Alice to Dan and another friendOf-labeled path from Dan to Bob. To produce a path from Alice to Eve, we use $\mathscr{C}|_{\mathfrak{G}}$:

$$Q|_{\texttt{AliceEve}} \rightarrow^{*}_{\mathcal{P}|_{\mathfrak{G}}} \{\text{Rewrite } Q|_{\texttt{AliceEve}} \mapsto Q|_{\texttt{AliceCarol}}\, Q|_{\texttt{CarolEve}}\}$$

$$Q|_{\texttt{AliceCarol}}\, Q|_{\texttt{CarolEve}} \rightarrow^{*}_{\mathcal{P}|_{\mathfrak{G}}} \{\text{Rewrite } Q|_{\texttt{CarolEve}} \mapsto Q|_{\texttt{CarolDan}}\, Q|_{\texttt{DanEve}}\}$$

$$Q|_{\texttt{AliceCarol}}\, Q|_{\texttt{CarolDan}}\, Q|_{\texttt{DanEve}} \rightarrow^{*}_{\mathcal{P}|_{\mathfrak{G}}} \{\text{Rewrite } Q|_{\texttt{AliceCarol}} \mapsto \texttt{friendOf}, \ldots\}$$

$$\text{friendOf} \circ \text{friendOf} \circ \text{friendOf}.$$

The annotations in each node-annotated non-terminal carry information that can be used to map strings in $\mathscr{C}|_{\mathfrak{G}}$ to paths in the underlying graph $\mathfrak{G}$. E.g., in this rewrite, we derived a path from Alice to Eve in graph $\mathfrak{G}$ of length three, namely the path "Alice friendOf Carol friendOf Dan friendOf Eve".

Using induction, we can prove that graph-annotated grammars can always be used as illustrated in Example 6:

Proposition 1. *Let $\mathscr{C} = (\mathcal{N}, \Sigma, \mathcal{P})$ be a grammar, let $\mathfrak{G} = (\mathcal{V}, \Sigma, \delta)$ be a graph, let $\mathscr{C}|_{\mathfrak{G}} = (\mathcal{N}|_{\mathfrak{G}}, \Sigma, \mathcal{P}|_{\mathfrak{G}})$ be the annotated grammar over $(\mathscr{C}, \mathfrak{G})$, let $m\pi n$ be a path in $\mathfrak{G}$, and let $A \in \mathcal{N}$ be a non-terminal. We have $\mathrm{trace}(\pi) \in \mathcal{L}(\mathscr{C}; A)$ if and only if we can derive π from $A|_{mn} \in \mathcal{N}|_{\mathfrak{G}}$.*

We note that annotated grammars can, on their own, be used in *interactive* data exploration tools in which users can explorer the query results by zooming in on certain paths in the dataset, e.g., for graph analysis and query debugging.

3.2 Deriving Shortest Strings of a Grammar

Next, we propose an efficient way to compute a shortest string in the language defined by a grammar. Mclean et al. [27] already proved that a shortest string can be computed effective given a grammar, but did not provide a practical algorithm for computing shortest strings. Toward such an algorithm, we introduce rewrites using *simple* production rules:

Definition 3. *Let $\mathcal{P}$ be a set of production rules. We define $\mathrm{heads}(\mathcal{P}) = \{A \mid (A \mapsto s) \in \mathcal{P}\}$ and we define the set of non-terminals derivable from A using the production rules in $\mathcal{P}$ by $\langle A \rangle_{\mathcal{P}} = \{B \in \mathcal{N} \mid \exists s_1 \exists s_2\ A \rightarrow^{+}_{\mathcal{P}} s_1 \circ B \circ s_2\}$.*

A set of production rules $\mathcal{P}$ is non-recursive if, for every $A \in \mathrm{heads}(\mathcal{P})$, we have $A \notin \langle A \rangle_{\mathcal{P}}$. A set of production rules $\mathcal{P}$ is deterministic if, for every $A \in \mathrm{heads}(\mathcal{P})$, there exists exactly one production rule $(A \mapsto s) \in \mathcal{P}$. Finally, a set of production rules $\mathcal{P}$ is effective if $A \in \mathrm{heads}(\mathcal{P})$ implies that there exists a string $s \in \Sigma^*$ such that $A \rightarrow^{*}_{\mathcal{P}} s$. We refer to a set of production rules that is non-recursive, deterministic, and effective as simple.

A simple set of production rules $\mathcal{P}$ over alphabet Σ can be used to rewrite every non-terminal $A \in \text{heads}(\mathcal{P})$ into a unique string $\text{ustring}_{\mathcal{P}}(A)$ over Σ in a straightforward manner, as $\mathcal{P}$ does not provide any choices during such a rewrite.

Example 7. Consider Example 6. For brevity, we restrict ourselves to Alice, Carol, Dan, and Eve. With respect to these four people, the following set of production rules in the annotated grammar is deterministic non-recursive:

$$Q|_{AC} \mapsto \text{friendOf}, \quad Q|_{CA} \mapsto \text{friendOf}, \quad Q|_{CD} \mapsto \text{friendOf}, \quad Q|_{DE} \mapsto \text{friendOf},$$

$$Q|_{AD} \mapsto Q|_{AC} \, Q|_{CD}, \quad Q|_{AE} \mapsto Q|_{AD} \, Q|_{DE}, \quad Q|_{CE} \mapsto Q|_{CA} \, Q|_{AE}.$$

We can use simple production rules derived from a grammar to represent shortest strings in that grammar:

Lemma 2. *Let $\mathscr{C} = (\mathcal{N}, \Sigma, \mathcal{P})$ be a grammar. There exists a simple set of production rules $\mathcal{P}' \subseteq \mathcal{P}$ such that, for every non-terminal $A \in \mathcal{N}$ with $\mathcal{L}(\mathscr{C}; A) \neq \emptyset$, $\text{ustring}_{\mathcal{P}'}(A)$ is a shortest string in $\mathcal{L}(\mathscr{C}; A)$.*

We say that a set of production rules that satisfies the conditions of Lemma 2 is *minimizing*. Unfortunately, not every simple set of production rules is minimizing:

Example 8. Consider Example 7. The provided simple set of production rules $\mathcal{P}'$ is not minimizing: we have $|\text{ustring}_{\mathcal{P}'}(Q|_{CE})| = 4$, while a shorter string of length two exists. By replacing the production rule for $Q|_{CE}$ in $\mathcal{P}'$ by $Q|_{CE} \mapsto Q|_{CD} \, Q|_{DE}$, we obtain a minimizing set of production rules.

Using a minimizing set of production rules, it is straightforward to produce shortest strings for $A \in \text{heads}(\mathcal{P})$. Moreover, the way to obtain these shortest strings, by rewriting A, also provides complete information on how these shortest strings can be obtained from the original grammar. Next, we propose the MINIMIZESET algorithm to construct a minimizing set of production rules. The pseudo-code of this algorithm can be found in Fig. 2, *left*.

The MINIMIZESET algorithm works rather intuitively. Let $\mathscr{C} = (\mathcal{N}, \Sigma, \mathcal{P})$ be a grammar. Production rules of the form $(A \rightarrow \sigma) \in \mathcal{P}$, $\sigma \in \Sigma$, produce the shortest possible strings: if $(A \rightarrow \sigma) \in \mathcal{P}$, then σ is a shortest string in $\mathcal{L}(\mathscr{C}; A)$. If such productions rules exist for A, then we choose one of them for the minimizing set of production rules (Line 3). Next, we process non-terminals A for which we have determined the length $cost[A]$ of the shortest strings in $\mathcal{L}(\mathscr{C}; A)$. We do so on increasing string length by using a min-priority queue new (Line 7). We process A by checking, for each production rule $(C \mapsto A \, B) \in \mathcal{P}$ or $(C \mapsto B \, A) \in \mathcal{P}$, whether using this production rule will allow us to rewrite C into a shorter string than the currently-found string with length $cost[C]$ (Line 10 and Line 12). We do so by rewriting—in this production rule—A to a string of length $cost[A]$ (Line 14).

Theorem 1. *Let $\mathscr{C} = (\mathcal{N}, \Sigma, \mathcal{P})$ be grammar. Execution of MINIMIZESET$(\mathscr{C})$ yields a minimizing set of production rules $\mathcal{P}'$ for $\mathscr{C}$ in $\mathcal{O}(|\mathcal{N}|(|\mathcal{N}|\log|\mathcal{N}| + |\mathcal{P}|))$.*

Algorithm MINIMIZESET($\mathscr{C} = (\mathcal{N}, \Sigma, \mathcal{P})$):

```
 1: P', cost := empty mapping, empty mapping.
 2: new is a min-priority queue.
 3: for all (A ↦ σ) ∈ P do
 4:     if A ∉ cost then
 5:         cost[A], P'[A] := 1, (A ↦ σ).
 6:         add A to new with priority 1.
 7: while new ≠ ∅ do
 8:     Take A with minimum priority in new.
 9:     Remove A from new.
10:     for all (C ↦ A B) ∈ P with B ∈ cost do
11:         PRODUCE(C ↦ A B).
12:     for all (C ↦ B A) ∈ P with B ∈ cost do
13:         PRODUCE(C ↦ B A).
14: return {P'[A] | A ∈ P'}.
```

Procedure PRODUCE($D \mapsto E\ F$):

```
15: if D ∉ cost then
16:     cost[D] := cost[E] + cost[F].
17:     P'[D] := D ↦ E F.
18:     Add D to new with priority cost[E] + cost[F].
19: else if cost[D] > cost[E] + cost[F] then
20:     cost[D] := cost[E] + cost[F].
21:     P'[D] := D ↦ E F.
22:     Lower priority of D ∈ new to cost[E] + cost[F].
```

Algorithm MINIMIZESETGG($\mathscr{C}, \eth$):

```
 1: P', cost := empty mapping, empty mapping.
 2: new is a min-priority queue.
 3: for all (A ↦ σ) ∈ P and (m, σ, n) ∈ δ do
 4:     if A|mn ∉ cost then
 5:         cost[A|mn], P'[A|mn] := 1, (A|mn ↦ σ).
 6:         Add A|mn to new with priority 1.
 7: while new ≠ ∅ do
 8:     Take A|mn with minimum priority in new.
 9:     Remove A|mn from new.
10:     for all (C ↦ A B) ∈ P with B|no ∈ cost do
11:         PRODUCEGG(C|mo ↦ A|mn B|no).
12:     for all (C ↦ B A) ∈ P with B|om ∈ cost do
13:         PRODUCEGG(C|on ↦ B|om A|mn).
14: return {P'[A|mn] | A|mn ∈ P'}.
```

Procedure PRODUCEGG($D|_{uw} \mapsto E|_{uv}\ F|_{vw}$):

```
15: if D|uw ∉ cost then
16:     cost[D|uw] := cost[E|uv] + cost[F|vw].
17:     P'[D|uw] := D|uw ↦ E|uv F|vw.
18:     Add D|uw to new with priority cost[E|uv] + cost[F|vw].
19: else if cost[D|uw] > cost[E|uv] + cost[F|vw] then
20:     cost[D|uw] := cost[E|uv] + cost[F|vw].
21:     P'[D|uw] := D|uw ↦ E|uv F|vw
22:     Lower priority of D|uw ∈ new to cost[E|uv] + cost[F|vw].
```

Fig. 2. On the *left*, the MINIMIZESET algorithm that constructs a minimizing set of production rules for the grammar $\mathscr{C}$. On the *right*, the MINIMIZESETGG algorithm that constructs a minimizing set of production rules for the annotated grammar $\mathscr{C}|_\eth$, of which only the necessary parts are implicitly constructed.

Using $\mathcal{P}'$, a set R of shortest strings s_A in $\mathcal{L}(\mathscr{C}; A)$, $A \in \mathcal{N}$, can be constructed in $\mathcal{O}(L)$, in which $L = \sum\{|s_A| \mid s_A \in R\}$ is the total length of these shortest strings.

Proof (sketch). The main *while*-loop maintains the following invariants:

1. The set $\{\mathcal{P}'[A] \mid A \in \mathcal{P}'\}$ is simple.
2. If $A \in \mathcal{P}'$ and $\mathcal{P}'[A] = (A \mapsto B\ C)$, then $cost[A] \geq cost[B] + cost[C]$, $cost[A] > cost[B]$, and $cost[A] > cost[C]$.
3. If $A \in \mathcal{P}'$ and s is a shortest string in $\mathcal{L}(\mathscr{C}; A)$, then $|s| \leq cost[A]$.
4. Let m be the priority of the last element removed from *new*. No new element is inserted in *new* with priority less than or equal to m.
5. Let m be the priority of the last element removed from *new*. For every $A \in \mathcal{N}$ and every shortest string s in $\mathcal{L}(\mathscr{C}; A)$ with $|s| \leq m$, we have $cost[A] = |s|$.

As each non-terminal is added to *new* at most once, the MINIMIZESET algorithm terminates. At termination, Invariants 1–5 guarantee that the resulting set of production rules is minimizing.

To obtain the stated complexity, we represent *costs* as an array holding $|\mathcal{N}|$ integers. The costs used in *cost* and *new* are integers in the range $1, \ldots, 2^{|\mathcal{N}|-1}$, which we can represent using $\log(2^{|\mathcal{N}|}) = |\mathcal{N}|$ bits. The initialization steps perform $\mathcal{O}(|\mathcal{P}|)$ steps. The *while*-loop, in the worst case, visit every non-terminal once. For each of these non-terminals, one insertion into and one removal from the priority queue *new* is performed. The inner *for*-loops will visit every production rule twice, causing at most $2|\mathcal{P}|$ decrease key operations on priority queue *new*. When using a Fibonacci heap for a priority queue holding at most e elements,

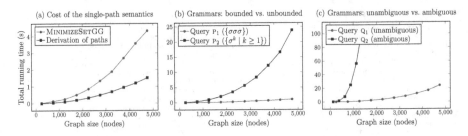

(a) Cost of the single-path semantics   (b) Grammars: bounded vs. unbounded   (c) Grammars: unambiguous vs. ambiguous

Fig. 3. Measurements on the performance of MINIMIZESETGG.

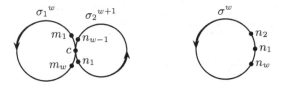

Fig. 4. On the *left*, the double-cyclic graph: two cycles, one having $w-1$ edges labeled with σ_1, and one having w edges labeled with σ_2. The two cycles are connected via a shared node c. On the *right*, the cyclic graph having w nodes labeled with σ.

each insert and removal costs $\mathcal{O}(\log e)$ and each decrease key operation costs an amortized $\mathcal{O}(1)$ heap operations [16]. Hence, a total of $\mathcal{O}(|\mathcal{N}| \log|\mathcal{N}| + |\mathcal{P}|)$ heap operations are performed. Taking the size of the integers representing priorities into account, the heap operations cost $\mathcal{O}(|\mathcal{N}|(|\mathcal{N}| \log|\mathcal{N}| + |\mathcal{P}|))$.   □

3.3 Deriving Shortest Paths for Path Query Results

Using the above results, we can already answer context-free path queries under the single-path semantics, this by applying MINIMIZESET on an annotated grammar. Unfortunately, this approach has high overhead due to the explicit construction and storing of the annotated grammar. Luckily, during the execution of MINIMIZESET, the relevant parts of $\mathscr{C}|_{\mathfrak{G}}$ can be implicitly derived from $\mathscr{C}$ and $\mathfrak{G}$. We obtain the MINIMIZESETGG algorithm by integrate these implicit derivation steps into MINIMIZESET. The resulting pseudo-code can be found in Fig. 2, *right*. We conclude:

Theorem 2. *Let* $\mathscr{C} = (\mathcal{N}, \Sigma, \mathcal{P})$ *be a grammar,* $\mathfrak{G} = (\mathcal{V}, \Sigma, \delta)$ *be a graph, and* $\mathrm{A} \in \mathcal{N}$ *a context-free path query. We can evaluate* $\mathrm{single}(\mathrm{A}|_{\mathfrak{G}})$ *using* MINIMIZESETGG *in* $\mathcal{O}(|\mathcal{N}||\mathcal{V}|^2(|\mathcal{N}||\mathcal{V}|^2 \log(|\mathcal{N}||\mathcal{V}|^2) + |\mathcal{P}|(|\mathcal{V}|^3 + |\delta|)) + L)$, *in which* $L = \sum\{|\pi| \mid \pi \in \mathrm{single}(q|_{\mathfrak{G}})\}$ *is total length of the shortest paths in the result.*

4 Empirical Evaluation

To show that the path-based semantics for context-free path are viable in practice, we implemented the MINIMIZESETGG algorithm of Fig. 2, *right*, and the straightforward path derivation algorithm in C++14. Open-source code of the full C++14 implementation of the data structures, algorithms, and supporting tooling used can be found at https://www.jhellings.nl/projects/cfpqpaths/. Using this implementation, we ran three different experiments to study the behavior of the MINIMIZESETGG algorithm. The programs were compiled and run on a workstation with an Intel Core i5-4670 CPU, running at a maximum of 3.8 GHz, and with 16 GiB of main memory. In each of our experiments, we test with synthetic graphs that are designed specifically to test extreme-case behavior of the algorithms. Visualizations of these graphs can be found in Fig. 4.

Cost of the Single-Path Semantics. As the first experiment, we study the cost of evaluating context-free path queries using the single-path semantics. To put MINIMIZESETGG to the test, we run these experiments with the grammar

$$Q \mapsto A\ Q', \qquad Q' \mapsto Q\ B, \qquad Q \mapsto A\ B, \qquad A \mapsto \sigma_1, \qquad B \mapsto \sigma_2,$$

which is context-free and cannot be expressed by a regular language. We use the double-cyclic graphs of Fig. 4, as this combination of query and graphs produces very large paths. More specifically, we have proven that, in this case, the longest shortest paths have a size that is *quadratic* in the size of the graph, whereas for all single-symbol grammars and regular grammars the maximum size is only *linear* in the size of the graph (details omitted due to space limitations). The results of the experiment can be found in Fig. 3(a). As is clear from the results, single-path evaluation is practically feasible: the query Q, evaluated on a double-cyclic graph of 4750 nodes, yields a set of $11 \cdot 10^6$ distinct paths, of which the longest (non-simple) path has $11 \cdot 10^6$ edges, and the average path has $5.6 \cdot 10^6$ edges. Hence, the query result is large. Still, MINIMIZESETGG finished in only 4.3 s and the longest path was constructed in 1.5 s. Hence, even for queries and graphs that produce very large results, the query costs are reasonable.

Grammars: Bounded vs. Unbounded. In the second experiment, we take a more in-depth look of the cost of context-free path query evaluation. In practice, many path queries are *bounded* in the sense that only paths of a limited length are inspected in the graph. E.g., to ask for friends-of-friends in a social network, one only has to inspect paths of length two. Some path queries, however, are *unbounded*, as context-free path queries can use recursion. This is of use, e.g., to query for pairs of indirect friends (Example 1). As unbounded queries can yield much larger result sets than bounded queries, we inspect the impact of the type of queries on the running time of MINIMIZESETGG. For this experiment, we use the queries P_1 (bounded) and P_2 (unbounded):

$$P_1 \mapsto S\ B \qquad\qquad B \mapsto S\ S \qquad\qquad S \mapsto \sigma;$$
$$P_2 \mapsto S\ P_2 \qquad\qquad P_2 \mapsto \sigma \qquad\qquad S \mapsto \sigma.$$

The language described by P_1 is $\mathcal{L}_1 = \{\sigma\sigma\}$, and the language described by P_2 is $\mathcal{L}_2 = \{\sigma^k \mid k \geq 1\}$. We use the cycle graphs with w nodes of Fig. 4, on which query P_1 will evaluate to a very sparse result set of w paths, whereas query P_2 will evaluate to a very dense result set of w^2 paths. We measured the running time of MINIMIZESETGG for both queries. The results of the experiment can be found in Fig. 3(b). As is clear from the results, the performance of single-path evaluation depends largely on the size of the query result. On the one hand, query evaluation for P_1, a bounded query yielding a small result set, finished within a second on all graphs. On the other hand, query evaluation for P_2, an unbounded query yielding large result sets, produced a result set $22 \cdot 10^6$ paths on the larges graph and did so in 22 s. We notice that the size of the result set is the limiting factor here: in the previous experiment, we already demonstrated that MINIMIZESETGG can easily deal with very large paths constructed by complex context-free path queries.

Grammars: Unambiguous vs. Ambiguous. In the third and final experiment, we look at the impact of the design of context-free path queries on the cost of their evaluation. This experiment is inspired by well-known results from parsing and compiler construction (see, e.g., [17]): for grammars that are deterministic and unambiguous, e.g., $LL(k)$ or $LR(k)$ grammars, simple high-performance parsers with a linear running time exist. For non-deterministic and for ambiguous grammars, such high-performance parsers do not exist, however. The MINIMIZE-SETGG algorithm we propose works on all grammars, even grammars that are non-deterministic and ambiguous. This raises the question whether the type of grammars impacts the overall performance. To answer this question, we construct two equivalent queries Q_1 (unambiguous) and Q_2 (ambiguous):

$$Q_1 \mapsto S\ Q_1 \qquad\qquad Q_1 \mapsto \sigma \qquad\qquad S \mapsto \sigma;$$
$$Q_2 \mapsto Q_2\ Q_2 \qquad\qquad Q_2 \mapsto \sigma.$$

Both queries specify the language $\mathcal{L} = \{\sigma^k \mid k \geq 1\}$. As in the previous experiment, we use cycle graphs. On these cycle graphs, both queries will evaluate to very dense results sets. We measured the running time of MINIMIZESETGG for both queries. The results of the experiment can be found in Fig. 3(c). As is clear from the results, evaluation of the unambiguous query Q_1 is magnitudes faster than evaluation of the ambiguous query Q_2, even though MINIMIZESETGG does not yet optimize for deterministic or unambiguous grammars. The reason for this is simple: for any shortest path in the graph, Q_2 has many different ways to derive the trace of this path, whereas Q_1 only has a single derivation. Consequently, MINIMIZESETGG will have to inspect many more choices while evaluating Q_2. Still, we believe that further optimizations for deterministic and unambiguous grammars are possible, a direction we leave open for future work.

5   Related Work

There is an abundant literature on graph queries, formal languages, and context-free grammars. There is only limited work toward answering graph queries with paths, however. Likewise, there is only limited work on the related problem of deriving shortest strings from grammars. Next, we give a brief overview.

As stated before, path-based semantics have only gained limited attention. For the regular expressions, Barceló et al. [6] introduced the extended regular path queries that have path variables for output. The main focus of Barceló et al. is, however, on the use of path variables for expressivity purposes, and path-based results are only studied in limited details. Recent work by Hofman et al. [21] provides an alternative to use path-based query semantics for debugging: to gain more insight in the behavior of regular path queries with respect to the expected behavior, Hofman et al. propose a technique based on separability. Although this approach addresses query debugging, it does not lift the other limitations of the traditional query semantics used to evaluate path queries. In practical graph database systems, path-based results can already be used in some limited settings [2]. E.g., SPARQL can return RDF graphs via CONSTRUCT queries [19], which can be used to encode fixed-size paths; whereas Gremlin can enumerate graph traversal steps (which can encode paths) via the .path() step, which comes at prohibitive high costs [29]. In the setting of model checking using CTL [12], path-based query semantics are widely used to produce witnesses and counterexamples that show why the graph does or does not meet the conditions expressed by the CTL formulae. Unfortunately, model checking languages lack the expressive power found in most path query languages used to query graph databases. This sharply contrasts our work, as we show that path-based results are viable both in theory and in practice, this even for complex context-free path queries. Hence, to the best of our knowledge, our work is the first to systematically formalize and study path results for complex graph query languages.

Barrett et al. [7] studies variations of the single-path semantics we propose in this work. They do so from a complexity-theoretical standpoint, however, by classifying the complexity of query evaluation using variations of our single-path semantics. E.g., they show that the single-path semantics is feasible for regular path queries and context-free path queries, but becomes unfeasible when only simple paths are to be returned. As their focus is on classifying the complexity of evaluation, Barret et al. do not provide practical algorithms for the evaluation of path queries using the single-path semantics. We improve on this work by providing the algorithm MINIMIZESETGG, an efficient algorithm for evaluating context-free path queries on graphs using the single-path semantics.

Finally, we have shown that the evaluation of context-free path queries on graphs using the single-path semantics can be reduced to the derivation of a shortest string from a grammar. Mclean et al. [27] proved that such a shortest string could be computed effective given a grammar, but failed to give a practical algorithm for doing so. We improve on these results by providing the algorithm MINIMIZESET, an efficient algorithm for computing the shortest string in a grammar. Other works, e.g. [13–15,26], provide ways to enumerate strings in a grammar, but these algorithms cannot effectively be used to quickly find the shortest such string.

6   Conclusions and Future Work

To address the limitations of the traditional semantics for evaluating path queries, such as the regular path queries and the context-free path queries, we proposed the single-path semantics. This path-based semantics is not only useful for end-users, but also enables new directions in the design of graph query languages and enables new tools for graph analytics, data exploration, data provenance, and debugging of complex path queries. To show the practical viability of the single-path semantics, we also propose algorithms that evaluate context-free path queries using the single-path semantics. Our initial results are promising: our experimental evaluation shows that queries can be evaluated using the single-path semantics with little effort, even in cases where the path-based query results are very large. Based on our initial results, we see several avenues for the further study of evaluating queries with path-based semantics:

1. The algorithms in our paper are *bottom-up* and are tuned toward evaluating a query over the entire graph. In many practical applications, the end-user is only interested in a part of the graph, e.g., paths that originate or end at a certain node. For such applications, we are interested in the development of *top-down* and *goal-oriented* algorithms.
2. Our measurements showed that the cost of evaluating a context-free path query depends heavily on the structure of the grammar used by the query: evaluating different grammars that express the same query can have widely different costs. This raises an interesting query optimization question: can we automatically optimize grammars to reduce the cost of evaluation?
3. Furthermore, it is open whether simpler, more efficient, query evaluation algorithms exist for restricted classes of context-free grammars (e.g., deterministic grammars or unambiguous grammars [17]). It is not directly clear if such algorithms exist: deterministic and unambiguous grammars will still face ambiguity and non-deterministic choices in their evaluation on graphs, as complex graphs can have many paths with the same traces.

References

1. Alon, U.: An Introduction to Systems Biology: Design Principles of Biological Circuits. Chapman and Hall/CRC, Boca Raton (2006)
2. Angles, R., Arenas, M., Barceló, P., Hogan, A., Reutter, J., Vrgoč, D.: Foundations of modern query languages for graph databases. ACM Comput. Surv. 50(5), 68:1–68:40 (2017)
3. Arenas, M., Conca, S., Pérez, J.: Counting beyond a yottabyte, or how SPARQL 1.1 property paths will prevent adoption of the standard. In: Proceedings of the 21st International Conference on World Wide Web, pp. 629–638. ACM (2012)
4. Bar-Hillel, Y., Perles, M.A., Shamir, E.: On formal properties of simple phrase structure grammars. Zeitschrift für Phonetik, Sprachwissenschaft und Kommunikationsforschung 14, 143–172 (1961)
5. Barceló, P.: Querying graph databases. In: Proceedings of the 32nd Symposium on Principles of Database Systems, pp. 175–188. ACM (2013)

6. Barceló, P., Libkin, L., Lin, A.W., Wood, P.T.: Expressive languages for path queries over graph-structured data. ACM Trans. Database Syst. **37**(4), 31:1–31:46 (2012)
7. Barrett, C., Jacob, R., Marathe, M.: Formal-language-constrained path problems. SIAM J. Comput. **30**(3), 809–837 (2000)
8. Berglund, A., et al.: XML path language (XPath) 2.0 (2nd edn). Technical report, W3C (2010). http://www.w3.org/TR/2010/REC-xpath20-20101214/
9. Bray, T., Paoli, J., Sperberg-McQueen, C.M., Maler, E., Yergeau, F., Cowan, J.: Extensible markup language (XML) 1.1 (2nd edn). Technical report, W3C (2006). http://www.w3.org/TR/2006/REC-xml11-20060816
10. Cheney, J., Chiticariu, L., Tan, W.C.: Provenance in databases: why, how, and where. Found. Trends Databases **1**(4), 379–474 (2009)
11. Clark, J., DeRose, S.: XML path language (XPath) version 1.0. Technical report, W3C (1999). http://www.w3.org/TR/1999/REC-xpath-19991116/
12. Clarke, E.M., Grumberg, O., Peled, D.: Model Checking. The MIT Press, Cambridge (1999)
13. Dömösi, P.: Unusual algorithms for lexicographical enumeration. Acta Cybern. **14**(3), 461–468 (2000)
14. Dong, Y.: Linear algorithm for lexicographic enumeration of CFG parse trees. Sci. China Ser. F: Inf. Sci. **52**(7), 1177–1202 (2009). https://doi.org/10.1007/s11432-009-0132-7
15. Florêncio, C.C., Daenen, J., Ramon, J., den Bussche, J.V., Dyck, D.V.: Naive infinite enumeration of context-free languages in incremental polynomial time. J. Univ. Comput. Sci. **21**(7), 891–911 (2015)
16. Fredman, M.L., Tarjan, R.E.: Fibonacci heaps and their uses in improved network optimization algorithms. J. ACM **34**(3), 596–615 (1987)
17. Grune, D., Jacobs, C.J.: Parsing Techniques: A Practical Guide, 2nd edn. Springer, New York (2008). https://doi.org/10.1007/978-0-387-68954-8
18. Harel, D., Pnueli, A., Stavi, J.: Propositional dynamic logic of nonregular programs. J. Comput. Syst. Sci. **26**(2), 222–243 (1983)
19. Harris, S., Seaborne, A.: SPARQL 1.1 query language. Technical report, W3C (2013). http://www.w3.org/TR/2013/REC-sparql11-query-20130321
20. Hellings, J.: Conjunctive context-free path queries. In: Proceedings of the 17th International Conference on Database Theory (ICDT 2014), pp. 119–130 (2014)
21. Hofman, P., Martens, W.: Separability by short subsequences and subwords. In: 18th International Conference on Database Theory. Leibniz International Proceedings in Informatics (LIPIcs), vol. 31, pp. 230–246. Schloss Dagstuhl-Leibniz-Zentrum fuer Informatik (2015)
22. Kozen, D.: Kleene algebra with tests. ACM Trans. Program. Lang. Syst. **19**(3), 427–443 (1997)
23. Lange, M.: Model checking propositional dynamic logic with all extras. J. Appl. Log. **4**(1), 39–49 (2006)
24. Libkin, L., Martens, W., Vrgoč, D.: Querying graph databases with XPath. In: Proceedings of the 16th International Conference on Database Theory, pp. 129–140. ACM (2013)
25. Losemann, K., Martens, W.: The complexity of evaluating path expressions in SPARQL. In: Proceedings of the 31st ACM SIGMOD-SIGACT-SIGAI Symposium on Principles of Database Systems, pp. 101–112. ACM (2012)
26. Mäkinen, E.: On lexicographic enumeration of regular and context-free languages. Acta Cybern. **13**(1), 55–61 (1997)

27. Mclean, M.J., Johnston, D.B.: An algorithm for finding the shortest terminal strings which can be produced from non-terminals in context-free grammars. In: Street, A.P., Wallis, W.D. (eds.) Combinatorial Mathematics III. LNM, vol. 452, pp. 180–196. Springer, Heidelberg (1975). https://doi.org/10.1007/BFb0069557

28. Robinson, I., Webber, J., Eifrem, E.: Graph Databases: New Opportunities for Connected Data, 2nd edn. O'Reilly Media Inc., Boston (2015)

29. Rodriguez, M.A.: The gremlin graph traversal machine and language (invited talk). In: Proceedings of the 15th Symposium on Database Programming Languages, pp. 1–10. ACM, New York (2015)

30. Schreiber, G., Raimond, Y.: RDF 1.1 primer. Technical report, W3C (2014). http://www.w3.org/TR/2014/NOTE-rdf11-primer-20140624

31. Sevon, P., Eronen, L.: Subgraph queries by context-free grammars. J. Integr. Bioinform. **5**(2), 157–172 (2008)

Software Foundations for Data Interoperability

NGNC: A Flexible and Efficient Framework for Error-Tolerant Query Autocompletion

Yukai Miao[1]([✉]), Jianbin Qin[2], Sheng Hu[3], Yuyang Dong[4], Yoshiharu Ishikawa[5], and Makoto Onizuka[6]

[1] University of New South Wales, Sydney, Australia
yukai.miao@unsw.edu.au
[2] Shenzhen Institute of Computing Sciences, Shenzhen University, Shenzhen, China
jqin@sics.ac.cn
[3] Hokkaido University, Sapporo, Japan
hu.sheng@icredd.hokudai.ac.jp
[4] NEC Corporation, Tokyo, Japan
y-dong@aj.jp.nec.com
[5] Nagoya University, Nagoya, Japan
ishikawa@i.nagoya-u.ac.jp
[6] Osaka University, Suita, Japan
onizuka@ist.osaka-u.ac.jp

Abstract. Query autocompletion (QAC) is an important feature that automatically completes a query and saves users' keystrokes. It has been widely adopted in Web search engines, desktop search, input method editors, etc. In some applications, especially for mobile devices, typing accurately is laborious and error-prone. Hence advanced QAC methods tolerate errors when users are typing. As such, some data integration tasks also adopt this feature to process string similarity searches. Most existing work uses edit distance to measure the similarity between the input and correct strings. These methods overlook the quality of the suggested completions, and the efficiency needs to be improved. In this paper, we present NGNC, a framework that supports error-tolerant QAC in a flexible and efficient way. The framework is designed on the basis of a noisy channel model which separates the query prediction to two estimations, one by a language model and the other by an error model. Many QAC ranking methods and spelling correction methods can be easily plugged into the framework. To address the efficiency issue, we devise a neighborhood generation method accompanied with a trie index to quickly find candidates for the error model, as well as a fast top-k retrieval method by caching and pruning. We develop a QAC system based on NGNC. It is able to evaluate the combinations of various ranking and spelling correction methods using query logs and automatically choose the best combination for online query workloads. We highlight research challenges, present our solutions, overview the system architecture, and perform an experimental evaluation on a real dataset to showcase how NGNC improves the state of the art of error-tolerant QAC.

L. Qin et al. (Eds.): SFDI 2020/LSGDA 2020, CCIS 1281, pp. 101–115, 2020.
https://doi.org/10.1007/978-3-030-61133-0_8

Keywords: Query autocompletion · Query suggestion · Spelling correction

1   Introduction

Query autocompletion (QAC) is an important feature that guides users to type the query correctly and efficiently. As a user types the query, it shows top-ranked suggestions that contain the currently input characters as a prefix, hence to save keystrokes. Due to the convenience it brings to users, it has become a standard feature in many applications, including Web search engines, command shells, input method editors (IMEs) [12], and integrated development environments (IDEs) [11]. It is well-known that misspelling is a common phenomenon when users are typing, especially when typing is tedious and error-prone, e.g., with a mobile phone. Thus, many studies on QAC target the case of error-tolerant QAC (a.k.a. fuzzy type-ahead search/online spelling correction), i.e., to tolerate a small number of errors in the input [4,5,7,8,16,17,23,24]. An example is shown in Fig. 1. As the user types `schwatzn`, an incorrect prefix of `schwarzenegger`, the system still suggests correct completions. As such, it also provides a way of coping with noise in textual data, and hence can be used for string similarity search in data integration tasks [22].

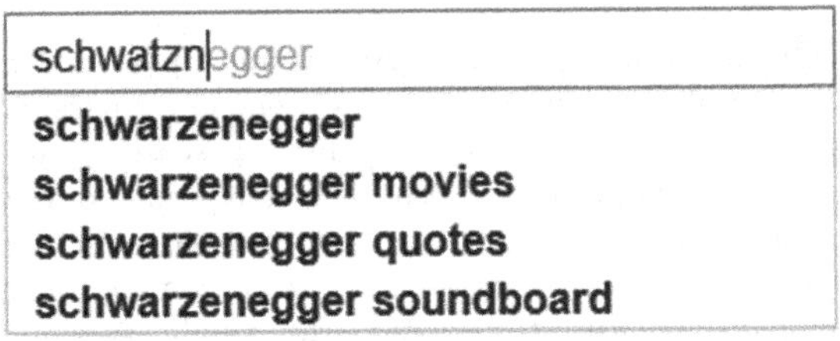

Fig. 1. Error-tolerant query autocompletion.

State-of-the-art solutions to error-tolerant QAC can be divided into two categories. The first category, which includes most studies, uses edit (Levenshtein) distance to measure the similarity between the user's input and a correct string's prefix [4,5,7,16,17,23,24]. Correct strings whose prefixes are within an edit distance threshold to the input are produced as candidates for further ranking. The second category [8] employs the noisy channel model [14], widely adopted for spelling correction, to estimate the probability of yielding the potentially misspelled query, using the combination of a language model and an error model. The language model is based on the maximum likelihood estimation of the distribution of queries from the query log. For the error model, the (completion, query) pair is cut into "transfemes" (the transformation from a substring to another, e.g., em → an), and then a Markov n-gram model is utilized to estimate the probability of a sequence of transfemes.

Despite many error-tolerant QAC solutions proposed in the last decade, two challenging issues remain. First, most existing work focuses on tolerating errors, yet it is unclear how the quality of QAC (i.e., accuracy and keystroke saving) can be improved by choosing QAC ranking methods [2,15] or spelling correction methods [9,14,19] for the target application. E.g., diversified results [3,6] are desirable for a search engine; while for an IDE or an IME, users may want recently chosen suggestions to be ranked higher and thus context-aware QAC [1,18] is more useful. Second, the efficiency of error-tolerant QAC still needs improvement. State-of-the-art edit distance-based methods spend around 0.1 s per query to produce candidates within an edit distance threshold of 3 to the input (as the standard setting in most aforementioned studies, also suggested by [19] for spelling correction). Although such speed is acceptable for single queries, it does not mean the response is efficient when multiple queries are invoked simultaneously, a common scenario for Web search engines, cloud IMEs, and online IDEs. Moreover, the candidates need to be ranked (e.g., by a support vector machine [9]) to present a set of good top-k suggestions to users, thereby consuming more query processing time. It is unknown how to efficiently compute top-k results under such ranking[1]. The Markov n-gram method is even slower – it spends 0.5 s per query if we seek a 90% recall and the time rapidly increases when a higher recall is needed [8] – thus less likely to be used for efficiency-demanding online services.

Seeing the above issues, we present a framework that processes error-tolerant QAC in a flexible and efficient way. Our framework is based on a weighted **noisy channel model**, which consists of a language model and an error model to evaluate the suggestions. The weight can be adjusted to reflect which model is more focused. As such, the framework becomes flexible in the sense that developers are able to *plug in* and *tune* a wide range of QAC ranking methods for the language model and spelling correction methods for the error model. Hence, an appropriate combination can be chosen to optimize the quality of QAC for the target application. To generate suggestions, we adopt an edit distance constraint to find a set of candidates first. To improve the efficiency, unlike existing methods that directly build a trie to index the strings in a lexicon, we resort to **neighborhood generation** and index the deletion neighbors of the strings, thereby obviating the cause of the inefficiency of existing methods. Then the noisy channel model is utilized to rank the candidates. To speed up this process, we propose a fast top-k retrieval method tailored to the noisy channel model. It caches previously computed probabilities and prunes unpromising evaluations. The two acceleration methods jointly achieve the overall efficiency of query processing.

We built a system based on the proposed framework, named NGNC (**N**eighborhood **G**eneration for **N**oisy **C**hannel). It consists of a module that evaluates the performances of combinations of different ranking and spelling correction methods and selects the best one for online query workloads. We

---

[1] Although there have been a few studies [5,7,17,24] on the top-k retrieval by edit distance ranking or its simple extensions, it was reported that the recall and the keystroke saving are inferior to learning methods [8].

evaluated its performance using the DBLP dataset of author names and titles. We implemented a series of state-of-the-art QAC and spelling correction methods and integrated them into the system. An experimental evaluation showcases how the system improves upon existing solutions.

The rest of the paper is organized as follows. Section 2 reviews the noisy channel model and introduces our NGNC framework, including candidate generation and top-k retrieval. Section 3 presents the system architecture based on NGNC. Section 4 reports our experimental results. Section 5 concludes this paper.

2 The NGNC Approach

Given a query string q, an error-tolerant query autocompletion is to return a list of k suggestions of correct completions, from which the user can select. To correct misspellings in the query, we assume that a lexicon of correct strings, denoted by S, is available.

2.1 Noisy Channel Model

The noisy channel model is a kind of Bayesian inference. Let c denote a completion. Given an observation q, we want to find correctly spelled completions ranked by descending order of probability $P(c|q)$. By applying Bayes' rule and dropping the constant $P(q)$, we have

$$P(c|q) = \frac{P(q|c)P(c)}{P(q)} \propto P(q|c)P(c). \tag{1}$$

$P(c)$ is computed by a language model that describes the prior probability of c as the intended completion. $P(q|c)$ is computed by an error model that estimates the probability of producing the observed input q when the intended completion is c. Equation 1 refers to a standard model that just multiples the two probabilities, yet often they are not commensurate. A remedy is to weight the two models. By using a weight $\lambda \in [0, 1]$, we parameterize the right side of Eq. 1 as[2] $P(q|c)^\lambda P(c)^{1-\lambda}$. By taking the log-probability, we have

$$\log P(c|q) \propto \lambda \log P(q|c) + (1 - \lambda) \log P(c). \tag{2}$$

The two probabilities can be estimated separately. E.g., we may use Lueck's method [20], the winner of Microsoft Speller Challenge 2011, to estimate the error probability $P(q|c)$. On the other hand, there has been quite some work on improving the quality of QAC, e.g., by returning context-aware [1,18] or diversified [3,6] results. They can be plugged in as the language model for $P(c)$. This setting also enables our framework to process previously unseen queries, in contrast to the existing noisy channel method [8] that only uses maximum likelihood estimation on the query log.

---

[2] The weighting scheme in [14], which only assigns weight to $P(c)$, is a special case of our ranking function.

Further, we notice that for query spelling correction, the language and error models are often put together, e.g., in a support vector machine [9] or a hidden Markov model [19]. To incorporate these models, we generalize the noisy channel model to the following form:

$$\log P(c|q) \propto \sum_i \mu_i f_i^{EM} + \sum_j \lambda_j f_j^{LM}, \tag{3}$$

where each f_i^{EM} is an error model feature, f_j^{LM} is a language model feature, and μ_i and λ_j are the weights of the two models.

As such, the QAC model becomes flexible as we may integrate any *linear* models for error and language, either separately or in a combined way. It can be seen that the standard noisy channel model (Eq. 1) is a special case such that there are only one error model feature and one language model feature, whose weights are both 1; while the improved noisy channel model (Eq. 2) has a weight $\lambda_j = \lambda$ on the language model.

2.2   Candidate Generation

We use the lexicon S to generate completions. Due to the large size of S, it is prohibitively expensive to generate completions by considering every string in S and comparing them with the input. As a result, a common practice is to generate a set of candidates similar to the input. Edit (Levenshtein) distance is a good measure for string similarity and has been widely adopted and studied for error-tolerant QAC. It measures the minimum number of edit operations, including insertion, deletion, and substitution of a character, to transform one string to another. It can be computed using dynamic programming.

Suppose n keywords have been input to the query q. Let $q[n]$ denote the last (partial) keyword of q^3. Then the candidate generation is to find the strings $s \in S$, such that there exists a prefix of s whose edit distance to $q[n]$ is no greater than a threshold τ. Each string s is then appended to the completions of previous keywords to produce a candidate completion c.

Existing methods for candidate generation [4,5,7,16,17,24] are mainly based on a trie index. The strings in S are offline indexed in a tri.e. For online query processing, they maintain the set of the strings whose prefixes are within edit distance τ from $q[n]$. The frontier of these prefixes in the trie are called *active nodes*. Whenever a character is appended to $q[n]$, the set of new active nodes is computed using current active ones. The strings stored under the active nodes are returned as candidates. The main drawback of these methods is the large active node size. E.g., consider $q[n] = $ abc and $\tau = 1$. The active nodes include all the prefixes in the pattern of ?bc, a?c, or ab?. Even for the method [24] that tries to alleviate this drawback by removing ancestor-descendant relationship among active nodes, the active node size is still typically 10^4 for a lexicon of

---

[3] For ease of exposition, we do not consider merging/splitting errors (e.g., power point for powerpoint) here. This case can be covered by inserting/deleting a space.

one million strings and theoretically $O(|q[n]|^\tau |\Sigma|^\tau)$, where $|\Sigma|$ is the size of the alphabet, thereby significantly affecting query response time and becoming even worse for applications with a large alphabet such as Unicode.

To solve the above issue, rather than index original strings, we employ the neighborhood generation technique and index in a trie the strings' deletion neighbors, which are generated by deleting at most τ characters from the strings. When the user inputs a query keyword, its deletion neighbors are also generated and searched in the trie for matching prefixes. This process can be performed incrementally (i.e., when a keystroke is input, we do not start from scratch but compute from existing active nodes) and efficiently by maintaining a small set of active nodes whose size is insensitive to the alphabet size. To understand how this works, consider the above example $q[n] =$ abc and $\tau = 1$. All the strings such as aba, abb, ..., abz can be represented as a deletion neighbor ab# (# means the character is deleted) which has an edit distance of 1 to $q[n]$. We prove that for the case of prefix match, the edit distance constraint can be equivalently converted to a constraint on deletion neighbors, and thus guarantee the correctness of the algorithm based on neighborhood generation.

The number of active nodes of our method is typically around 10^3 and can be further reduced to the order of 10 by a series of optimizations. Our experiments show that the time spent on candidate generation can be reduced by up to two orders of magnitude from existing methods. One may notice that the index size could be large due to neighborhood generation. Hence, we eliminate various kinds of redundancy in the index to reduce the size to an acceptable level – several GB for a lexicon of 1M strings, so the index can fit in main memory for real applications. We refer readers to our recent work [21] for the details of the candidate generation algorithm.

2.3   Top-k Retrieval

Given a set of candidate completions that satisfy the edit distance constraint, we rank them by Eq. 2 and pick the top-k completions. Due to the potentially large number of candidate completions (e.g., when the query length is 5, the number of candidate completions that pass the $\tau = 3$ edit distance filter is usually in the order of 10^4 for a lexicon of 1M strings), this step needs acceleration as well. Traditional top-k query processing algorithms that are based on sorted lists, such as the TA algorithm [10], do not apply here because both $P(q|c)$ and $P(c)$ need online evaluation, meaning that there is no sorted list available. To address this problem, we propose a fast top-k retrieval algorithm based on two observations:

Caching. As the user incrementally types characters, given a query q' which appends a character to q, many candidate completions may be shared with q. In Eq. 2, the language model $P(c)$ is independent of the query; i.e., for a completion c shared by q and q', the value of $P(c)$ is constant. Thus, we cache the value of $P(c)$ when processing q, and skip evaluating it again if c is a completion for q'.

Pruning. This is to deal with the case when $P(c)$ is not in the cache. Although we need both $P(q|c)$ and $P(c)$ to obtain the overall score for ranking, some

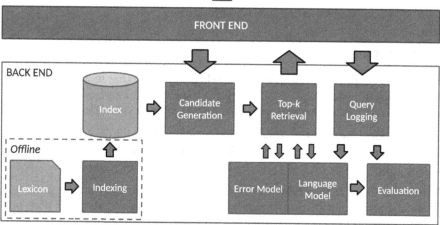

Fig. 2. System architecture.

evaluations can be skipped when c is unpromising. We first compute the model with the higher weight, say the language model $P(c)$. Since the log-probability of the error model is in the range of $(-\infty, 0]$, by Eq. 2, if $(1-\lambda)\log P(c)$ is less than the score of the current k-th completion, then we can safely discard c without computing $P(q|c)$.

So far we have treated both $P(q|c)$ and $P(c)$ as black boxes. The performance can be further accelerated for the white box case. For caching, we may keep the features used for evaluating $P(q|c)$, and reuse them when we evaluate $P(q'|c)$, provided that they share these features. For pruning (suppose the language model has more weight), we take the difference between the current k-th completion's score and $(1-\lambda)\log P(c)$ as an input of the error model, so as to achieve early termination when computing $P(q|c)$. E.g., suppose $P(q|c)$ is a product of two components and both can be upper-bounded. After computing the first component, we use the upper bound of the second component and the input difference to check if it is possible to achieve a higher score than the current k-th completion, and stop if this check fails.

3   System Architecture

Figure 2 shows our system architecture. The system is comprised of two components: a front-end user interface that handles user interactions and a back-end infrastructure that processes input queries.

3.1   Front End

The front end of the system is a user interface similar to a Web search engine. The user may type in a query in the search box. The system returns a list of top suggestions that completes the query and corrects any misspelling. The user can navigate through the suggestions. The user may also click a suggestion, and then the system directs to the corresponding result.

3.2 Back End

The back end consists of the following modules: (1) indexing module, (2) candidate generation module, (3) top-k retrieval module, (4) language/error evaluation module, (5) query logging module, and (6) online evaluation module.

Indexing Module. This module generates deletion neighbors of each string in the lexicon and indexes them in a trie in an offline manner. Strings are stored at the leaf nodes of the trie index, so the lexicon does not have to be loaded again.

Candidate Generation Module. It takes the input query from the front end. For each (partial) keyword in the query, it finds the indexed strings whose prefixes are within edit distance τ from the keyword. We use the method presented in Sect. 2.2 to find the strings satisfying the edit distance constraint, and concatenate them as candidate completions.

Top-k Retrieval Module. It takes candidate completions as input and interacts with the language/error evaluation module to compute top-k suggestions, using the method presented in Sect. 2.3. The top-k suggestions are output to the front end.

Language/Error Evaluation Module. It evaluates the $P(c)$ and $P(q|c)$ probabilities of a candidate completion using the selected language and error models.

Query Logging Module. This is to log the queries that have been input by the user. The language model can use the log to improve the result quality, e.g., by considering search context or user behavior.

Online Evaluation Module. This module evaluates the top-k ranking performance of all the combinations of language/error modules to help users tune the system and find the best one to use for online query workloads. We assume that users may vary across typing habits and preferences on the query results. So the online evaluation is based on user-specific query logs. We first extract the query logs for the user requesting the evaluation and obtain the matched result for each query, i.e. what is eventually clicked by the user. Then, we process these queries using all the model combinations and evaluate the quality of their suggestions. The evaluation results can be used for automatic model selection as well.

4 Experiments

We performed an experimental evaluation on several real datasets. All the modules in the front and back ends were implemented in Python.

Table 1. Online evaluation results (DBLP).

	MPC + Lueck	MPC + Markov	MPC + SVM	CA + Lueck	CA + Markov	CA + SVM	Div + Lueck	Div + Markov	Div +SVM
MRR	0.756	0.763	0.765	0.764	0.765	0.767	0.542	0.550	0.545
SK@1	0.733	0.743	0.743	0.750	0.753	0.751	0.483	0.502	0.495
SK@2	0.767	0.770	0.782	0.767	0.770	0.779	0.567	0.567	0.567
SK@3	0.783	0.788	0.788	0.783	0.788	0.788	0.617	0.617	0.617

4.1 Experiment Setup

We choose DBLP, a dataset of author names and titles of computer science bibliography records from the DBLP website, as the lexicon for evaluation. It has been used in many studies on error-tolerant QAC [4,5,16,17,23,24]. The dataset was tokenized into terms using white space and punctuation. When a term is clicked, the system directs to the corresponding page on DBLP. After preprocessing, the dataset has 319,690 strings, with an average length of 8.6 and an alphabet of 38 characters.

Users may experience the QAC quality by interacting with the system. In addition to quickly completing users' queries, the system also evaluates the query response time to reflect the efficiency of our method.

The following settings are available in our experiments:

- Edit distance threshold τ for candidate generation: The available range is $[0,3]$, and the default value is 3. A larger τ indicates more errors in the input are tolerated. Note that when $\tau = 0$, the QAC becomes an exact prefix match.
- The number of suggestions k: The default setting is 5. A list of up to 25 suggestions is available.
- The parameter λ in the noisy channel model: The default setting is 0.5. The available range is $[0,1]$.
- Language model: The default language model is most popular completion (MPC), i.e., the probability is given by the popularity in historical queries. Users may replace it with context-aware QAC [1] (CA) that memorizes the suggestions clicked by the user and gives them higher ranks for succeeding search, or diversified QAC [3] (Div) that returns diversified results.
- Error model: The default model is Lueck's method [20] (Lueck), which evaluates the probability by normalized edit distance. Other options include Markov n-gram model [8] (Markov) and support vector machine [9] (SVM).
- Online model evaluation: We use $k = 2$ as the default setting for automatic model selection. It can be tuned by users.

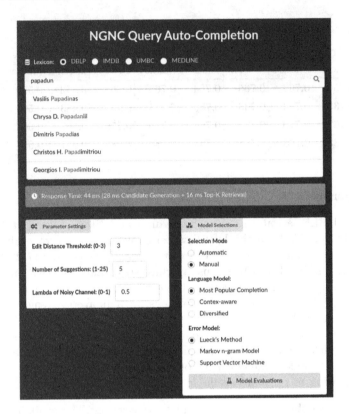

Fig. 3. Query results with default setting, $q = $ **papadun**.

Changing the settings affects not only QAC results but also query processing time, which can be seen from the front end of the system.

4.2 Experiment Results

Online Evaluation and Automatic Model Selection. The online evaluation module provides the latest performance metrics of different model combinations for top-k ranking based on the existing user query log. As shown in Table 1, we measure the performance on the DBLP dataset via commonly-used quality metrics, including Mean Reciprocal Rank (MRR) and Success Rate at top-k (SR@k) [13].

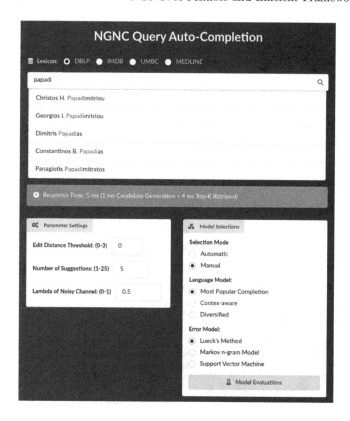

Fig. 4. Query results with $\tau = 0$ (errors not allowed), $q = $ `papadi`.

The combination of CA + SVM achieves the highest MRR. For SR@k, the best competitors are CA + Markov when $k = 1$ and MPC + SVM when $k = 2$ or 3. In general, CA is the best language model for top-1 results because it remembers what users clicked recently. When we consider results with lower ranks, MPC becomes the best. For error models, SVM is generally the best option, though outperformed by Markov in a few cases. Both are better than Lueck because they consider more factors than the normalized edit distance used in Lueck. This result has also been witnessed by previous studies [8,9].

Given such results, users can opt for the automatic model selection which chooses the best model combination that achieves the highest SR@k, though this feature does not work well in a cold start when the user log is very scarce.

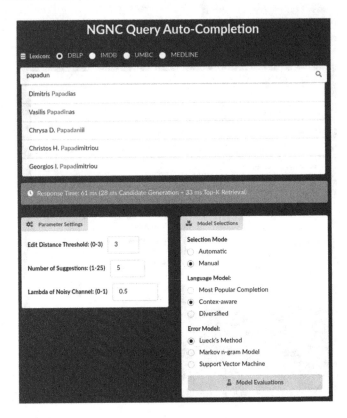

Fig. 5. Query results with context-aware language model (`Dimitris Papadias` recently clicked), $q = $ `papadun`.

4.3   Query Result Examples

Figure 3 shows the user interface. We use the default setting. Results are shown in the list for a query `papadun`.

Figure 4 shows the results of a query `papadi` if we set $\tau = 0$. It can be seen that the QAC becomes exact prefix match.

We may use CA as language model. Suppose that `Dimitris Papadias` was just clicked by the user. Then for the query `papadun`, we have the results given in Fig. 5. `Dimitris Papadias` is ranked first.

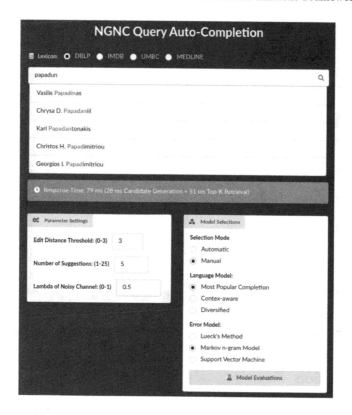

Fig. 6. Query results with Markov n-gram error model, $q =$ papadun.

By choosing Markov to estimate the error, the results of the query papadun are given in Fig. 6. Vasilis Papadinas is ranked first because the transfeme i → u is more probable due to keyboard adjacency.

Figure 7 shows the results of query papadun with the automatic model selection. In this scenario, the system automatically selects MPC as language model and SVM as error model, because they collectively achieve the highest SR@2 for the current user query log.

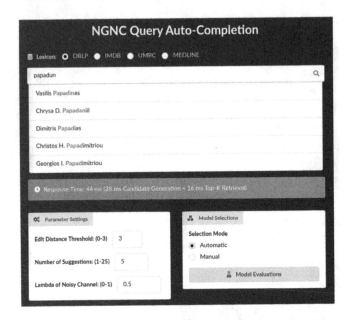

Fig. 7. Query results with automatically selected models, $q =$ papadun.

5   Conclusion

In this paper, we proposed NGNC, a flexible and efficient framework for error-tolerant QAC. By analyzing existing methods for error-tolerant QAC, we considered a framework design composed of a noisy channel model which separates the query prediction to two estimations, one by a language model and the other by an error model. In consequence, many existing QAC ranking methods and spelling correction methods can be plugged into the framework. To address the efficiency issue, we first devised a neighborhood generation method plus a trie index to find candidates for the error model, and then we proposed a fast top-k retrieval method through caching and pruning. Based on NGNC, we developed a QAC system, which is able to evaluate the combinations of various ranking and spelling correction methods using query logs and automatically choose the best combination to process online query workloads. We performed experiments on a real dataset to evaluate NGNC and showed how it improves the state of the art of error-tolerant QAC.

References

1. Bar-Yossef, Z., Kraus, N.: Context-sensitive query auto-completion. In: WWW, pp. 107–116 (2011)
2. Cai, F., de Rijke, M.: A survey of query auto completion in information retrieval. Found. Trends Inf. Retrieval **10**(4), 273–363 (2016)

3. Cai, F., Reinanda, R., de Rijke, M.: Diversifying query auto-completion. ACM Trans. Inf. Syst. **34**(4), 25:1–25:33 (2016)
4. Cetindil, I., Esmaelnezhad, J., Kim, T., Li, C.: Efficient instant-fuzzy search with proximity ranking. In: ICDE, pp. 328–339 (2014)
5. Chaudhuri, S., Kaushik, R.: Extending autocompletion to tolerate errors. In: SIG-MOD, pp. 707–718 (2009)
6. Chen, W., Cai, F., Chen, H., de Rijke, M.: Personalized query suggestion diversi-fication. In: SIGIR, pp. 817–820 (2017)
7. Deng, D., Li, G., Wen, H., Jagadish, H.V., Feng, J.: META: an efficient matching-based method for error-tolerant autocompletion. PVLDB **9**(10), 828–839 (2016)
8. Duan, H., Hsu, B.P.: Online spelling correction for query completion. In: WWW, pp. 117–126 (2011)
9. Duan, H., Li, Y., Zhai, C., Roth, D.: A discriminative model for query spelling correction with latent structural SVM. In: EMNLP-CoNLL, pp. 1511–1521 (2012)
10. Fagin, R., Lotem, A., Naor, M.: Optimal aggregation algorithms for middleware. In: PODS (2001)
11. Hu, S., Xiao, C., Ishikawa, Y.: Scope-aware code completion with discriminative modeling. J. Inf. Process. **27**, 469–478 (2019)
12. Hu, S., Xiao, C., Qin, J., Ishikawa, Y., Ma, Q.: Autocompletion for prefix-abbreviated input. In: SIGMOD, pp. 211–228 (2019)
13. Jiang, J.-Y., Ke, Y.-Y., Chien, P.-Y., Cheng, P.-J.: Learning user reformulation behavior for query auto-completion. In: SIGIR (2014)
14. Jurafsky, D., Martin, J.H.: Speech and Language Processing, vol. 3. Pearson, Lon-don (2014)
15. Krishnan, U., Moffat, A., Zobel, J.: A taxonomy of query auto completion modes. In: ADCS, pp. 6:1–6:8 (2017)
16. Li, G., Ji, S., Li, C., Feng, J.: Efficient fuzzy full-text type-ahead search. VLDB J. **20**(4), 617–640 (2011)
17. Li, G., Wang, J., Li, C., Feng, J.: Supporting efficient top-k queries in type-ahead search. In: SIGIR, pp. 355–364 (2012)
18. Li, L., Deng, H., Dong, A., Chang, Y., Baeza-Yates, R.A., Zha, H.: Exploring query auto-completion and click logs for contextual-aware web search and query suggestion. In: WWW, pp. 539–548 (2017)
19. Li, Y., Duan, H., Zhai, C.: A generalized hidden Markov model with discriminative training for query spelling correction. In SIGIR, pp. 611–620 (2012)
20. Lueck, G.: A data-driven approach for correcting search queries. In: Spelling Alter-ation for Web Search Workshop, p. 6 (2011)
21. Qin, J., et al.: Efficient query autocompletion with edit distance-based error toler-ance. VLDB J. **29**(4), 1–25 (2020)
22. Qin, J., Zhou, X., Wang, W., Xiao, C.: Trie-based similarity search and join. In: EDBT/ICDT Workshops, pp. 392–396 (2013)
23. Xiao, C., Qin, J., Wang, W., Ishikawa, Y., Tsuda, K., Sadakane, K.: Efficient error-tolerant query autocompletion. PVLDB **6**(6), 373–384 (2013)
24. Zhou, X., Qin, J., Xiao, C., Wang, W., Lin, X., Ishikawa, Y.: BEVA: an effi-cient query processing algorithm for error-tolerant autocompletion. ACM Trans. Database Syst. **41**(1), 5:1–5:44 (2016)

A Cheap Implementation of Resugaring in BIRDS Based on Bidirectional Transformation

Xing Zhang[1]([⊠]), Van-Dang Tran[2,4]([⊠]), and Zhenjiang Hu[2,3]([⊠])

[1] Nankai University, Tianjin, China
1612945@mail.nankai.edu.cn
[2] National Institute of Informatics, Tokyo, Japan
dangtv@nii.ac.jp
[3] Peking University, Beijing, China
[4] The Graduate University for Advanced Studies, SOKENDAI, Hayama, Japan
huzj@pku.edu.cn

Abstract. Syntactic sugar refers to a certain syntactic structure added to the programming language. This syntactic structure has no effect on the function of the language, but is more convenient for programmers to use. Since syntactic sugar will be translated to the basic syntactic structure of the core language at the compilation stage, the relationship between the source program written with syntactic sugar and the execution of the core program is masked, and the compiled program is unfamiliar to programmers. It is not convenient for programmers to learn and debug source programs written with syntactic sugar. To solve that problem, this paper adopts the idea of resugaring for automatically transforming the evaluation sequence of the core language into the evaluation sequence of the surface language, and gives a cheap implementation using the existing bidirectional transformation tool BIRDS. The resugaring algorithms for both non-recursive and recursive desugaring transformations are implemented using Datalog, and the solutions to maintain two important properties of emulation and abstraction in the process of resugaring are studied.

Keywords: Desugaring · Resugaring · Bidirectional transformation · BIRDS

1 Introduction

Syntactic sugar plays an important role in extending a core language to a surface language with more user-friendly language constructs. The core language may be a small language with a simple syntactic structure but powerful functions, and it can be enriched to a surface language with additional syntactic sugars. A syntactic sugar can be defined by a set of desugaring rules, describing how it

This work is partially supported by the Japan Society for the Promotion of Science (JSPS) Grant-in-Aid for Scientific Research (S) No. 17H06099.

L. Qin et al. (Eds.): SFDI 2020/LSGDA 2020, CCIS 1281, pp. 116–130, 2020.
https://doi.org/10.1007/978-3-030-61133-0_9

can be mapped to the core language. For instance, the following desugaring rule defines the syntax sugar Or, showing how to transform a surface term with Or to a core term with Let.

$$\mathrm{Or}([x, y, ys...]) \rightarrow \mathrm{Let}([\mathrm{Bind}(\text{``}t\text{''}, x)], [\mathrm{If}(\mathrm{Id}(\text{``}t\text{''}), \mathrm{Id}(\text{``}t\text{''}), \mathrm{Or}([y, ys...]))])$$

One problem with syntactic sugars is that after the desugaring, the resulting programs (in the core language) become unfamiliar to programmers, and it obscures the relationship between the user's source program and the program being evaluated. To resolve this problem, the resugaring technique was proposed to lift the core evaluation sequence into one for the surface [17]. Given a surface term which can be desugared to a core term, resugaring is the process of adding syntactic sugars each step after the reduction of the corresponding desugared core term, in order to obtain an evaluation sequence expressed in surface language. When applied debugging and comprehension tools to core language terms resulting from desugaring, their output is also in terms of the core language. Resugaring can establish correspondence with the surface language that the user employs, so as to facilitate the use of those tools on the surface language [17]. Resugaring should satisfy the following two properties.

– **Emulation**. Each term in the generated surface evaluation sequence desugars into the core term which it is meant to represent.
– **Abstraction**. Code introduced by desugaring is never revealed in the surface evaluation sequence, and code originating from the original input program is never hidden by resugaring.

However, implementation of resugaring needs much effort. We need to implement both desugaring and resugaring carefully to make sure that they are consistent satisfying the emulation property. As pointed out in [17], this pair of transformations between terms of the core and the surface languages forms a bidirectional transformation; taking the surface program as the source and the core language as the view, then the forward transformation is desugaring, and the putback transformation is resugaring. This inspired us to consider a direct use of a bidirectional transformation language to implement resugaring (together with desugaring) so that the consistency between desugaring and resugaring is guaranteed for free. Furthermore, if we adopt to use a putback-based bidirectional language, where the forward transformation can be automatically derived from the putback transformation, by writing a resugaring program, a desugaring program can be automatically generated.

In this paper, we present a new implementation of resugaring using the putback-based bidirectional transformation tool called BIRDS (Bidirectional Transformation for Relational View Update Datalog-based Strategies) [20]. We use the BIRDS tool to develop the resugaring transformation, and automatically generate the corresponding desugaring transformation. Our main technical contributions are summarized as follows.

– We present a new implementation of resugaring using BIRDS based on bidirectional transformation. Our method is simpler and only needs to develop

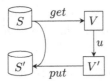

Fig. 1. Bidirectional transformation

and maintain resugaring, which is in sharp contrast to the traditional method that needs to develop and maintain both desugaring and resugaring. Furthermore, our implementation satisfies the emulation property for free, and meets the abstraction property.

- We show how syntax trees can be uniformly represented by relational tables, and how tree transformations (including pattern matching and substitution) can be efficiently implemented over relational operations in Datalog. This enables us to use BIRDS to implement a resugaring system, which integrates rule checking, desugaring and resugaring, and algebraic stepper [5,6].
- Compared to the traditional implementation method, which uses about 1000 lines of codes in Haskell, our new method successfully implements the resugaring transformation using less than 200 lines of codes in Datalog for the same algorithm. Our method is powerful enough to deal with many difficult cases such as recursive syntactic sugars.

The remainder of this paper is organized as follows. After presenting some basic notions in Sect. 2, we propose an algorithm for performing resugaring using a view update strategy in Sect. 3. Section 4 shows how to maintain the emulation and abstraction in our implementation. Section 5 gives some examples, Sect. 6 summarizes related works, and Sect. 7 concludes this paper.

2   Preliminaries

2.1   Bidirectional Transformation

A bidirectional transformation (BX) [11] is a pair of a forward transformation *get* and a backward (putback) transformation *put* (see Fig. 1). The forward transformation *get* is a query over a source S that results in a view V. The putback transformation *put* takes the original S and an updated view V' as input to produce a new source S'. To ensure consistency between the source database and the view, *get* and *put* must satisfy the following round-tripping properties, called GetPut and PutGet:

$$\forall S, put(S, get(S)) = S \qquad \text{(GetPut)}$$
$$\forall S, V', get(put(S, V')) = V' \qquad \text{(PutGet)}$$

The GetPut property ensures that unchanged views correspond to unchanged sources. The PutGet property ensures that all view updates are completely embedded into the source such that the updated view can be computed again from the forward transformation *get* over the updated source.

```
1   % Schema declaration
2   source s₁('X':int, 'Y':int).
3   source s₂('X':int, 'Y':int).
4   view v('X':int, 'Y':int).
5   % View update strategy rules
6   -s₁(X,Y) :- s₁(X,Y), not v(X,Y).
7   -s₂(X,Y) :- s₂(X,Y), not v(X,Y).
8   +s₁(X,Y) :- v(X,Y), not s₁(X,Y), not s₂(X,Y).
```

Fig. 2. A program in BIRDS

2.2 Bidirectional Programming with Datalog

We follow [20] and employ the BIRDS framework [1] to use the Datalog language with extensions for programming putback transformations, i.e. view update strategies. BIRDS [20] supports putback-based bidirectional programming [10,12,13]. In other words, the framework automatically checks the well-behavedness of a putback program written by the user and generates the corresponding forward (*get*) one for free. BIRDS further optimizes the user-written programs before compiling them into lower-level code.

Consider two base tables $s_1(X, Y)$ and $s_2(X, Y)$ and a view $v(X, Y)$, which is expected to be a union over s_1 and s_2. A program of view update strategy accepted by BIRDS consists of two essential parts: schema declaration and view update strategy rules. Figure 2 shows an example of the program, where s_1, s_2 and v are all binary relations with the same attributes 'X' and 'Y'. The first two rules (Lines 6 and 7) of the view update strategy say that if a tuple (X, Y) is in s_1 or s_2 but not in v, it will be deleted from s_1 or s_2, respectively. The last rule says that if a tuple (X, Y) is in v but in neither s_1 nor s_2, it will be inserted to s_1. BIRDS will automatically check the validity of the program and generate a view definition, i.e., forward transformation, as the following.

$$v(X, Y) :- s_1(X, Y).$$
$$v(X, Y) :- s_2(X, Y).$$

3   Resugaring as Putback Transformation

In this section, we shall explain how to write resugaring as a putback transformation (view update strategy), and how to use the BIRDS tool to run it and to automatically generate the corresponding desugaring program. We have implemented the complete putback program[1] using Datalog.

---

[1] https://github.com/nksezx/ResugaringAsPutback/blob/master/putback.dl.

3.1 Converting Syntax Trees to Relational Tables

Since BIRDS works only on relational database, the first step to use BIRDS is to convert syntax trees into relations (tables). This can be done straightforwardly, because syntax trees can be considered as graphs, and graphs can be naturally represented by edge tables describing relationship between nodes. In order to facilitate the traversal and compress tables, we convert each abstract syntax tree into a binary tree, because the binary tree will have a fixed number of columns after it is expressed as a relational table.

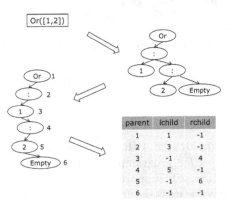

Fig. 3. Converting syntax trees to relational tables

As shown in Fig. 3, the syntax tree of Or([1,2]) is first converted into a binary tree. Then, we give each node a unique number and use the relational table to record the left and right child of each node. In this way, the relational table can be used to concisely represent syntax trees.

3.2 Designing Source and View Tables

To use BIRDS, we need to design source tables that represent the surface programs (surface terms) and transformation rules and the view tables that represent the core programs (core terms). A good relational table design can make the update strategy easier to write. In our system, we have the following five tables.

Node. The node table records the information of all nodes in the patterns and terms. As shown in Table 1, *Id* is a unique key assigned to the created node in the semantic analysis. There are three types of nodes: keyword nodes, constant nodes, and variable nodes. There are three types of nodes in patterns (terms with variables) and only two in terms, which are keyword nodes and constant nodes. *Name* is the value of the node, which is a string. *Root* means the id of the root in the syntax tree.

Table 1. The node table

id:number	name:string	type:string	root:number
1	Or/And/:	keyword	1
2	123/Empty/true	constant	1
3	x/y/z	variable	1

Table 2. The pAst table

par:number	lchild:number	rchild:number
5	6	−1
6	−1	−1

pAst, sAst and cAst. These three tables are used to record the edge relationships of the syntax tree for patterns, surface syntax trees and core syntax trees. They are of the same schema as shown in Table 2: *Par* is the id of the parent node of each group, while *lchild* is the id of its left child and *rchild* is the id of its right child. *-1* means the node is missing.

The **pAst** table is to store all patterns. Consider the pattern of (Delay x). It is shown in Fig. 4, where only two nodes *Delay* and *x* are included, and the ids of the two nodes are 1 and 2, respectively. The x node is the left child node of *Delay*, so we have (1, 2, −1) and (2, −1, −1) in Table 2. The cAst view and the sAst source respectively record the edge relationships in the core term and the generated surface term. And their fields are exactly the same as the pAst source, which represents the two patterns before and after transformation in all rules.

Rule. The transformation rules are recorded in the rule table as shown in Table 3. The id of the root in the syntax tree uniquely represents the corresponding pattern. Let LHS represent the surface syntax pattern on the left side of the transformation rule, and RHS the core syntax pattern on the right side. Then, for the rule described in Fig. 5, the id of the LHS is 1, and the id of the RHS is 5, so we store (1, 5) in rule table in Table 3.

3.3   Non-recursive Resugaring

Resugaring is to turn a core term back to a surface term by reversely applying transformation rules. Non-recursive resugaring refers to the case where the core term will be transformed back to at most one syntactic sugar and at most once.

Matching. Matching is to match the core term with the RHSs of the transformation rules, so as to obtain the rules used in the resugaring and the mapping relationship between variables in patterns and bindings in the core term.

There are three types of nodes in the pattern, but there are only two types in the term. Therefore, after a simple combination, there are four cases (in Table 4)

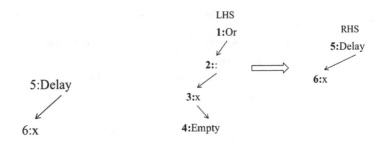

Fig. 4. A pattern   Fig. 5. A transformation rule

Table 3. Rule source

lhs:number	rhs:number
1	5

that meet the matching conditions. If the types of the pattern node and the term node are constants or keywords, then the matching succeeds when the names of the two are the same. If the pattern node is a variable, then the term node can be a constant node or a keyword node, because the variable can match a constant or sub-expression.

The matching algorithm consists of three steps: the first step is to recursively try to match starting from the root of the core term and the root of all RHS patterns; the second step is to determine the RHS that the core term completely matched, thereby we can determine the transformation rule that can be used; the third step is to extract the information needed for the subsequent substitution algorithm. Algorithm 1 describes the matching algorithm in detail with a specific example. The core term and related transformation rule are shown in Fig. 6.

As shown in Fig. 7, when the root of the term matches the root of the RHS, we will continue matching their left child and right child respectively, so the first step of matching is a recursive process. In the second step, we found that all the nodes of the above RHS were successfully matched to the term node in the first step, so we think that the matching was successful. So in the third step, we determined the corresponding LHS and the bindings corresponding to the variables in the LHS, namely $\{x \rightarrow 1,\ y \rightarrow 2\ ys \rightarrow Empty\}$.

Substitution. Substitution refers to the process of replacing the variables in the LHS determined in the matching with the corresponding bindings to obtain the final surface term.

3.4   Recursive Resugaring

Recursive resugaring refers to the case where the core term will use multiple syntactic sugars.

Table 4. Matching conditions

Pattern node	Term node
Keyword	Keyword
Constant	Constant
Variable	Keyword
Variable	Constant

Algorithm 1. Matching Algorithm

```
def matching(CoreTerm)
    // step 1
    foreach RHS in RHSs
        PROOT = Root ID of RHS
        TROOT = Root ID of CoreTerm
        trymatch(PROOT, TROOT)
    // step 2
    check()
    // step 3
    insert rule which RHS is 'completely matched' into 'state'
    if size of 'state' == 0:
        Raise('match failed!')
        return
    foreach (PID, TID, RHS) in 'matched':
        if RHS is 'completely matched' and type of PID is 'variable'
            insert (PID, TID) into 'env'
    foreach TID exists in 'env'
        insert subtree of TID into 'value'
```

Matching. Sub-term is a collection of partial nodes in the binary tree of the core term. These nodes can reach each other through their common edges. The meta term is a special sub-term, and its nodes can be bijective with all the nodes of a certain pattern. Therefore, the object of recursive resugaring is a core term with multiple meta terms. The core idea of the recursive transformation algorithm is to match each sub-term in parallel, so the matching should not only start from the root of the binary tree of the core term, but should try from each node. Starting from a certain node, the part of the nodes that successfully matches a pattern is a meta term.

The following uses an example to explain the recursive resugaring process in detail. As shown in Fig. 8, The nodes of the three colors of blue, gray and orange are the meta terms matching three different patterns respectively. We no longer only match from the root If, but each node of the core term can be used as the root to match with roots of patterns. From this, we can determine that the following rules will be used in transformation.

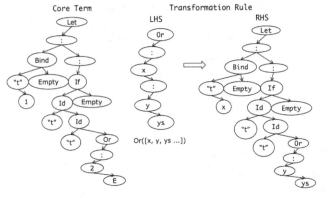

Fig. 6. A core term and a transformation rule

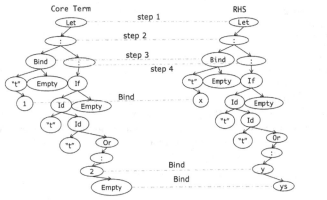

Fig. 7. Matching

And([x, y, ys ...]) → If(x, And([y, ys ...]), False)
Or([x, y, ys ...]) → Let([Bind("t", x)], [If(Id("t"), Id("t"), Or([y, ys ...]))])
If(x,y,z) → If(x,y,z) (a special rule, see 4.2)

Expansion. In Matching, we can determine the patterns to be converted from the patterns which meta terms successfully matched. In the expansion, we combine the determined patterns according to the positional relationship suggested by the core term into a combined pattern. In the previous example, we combined the target patterns as shown in Fig. 9.

Substitution. The substitution process here is consistent with non-recursive resugaring which replaces variables in the combined pattern with bindings.

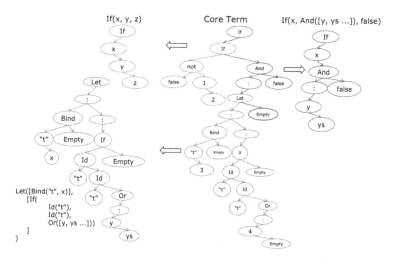

Fig. 8. Matching

4 Two Properties

4.1 Checking Transformation Rules for Preserving Emulation

Emulation means that the surface terms obtained by resugaring maintain the same semantics as the corresponding core terms. In other words, the surface term obtained after resugaring can be desugared to the corresponding core term again. In fact, this is also the PutGet property that the bidirectional transformation program needs to satisfy. Therefore, BIRDS can ensure that a single transformation rule satisfies emulation, but cannot guarantee the situation of multiple transformation rules. Some transformation rules will violate the emulation. For example, we use the following transformation rules to resugar $Max([-\infty])$.

$$Max([]) \rightarrow Raise(\text{``empty list''});$$
$$Max(xs) \rightarrow MaxAcc(xs, -\infty);$$

The following core language evaluation sequence will be obtained.

$$MaxAcc([-\infty], -\infty) \Rightarrow MaxAcc([], -\infty)$$

After adding sugar to them, we will obtain the following surface language evaluation sequence:

$$Max([-\infty]) \Rightarrow Max([])$$

But $Max([])$ should be desugared to the error message, instead of the second step of the core language evaluation sequence. But with the following transformation rules, the above problems will not occur.

$$Max([]) \quad \rightarrow Raise(\text{``empty list''});$$
$$Max(x : xs) \rightarrow MaxAcc([x, xs, ...], -\infty)$$

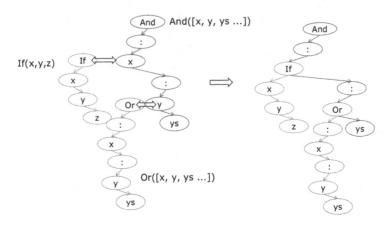

Fig. 9. Expansion

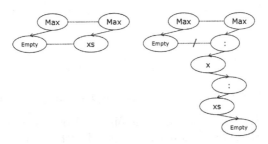

Fig. 10. Match the LHSs with each other

Therefore, we need to check whether there is any overlap among the transformation rules. If there is any overlap, the rules are invalid, otherwise they are valid. In Fig. 10, the first group has overlap, but the second group does not have any overlap.

4.2   Maintaining Abstraction

Abstraction means that the code obtained by desugaring will not be leaked in the output surface language program, and at the same time, the program in the original input cannot be resugared. If the surface term itself uses some core language syntax, such as "If":

$$\text{Let}([\text{Bind}(\text{``}t\text{''}, not(false))], [\text{If}(\text{Id}(\text{``}t\text{''}), \text{Id}(\text{``}t\text{''}), \text{Or}([true]))]).$$

After reduction, we hope that it will not be converted during resugaring, that is, Or ([not(true), true]) cannot be obtained.

Our solution is to treat the core syntax rules as special transformation rules with the same LHS and RHS. We mark the roots that match the core syntax rules with a "fixed" label, and the stepper will retain the labels during the reduction.

Num	Surface Language Evaluation Sequence	Core Language Evaluation Sequence

1	And([If(not(false), 1, 2), Or([3, 4])])	If(
		  (Tag Fixed If(not(false), 1, 2)),
		  And([
		    Let([Bind("t", 3)], [If(Id("t"), Id("t"), Or([4])])])
		  ]),
		  false
		)

2	And([If(true, 1, 2), Or([3, 4])])	If(
		  (Tag Fixed If(true, 1, 2)),
		  And([
		    Let([Bind("t", 3)], [If(Id("t"), Id("t"), Or([4])])])
		  ]),
		  false
		)

3	And([1, Or([3, 4])])	If(
		  1,
		  And([
		    Let([Bind("t", 3)], [If(Id("t"), Id("t"), Or([4])])])
		  ]),
		  false
		)

4	/	And([Let([Bind("t", 3)], [If(Id("t"), Id("t"), Or([4])])])])
5	Or([3,4])	Let([Bind("t", 3)], [If(Id("t"), Id("t"), Or([4])])])
6	/	If(3, 3, Or([4]))
7	3	3

Fig. 11. Resugaring

In the above example, since this surface language will match core syntax rule of *Let*, we add "fixed" tag in front of *Let*. Then, in resugaring, the marked nodes will not be used to match with RHSs. That is to say, the above core term will not match the RHS of Or syntactic sugar, so we can maintain abstraction during transformation.

5 An Example

We show an example of our resugaring. As shown in Fig. 11, except for the fourth and sixth steps, other core terms have the corresponding surface terms after resugaring, and satisfy emulation and abstraction. For example, the second step of the core language evaluation sequence is the result after *not(false)* is evaluated as *true*. Resugaring adds *And* and *Or* syntactic sugar to the second step of core to get the second step of surface.

6 Related Work

Bidirectional transformation (*bx*) is a mechanism used to maintain the consistency of two (or more) related sources of information. Researchers from many different fields, including software engineering [2,18], programming languages [7,15], databases [3,4] and document engineering, are actively studying the use of *bx* to solve various problems [8]. Our work shows the application of *bx* in programming language transformation.

The view update problem is a classical problem that has a long history in database research. A typical language of the putback-based approach is BiGUL [12,14], which supports programming putback functions declaratively while automatically deriving the corresponding unique forward transformation. Based on BiGUL, Zan et al. [21] design a putback-based Haskell library for bidirectional transformations on relations. But only [20] can run in database environments, which provides us with great convenience for language transformation on relational tables.

Data interoperability addresses the ability of systems and services that create, exchange and consume data to have clear, shared expectations for the contents, context and meaning of that data [9]. Because our approach solves the problem of correlation between the surface language and the core language being executed, the above problem is a typical problem of maintaining data interoperability. Many methods have been proposed to solve the problem. One method is to manually redefine the semantics based on the surface language, which undermines the benefits provided by the small core. The other is to use source tracking [19], but this is actually not a solution: users will still only see the core language after desugaring. In addition, creating a one-time solution for a given language is not suitable for those languages where users can create other syntactic sugar in the program itself, such as Lisp language [16].

Resugaring [17] is currently the most effective method. The traditional implementation method is to write two programs, namely, desugaring and resugaring, and then use string processing to transform the programming language. And we use the BIRDS [20] to automatically generate the desugaring program through the resugaring program, and convert the processing of the string into the operation of the relational table.

7   Conclusions

In this paper, we propose a new implentation method for resugaring, which can greatly reduce the difficulty of implementation. Not only did we propose to use the bidirectional transformation tool BIRDS to write the resugaring algorithm, but also presented a new solution to maintain emulation and abstraction during the transformation.

In the future, firstly, we intend to generalize the transformation algorithms on syntax trees by using more general bidirectional transformation on trees. Secondly, the tree is a special case of graph, and the relational table operation for the graph pattern and the tree pattern is not much different, so we intend to generalize the algorithm to the bidirectional transformation of the graph pattern.

References

1. BIRDS. https://dangtv.github.io/BIRDS/
2. Antkiewicz, M., Czarnecki, K.: Design space of heterogeneous synchronization. In: Lämmel, R., Visser, J., Saraiva, J. (eds.) GTTSE 2007. LNCS, vol. 5235, pp. 3–46. Springer, Heidelberg (2008). https://doi.org/10.1007/978-3-540-88643-3_1
3. Bancilhon, F., Spyratos, N.: Update semantics of relational views. ACM Trans. Database Syst. **6**(4), 557–575 (1981)
4. Bohannon, A., Pierce, B., Vaughan, J.: Relational lenses: a language for updatable views, pp. 338–347, January 2006
5. Clements.: Portable and high-level access to the stack with Continuation Marks. Ph.D. thesis, Northeastern University (2006)
6. Clements, J., Flatt, M., Felleisen, M.: Modeling an algebraic stepper. In: Sands, D. (ed.) ESOP 2001. LNCS, vol. 2028, pp. 320–334. Springer, Heidelberg (2001). https://doi.org/10.1007/3-540-45309-1_21
7. Culpepper, R., Felleisen, M.: Debugging hygienic macros. Sci. Comput. Programm. **75**(7), 496–515 (2010). Generative Programming and Component Engineering (GPCE 2007)
8. Czarnecki, K., Foster, J.N., Hu, Z., Lämmel, R., Schürr, A., Terwilliger, J.F.: Bidirectional transformations: a cross-discipline perspective. In: Paige, R.F. (ed.) ICMT 2009. LNCS, vol. 5563, pp. 260–283. Springer, Heidelberg (2009). https://doi.org/10.1007/978-3-642-02408-5_19
9. Dell'Erba, M., Fodor, O., Ricci, F., Werthner, H.: Harmonise: a solution for data interoperability. In: Monteiro, J.L., Swatman, P.M.C., Tavares, L.V. (eds.) Towards the Knowledge Society. ITIFIP, vol. 105, pp. 433–445. Springer, Boston, MA (2003). https://doi.org/10.1007/978-0-387-35617-4_28
10. Fischer, S., Hu, Z., Pacheco, H.: A clear picture of lens laws. In: Hinze, R., Voigtländer, J. (eds.) MPC 2015. LNCS, vol. 9129, pp. 215–223. Springer, Cham (2015). https://doi.org/10.1007/978-3-319-19797-5_10
11. Foster, J.N., Greenwald, M.B., Moore, J.T., Pierce, B.C., Schmitt, A.: Combinators for bi-directional tree transformations: a linguistic approach to the view update problem. In: Proceedings of the 32nd ACM SIGPLAN-SIGACT Symposium on Principles of Programming Languages, POPL 2005, Long Beach, California, USA, 12–14 January, pp. 233–246 (2005)
12. Ko, H.S., Hu, Z.: An axiomatic basis for bidirectional programming. Proc. ACM Program. Lang. **2**(POPL), 1–29 (2017). https://doi.org/10.1145/3158129
13. Ko, H., Zan, T., Hu, Z.: Bigul: a formally verified core language for putback-based bidirectional programming. In: Proceedings of the 2016 ACM SIGPLAN Workshop on Partial Evaluation and Program Manipulation, PEPM 2016, St. Petersburg, FL, USA, 20–22 January 2016, pp. 61–72 (2016)
14. Ko, H.S., Zan, T., Hu, Z.: Bigul: a formally verified core language for putback-based bidirectional programming. In: Proceedings of the 2016 ACM SIGPLAN Workshop on Partial Evaluation and Program Manipulation, PEPM 2016, pp. 61–72 (2016)
15. Krishnamurthi, S., Erlich, Y.-D., Felleisen, M.: Expressing structural properties as language constructs? In: Swierstra, S.D. (ed.) ESOP 1999. LNCS, vol. 1576, pp. 258–272. Springer, Heidelberg (1999). https://doi.org/10.1007/3-540-49099-X_17
16. Lapalme, G.: Implementation of a "lisp comprehension" macro. SIGPLAN Lisp Pointers **4**(2), 16–23 (1991). https://doi.org/10.1145/121983.121985

17. Pombrio, J., Krishnamurthi, S.: Resugaring: lifting evaluation sequences through syntactic sugar. In: ACM SIGPLAN Conference on Programming Language Design and Implementation, PLDI 2014, Edinburgh, United Kingdom, 09–11 June 2014, pp. 361–371. ACM (2014)
18. Schürr, A.: Specification of graph translators with triple graph grammars. In: Mayr, E.W., Schmidt, G., Tinhofer, G. (eds.) WG 1994. LNCS, vol. 903, pp. 151–163. Springer, Heidelberg (1995). https://doi.org/10.1007/3-540-59071-4_45
19. Tirkel, A., Rankin, G., van Schyndel, R., Ho, W., Osborne, C.: Electronic watermark, December 1993
20. Tran, V.D., Kato, H., Hu, Z.: Programmable view update strategies on relations. PVLDB **13**(5), 726–739 (2020)
21. Zan, T., Liu, L., Ko, H.S., Hu, Z.: Brul: a putback-based bidirectional transformation library for updatable views. In: Bx@ETAPS (2016)

Toward Appropriate Data Publishing in Relational Data Exchange Framework

Yasunori Ishihara[✉]

Nanzan University, Nagoya, Japan
`yasunori.ishihara@nanzan-u.ac.jp`

Abstract. We consider a data exchange setting with three kinds of participants, where the source has its data publishing policy. We formalize appropriate policies at the target with respect to the policy at the source. We also provide a heuristic algorithm to find an appropriate policy.

Keywords: Data exchange · Data publishing policy · Query rewriting

1 Introduction

In usual data exchange settings, participants are only two, namely, the source and the target. However, in practical situations, there are other participants to which the source and the target publish the exchanged data. In this paper, we consider such a data exchange setting. See Fig. 1. There are three kinds of participants: the *primary data provider*, *secondary data providers*, and *data users*. The primary data provider supplies a part of its data to each of secondary data providers and data users, through some mechanism such as views, schema mappings, etc. Moreover, secondary data providers supply parts of their data, which are originally supplied from the primary data provider, to their data users.

Example 1. Suppose that a world-wide medical institute (WMI for short) gathers data on some disease all over the world, and supplies the data related to Japanese people to a Japanese medical institute (JMI for short). WMI publishes a part of its data to world-wide news media, and JMI does a part of its data to news media in Japan. In this example, WMI is the primary data provider, JMI is a secondary data provider, and the news media are data users.

In general, the primary data provider has its *data publishing policy* to its users. For instance, in Example 1, WMI may want to hide the information on patients' nationality from news media to avoid nationality discrimination. When secondary data providers publish their data to their users, they should follow the policy of the primary data provider.

Example 2 (Continued from Example 1). Suppose that WMI has relational data with its schema $S(\text{ID}, \text{Age}, \text{Gender}, \text{Nationality}, \text{Severity})$. Then, data exchange mechanism $\mathbf{M}$ between WMI and JMI will be the following conjunctive query:

$$\mathbf{M}: \quad T(ID, Age, Gen, Sev) \text{:-} S(ID, Age, Gen, \text{"JPN"}, Sev).$$

© Springer Nature Switzerland AG 2020
L. Qin et al. (Eds.): SFDI 2020/LSGDA 2020, CCIS 1281, pp. 131–137, 2020.
https://doi.org/10.1007/978-3-030-61133-0_10

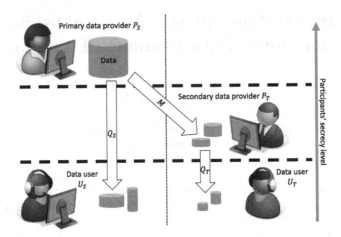

Fig. 1. The problem setting. Participants are classified into three secrecy levels.

If WMI wants to hide the information on patients' nationality as well as ID from news media, Q_S will be the following conjunctive query:

$$Q_S: \quad V(Age, Gen, Sev) :\text{-} S(ID, Age, Gen, Nat, Sev).$$

Now, suppose that JMI adopts the following conjunctive query Q_T as its data publishing policy:

$$Q_T: \quad W(Age, Gen, Sev) :\text{-} T(ID, Age, Gen, Sev).$$

At first glance, Q_T seems an "appropriate" policy in the sense that Q_T reveals only the attributes that Q_S does, namely, Age, Gender, and Severity. However, Q_T discloses some information that Q_S does not. To be specific, data user U_T of JMI can obtain the information on Japanese patients, while data user U_S of WMI can obtain patient data all over the world but U_S cannot identify which parts of the data are on Japanese patients.

In this paper, we formalize an *appropriate data publishing policy* Q_T at the secondary data provider for given policy Q_S at the primary data provider and given data exchange mechanism **M**, provided that all of **M**, Q_S, and Q_T are conjunctive queries. Then, we provide a heuristic algorithm to find such Q_T.

In the context of data integration, naturally there exist three kinds of participants, namely, data owners/providers, the data integrator, and data users. However, in this context, the main concern is often how to preserve the privacy of data owners, not how to follow their data publishing policies (e.g., [4]). In the setting of outsourcing network log analysis [3], the policy of the log owner is often fixed, e.g., the owner does not want the outsourcing company to identify the connection between network IDs and IP addresses. To the best of our knowledge, there is no research on how to incorporate three-participant model into data exchange framework, where the source has flexible data publishing policies.

2   Definitions

A *relation schema* $R[n]$ consists of a *relation name* R and its *arity* n. Fix a countable set DOM of *values*. A *tuple* t over $R[n]$ is an element in DOM^n. A *relation instance* I over $R[n]$ is a finite set of tuples over $R[n]$. A *database schema* $\mathbf{R}$ is a finite list $\langle R_1[n_1], \ldots, R_k[n_k]\rangle$ of relation schemas. A *database instance* $\mathbf{I}$ over a database schema $\mathbf{R} = \langle R_1[n_1], \ldots, R_k[n_k]\rangle$ is a list $\langle I_1, \ldots, I_k\rangle$, where each I_i is a relation instance of $R_i[n_i]$. We write $R_i(a_i, \ldots, a_{n_i}) \in \mathbf{I}$ if the i-th relation instance of $\mathbf{I}$ contains a tuple $(a_i, \ldots, a_{n_i})$.

Let $\mathbf{R} = \langle R_1[n_1], \ldots, R_k[n_k]\rangle$ be a database schema. Fix a countable set VAR of *variables*. An *atomic formula* over $\mathbf{R}$ is in the form of $R_i(x_1, \ldots, x_{n_i})$, where each x_j is in DOM∪VAR. A *conjunctive formula* over $\mathbf{R}$ is a possibly empty list of atomic formulas. The empty conjunctive formula is denoted by $\top$. A *conjunctive query* (CQ for short) Q over $\mathbf{R}$ is a rule in the following form:

$$Q: \quad V(y_1, \ldots, y_m) :- \varphi,$$

where V is a new relation name with arity m not in $\mathbf{R}$, each y_j is in DOM∪VAR, and φ is a conjunctive formula over $\mathbf{R}$. Q is said to be *safe* if all of $y_1, \ldots, y_m$ are in VAR and also appear in φ. A *safe version* of Q is a CQ obtained by eliminating, from its head, all the constants and all the variables not appearing in its body. Let $\mu : \text{VAR} \to \text{DOM}$ denote a variable assignment. The *answer* $Q(\mathbf{I})$ to Q on $\mathbf{I}$ over $\mathbf{R}$ is:

$$Q(\mathbf{I}) = \{(\mu(y_1), \ldots, \mu(y_m)) \mid$$
$$R_i(\mu(x_1), \ldots, \mu(x_{n_i})) \in \mathbf{I} \text{ for each } R_i(x_1, \ldots, x_{n_i}) \in \varphi\}.$$

If Q is safe, $Q(\mathbf{I})$ is finite and hence it is a relation instance over $V[m]$. The *output relation schema* of Q refers to the relation schema of $Q(\mathbf{I})$. Similarly, for a list $\mathbf{Q} = \langle Q_1, \ldots, Q_k\rangle$ of CQs, the *output database schema* of $\mathbf{Q}$ is the database schema of $\langle Q_1(\mathbf{I}), \ldots, Q_k(\mathbf{I})\rangle$.

Let $\mathcal{I}(\mathbf{R})$ denote the set of all database instances over $\mathbf{R}$, and Q_1 and Q_2 be CQs over $\mathbf{R}$. Q_1 is *contained* in Q_2, denoted $Q_1 \sqsubseteq Q_2$, if $Q_1(\mathbf{I}) \subseteq Q_2(\mathbf{I})$ for all $\mathbf{I} \in \mathcal{I}(\mathbf{R})$. Q_1 and Q_2 are *equivalent*, denoted $Q_1 \equiv Q_2$, if $Q_1 \sqsubseteq Q_2$ and $Q_2 \sqsubseteq Q_1$.

Let Q be a CQ and $\mathbf{M}$ be a list of CQs. A *CQ-rewriting* of Q using $\mathbf{M}$ is a CQ Q' such that

- the body of Q' contains only relations in the output schema of $\mathbf{M}$, and
- $Q' \circ \mathbf{M} \equiv Q$, where $\circ$ denotes query composition.

In this paper, we focus on the technique called canonical rewriting [1], which is used for deciding the existence of a CQ-rewriting. A *canonical rewriting* R_{can} of Q using $\mathbf{M}$ is a CQ such that:

- the head of R_{can} is the same as that of Q, and
- the body of R_{can} consists of all the answers to $\mathbf{M}$ on the body of Q.

If there is a CQ-rewriting of Q using $\mathbf{M}$, then R_{can} is a CQ-rewriting [1].

3   Appropriate Policies

Let Q_S be a safe CQ representing the data publishing policy at the primary data provider. Let $\mathbf{M}$ be a list of safe CQs representing data exchange mechanism between primary and secondary data providers. An *appropriate* policy Q_T at the secondary data provider for Q_S and $\mathbf{M}$ is a safe CQ satisfying confidentiality and availability defined below:

Confidentiality. There is a CQ-rewriting of $Q_T \circ \mathbf{M}$ using Q_S.

Availability. $Q_T \circ \mathbf{M}$ gives maximal information with respect to the existence of CQ-rewriting. That is, for any Q_T' satisfying confidentiality, if there is a CQ-rewriting of Q_T using Q_T', then there is a CQ-rewriting of Q_T' using Q_T.

Note that the following "information-collapsing" CQ $Q_\perp$ satisfies confidentiality for any Q_S and $\mathbf{M}$:

$$Q_\perp : \quad W() :\text{-} \top.$$

Example 3 (Continued from Examples 1 and 2). In this case, the information-collapsing CQ $Q_\perp$ is the unique, appropriate policy of JMI. As already stated, $Q_\perp$ always satisfies confidentiality. To see that $Q_\perp$ satisfies availability, we show that if Q_T' discloses some information, then Q_T' does not satisfy confidentiality.

Suppose that Q_T' discloses some information, i.e., there are instances $\mathbf{J}_1$ and $\mathbf{J}_2$ at JMI such that $Q_T'(\mathbf{J}_1) \neq Q_T'(\mathbf{J}_2)$. Now construct two instances $\mathbf{I}_1$ and $\mathbf{I}_2$ at WMI as follows:

$$\mathbf{I}_1 = \{(ID, Age, Gen, \text{"JPN"}, Sev) \mid (ID, Age, Gen, Sev) \in \mathbf{J}_1\} \cup$$
$$\{(ID, Age, Gen, \text{"CHN"}, Sev) \mid (ID, Age, Gen, Sev) \in \mathbf{J}_2\},$$
$$\mathbf{I}_2 = \{(ID, Age, Gen, \text{"CHN"}, Sev) \mid (ID, Age, Gen, Sev) \in \mathbf{J}_1\} \cup$$
$$\{(ID, Age, Gen, \text{"JPN"}, Sev) \mid (ID, Age, Gen, Sev) \in \mathbf{J}_2\}.$$

Since $\mathbf{M}(\mathbf{I}_1) = \mathbf{J}_1$ and $\mathbf{M}(\mathbf{I}_2) = \mathbf{J}_2$, we have $Q_T' \circ \mathbf{M}(\mathbf{I}_1) \neq Q_T' \circ \mathbf{M}(\mathbf{I}_2)$. On the other hand, we have $Q_S(\mathbf{I}_1) = Q_S(\mathbf{I}_2)$, and hence, there is no CQ-rewriting of $Q_T' \circ \mathbf{M}$ using Q_S.

Example 4. Let $\mathbf{R} = \langle S_1[2], S_2[4] \rangle$ be a database schema at the primary data provider. Suppose that $\mathbf{M}$ consists of the following two CQs:

$$\mathbf{M} : \quad T_1(A, B) :\text{-} S_1(A, B) \quad T_2(C) :\text{-} S_2(b, C, D, e).$$

Also, let Q_S be the following CQ:

$$Q_S : \quad V_S(A, C, D, E) :\text{-} S_1(A, b), S_2(b, C, D, E).$$

Consider the following CQ Q_T:

$$Q_T : \quad V_T(A, C) :\text{-} T_1(A, b), T_2(C).$$

Q_T satisfies confidentiality because N defined below is a CQ-rewriting of $Q_T \circ \mathbf{M}$ using Q_S:

$$N : \quad W(A, C) :\text{-} V_S(A, C, D, e).$$

To see that Q_T satisfies availability, consider an arbitrary CQ Q'_T such that there is a CQ-rewriting of Q_T using Q'_T. Then, a canonical rewriting R_{can} of Q_T using Q'_T satisfies $R_{can} \circ Q'_T \equiv Q_T$. Since R_{can} is not information collapsing, the body of Q'_T must match the body of Q_T, i.e., each atomic formula in the body of Q'_T must be one of $T_1(X, Y)$, $T_1(X, b)$, $T_2(Z)$ or isomorphic to one of them. Moreover, the head of Q'_T must contain variables X and Z (since they are corresponding to A and C in Q_T), and for R_{can} to be safe, the body of Q'_T must contain these two variables. In summary, Q'_T must be one of the following form, where φ denotes atomic formulas isomorphic to the preceding ones:

1. $V'_T(X, Z) :\text{-} T_1(X, Y), T_2(Z), \varphi$
2. $V'_T(X, Z) :\text{-} T_1(X, b), T_2(Z), \varphi$
3. $V'_T(X, Z) :\text{-} T_1(X, Y), T_1(X, b), T_2(Z), \varphi$
4. $V'_T(X, Y, Z) :\text{-} T_1(X, Y), T_2(Z), \varphi$
5. $V'_T(X, Y, Z) :\text{-} T_1(X, Y), T_1(X, b), T_2(Z), \varphi$

The second and the third are equivalent to Q_T. We can see that the others do not satisfy confidentiality.

4   Policy Derivation

In this section, we propose a heuristic algorithm for deriving Q_T that satisfies confidentiality. Currently, we have no proof that Q_T also satisfies availability in general, but we can see that for the example cases above Q_T satisfies availability.

A *partial instantiation* θ of Q_S with respect to $\mathbf{M}$ is a partial mapping that maps a variable appearing in the head of Q_S to a constant appearing in the body of $\mathbf{M}$. The CQ obtained by applying θ to Q_S is denoted by $Q_S\theta$. For example, consider $\mathbf{M}$ and Q_S in Example 4. $\theta = [E \mapsto e]$ is a partial instantiation of Q_S with respect to $\mathbf{M}$, and $Q_S\theta$ is:

$$Q_S\theta : \quad V_S(A, C, D, e) :\text{-} S_1(A, b), S_2(b, C, D, e).$$

$\theta' = [B \mapsto e]$ is not a partial instantiation because B does not appear in the head of Q_S. $\theta'' = [E \mapsto c]$ is not because c does not appear in the body of $\mathbf{M}$.

Our heuristic algorithm consists of the following three steps:

1. Given $\mathbf{M}$ and Q_S, compute the set Θ of all partial instantiations of Q_S with respect to $\mathbf{M}$.
2. For each $\theta \in \Theta$,
   (a) compute a safe version Q^θ_{can} of a canonical rewriting of $Q_S\theta$ using $\mathbf{M}$; and
   (b) decide whether there is a CQ-rewriting of $Q^\theta_{can} \circ \mathbf{M}$ using $Q_S\theta$.

Let $\mathcal{Q}$ be the set of all Q_{can}^{θ} such that the decision at step (b) is affirmative.
3. Output $Q_{\perp}$ if $\mathcal{Q}$ is empty. Otherwise, output $Q_T \in \mathcal{Q}$ such that for any $Q_T' \in \mathcal{Q}$, if there is a CQ-rewriting of Q_T using Q_T', then there is a CQ-rewriting of Q_T' using Q_T.

Example 5 (Continued from Example 4). We demonstrate the second and third steps of our algorithm. First, consider the partial instantiation undefined everywhere. A safe version Q_{can} of a canonical rewriting of Q_S using $\mathbf{M}$ is:

$$Q_{can}: \quad V_T(A) :\text{-} T_1(A, b).$$

We can check that there is no CQ-rewriting of $Q_{can} \circ \mathbf{M}$ using Q_S.

Next, consider a partial instantiation $\theta = [E \mapsto e]$. A safe version Q_{can}^{θ} of a canonical rewriting of $Q_S\theta$ using $\mathbf{M}$ is:

$$Q_{can}^{\theta}: \quad V_T(A, C) :\text{-} T_1(A, b), T_2(C).$$

There is a CQ-rewriting N of $Q_{can}^{\theta} \circ \mathbf{M}$ using Q_S:

$$N: \quad W(A, C) :\text{-} V_S(A, C, D, e).$$

$\mathcal{Q}$ is the set of Q_{can}^{θ} such that θ maps E to e. At the third step, the algorithm will output Q_{can}^{θ} with $\theta = [E \mapsto e]$, which has been shown to be appropriate in Example 4.

The algorithm always finds Q_T with confidentiality because by step 2(b), $\mathcal{Q}$ contains only CQs that satisfy confidentiality. We are trying to prove that the output of the algorithm also satisfies availability.

5   Future Work

We are planning to extend $\mathbf{M}$ to target generating dependencies (tgds), which are commonly used in relational data exchange framework [2]. In this case, the behavior of $\mathbf{M}$ becomes nondeterministic because the secondary data providers can add their data to the supplied data from the primary data provider. We will have to redefine the appropriateness based on the semantics (e.g., certain answer semantics) that can handle such nondeterministic behavior.

Acknowledgment. The author is thankful to Prof. Toru Fujiwara, Prof. Hiroyuki Seki, Dr. Kenji Hashimoto, Mr. Keiji Fukushima, and Mr. Seiya Aizaki for their helpful discussion. The author also appreciates constructive comments and suggestions by the anonymous reviewers. This work is partially supported by JSPS Grant-in-Aid for Scientific Research (S) No. 17H06099 and (C) No. 19K11912.

References

1. Afrati, F.: Determinacy and query rewriting for conjunctive queries and views. Theor. Comput. Sci. **412**(11), 1005–1021 (2011)
2. Fagin, R., Kolaitis, P.G., Miller, R.J., Popa, L.: Data exchange: semantics and query answering. Theor. Comput. Sci. **336**(1), 89–124 (2005)
3. Furuta, Y., Yanai, N., Karasaki, M., Eguchi, K., Ishihara, Y., Fujiwara, T.: Towards efficient and secure encrypted databases: extending message-locked encryption in three-party model. In: Garcia-Alfaro, J., Navarro-Arribas, G., Hartenstein, H., Herrera-Joancomartí, J. (eds.) ESORICS/DPM/CBT -2017. LNCS, vol. 10436, pp. 55–69. Springer, Cham (2017). https://doi.org/10.1007/978-3-319-67816-0_4
4. Jabeen, F., et al.: Enhanced architecture for privacy preserving data integration in a medical research environment. IEEE Access **5**, 13308–13326 (2017)

Toward Programmable Strategy
for Co-existence of Relational Schemes

Jumpei Tanaka[1,2(✉)], Van-Dang Tran[1,2], and Zhenjiang Hu[2,3]

[1] The Graduate University for Advanced Studies, SOKENDAI, Shonan Village,
Hayama, Kanagawa, Japan
[2] National Institute of Informatics, 2-1-2 Hitotsubashi, Chiyoda-ku, Tokyo, Japan
{jumpeitanaka,dangtv}@nii.ac.jp
[3] Peking University, No. 5 Yiheyuan Road, Haidian District,
Beijing, People's Republic of China
huzj@pku.edu.cn

Abstract. The co-existence of relational schemas is an important feature of a database. A schema evolves to new versions, and then these multiple schema versions concurrently serve to multiple application versions evolving in the real world. We propose a programming framework for co-existence of relational schemas. The existing work shows a view based co-existence of relational schemas by giving a predefined strategy to propagate view update across schemas for data sharing. A co-existence strategy consists of a view definition for a new schema and rules of view update to propagate it from a new schema to an old schema. The existing work has three problems in practice; limited expressive power for co-existing strategies, a tricky design of auxiliary tables, and a necessity of global id. To resolve these problems, we propose a language for describing how an update is propagated across schemas and present a mechanism to derive auxiliary tables and other all equipment to run on an existing RDBMS. Our approach can be implemented by using the existing bidirectional transformation engine, BIRDS.

Keywords: Co-existence of schemas · Bidirectional transformation · Data sharing

1 Introduction

The co-existence of relational schemas is an important feature of a database. Today the information system is continuously evolved to follow ever-changing demands in the real world. Most of the information systems consist of applications and relational databases. In an application, its evolution is strongly supported by the tools, SVN and GIT, which maintain multiple versions of an application and deploys several versions of them to run concurrently. In a database, database schema and data are also continuously evolved to multiple versions [4]. However, the current database management systems do not support an efficient evolution of a schema and running multiple versions concurrently. As

© Springer Nature Switzerland AG 2020
L. Qin et al. (Eds.): SFDI 2020/LSGDA 2020, CCIS 1281, pp. 138–151, 2020.
https://doi.org/10.1007/978-3-030-61133-0_11

a notable work, Herrmann proposes MSVDB (Multi-Schema-Version Database Management System) that achieves a co-existence of relational schemas in the evolutional process of a database [13,14]. MSVDB composes a relational schema by views on top of shared physical data in one database. It provides a set of schema modification operations (SMOs) to show how to make an old schema evolved to a new one. It automatically gives a co-existence strategy for data sharing between these two schemas, i.e., a strategy for propagating updates between schemas through physical data. Despite the user-friendly description of schema evolution and fully automatic mechanism, the MSVDB approach based on SMO has limited expressive power for users to describe co-existence strategies between two schemas. It prevents a user from solving many practical problems in a co-existence of schemas.

- First, in the MSVDB approach, SMO describes a static relationship between the old and the new schemas, but it does not specify the strategy for data propagation (or data sharing) between the users of different schemas. The users may wish to share as many new information as possible even after evolution, or, to the other extreme, to do independently even if the two schemas co-exist. However, SMO cannot describe such an intended co-existing strategy; rather, it just provides a predefined strategy.
- Second, for the predefined strategy for each SMO given in the MSVDB approach, its implementation requires a tricky design of auxiliary tables that compensate supplemental information from physical data to an instance of a view. It lacks a systematical method to design these auxiliary tables, in which it is challenging to introduce new SMOs or change old SMOs even if we wish.
- Third, the MSVDB approach requires a global id system among schemas before and after the evolution to record the correspondence among tuples for traceability. In practice, such a global id system is system-oriented, but not what the end-users wish to see. Moreover, the management of global id's uniqueness would cause performance bottleneck and unfavorable complexity of information systems.

In this paper, we resolve the above problems by proposing a new framework. Rather than using SMO to describe static relation between two schemas, we provide a new view-embedding method to describe both static and dynamic relationships, use it to specify declaratively intended strategies for co-existence of relational schemas, and automatically derive necessary auxiliary tables for strategy implementation. Our technical contributions are summarized as follows.

- We provide, as far as we are aware, the first programming framework for describing intended strategies for data sharing/reuse between the users of the co-existing schemas. The description is declarative without global id, and powerful enough to cover all strategies that SMO provides and can do more.
- We show that all auxiliary tables for implementing the strategies can be done entirely automatically through a derivation of view definition and ensuring arbitrary updates on a view.
- We design our framework over BIRDS, a bidirectional relational description system, and illustrate our system's usefulness through examples.

The rest of the paper is organized as follows. After introducing preliminary in Sect. 2, we show an overview of our framework in Sect. 3. We define a language for the co-existence strategy of relational schemas in Sect. 4 and show implementation of the framework in Sect. 5. Finally, we discuss related work in Sect. 7 and conclude the paper in Sect. 8.

2   Preliminary

In this section, we briefly review the basic concepts that will serve our approach.

2.1   Co-existence of Relational Schemas

The co-existence of relational schemas is to maintain and run multiple schemas concurrently in one database. Figure 1 depicts its high-level architecture. A table in each schema is a view on top of physical data. A source schema (e.g., schema1) is modified to a target schema (e.g., schema2) by a user for several reasons. Each schema acts like a regular single-schema database (e.g., DB1 and DB2). Arbitrary updates from each application (e.g., application1 and application2) are handled and shared across schemas for needs through forward and backward transformations against physical data. A co-existence strategy controls how data is shared/reused by specifying what is propagated across schemas or what is not. MSVDB approach [13,14] introduces SMO for atomic schema modification, e.g., union of tables, paired with one predefined co-existence strategy. To be concrete, consider the following example borrowed from [13].

Example 1. Suppose schema1 is defined with a view task($id, auth, task, prio$) by giving identity mapping between the view and a base table task_base of physical data. Let us suppose the SMO modifies a view task of schema1 to a view todo($id, auth, task, prio$) of schema2 by selecting those tuples satisfying $prio=1$. A given forward transformation realizes this selection by a view definition on RDBMS. Figure 2(a) shows that it results in a tuple $(2, \text{Ann}, \text{write paper}, 1)$ in todo.

This SMO accompanies a co-existence strategy which propagates view updates of schema2 to schema1 through one-to-one mapping of tuples via id. Figure 2(b) illustrates its behavior of insertions. When a tuple of $prio=1$, $(3, \text{Ada}, \text{clean room}, 1)$, is inserted to todo, a given backward transformation as trigger on RDBMS propagates it to task as an insertion of a new tuple. Even if this insertion initially occurs over task, the forward transformation of selection computes $(3, \text{Ada}, \text{clean room}, 1)$ of todo from an updated instance of task. Differently, when a tuple of $prio \neq 1$, $(4, \text{Ron}, \text{buy book}, 4)$, is inserted to todo, the backward transformation propagates it to both a view task and an auxiliary table task* of physical data. Even though the forward transformation of selection does not compute $(4, \text{Ron}, \text{buy book}, 4)$ from task to todo, another rule of the forward transformation is prepared to compute it from task* to todo. Finally, all propagated tuples to task are stored in task_base of physical data by the identity mapping. Figure 2(c) shows a behavior of deletions. Regardless of either cases of insertion propagation, a deletion of a tuple in a source schema deletes a corresponding tuple in a target schema, and vice versa.   □

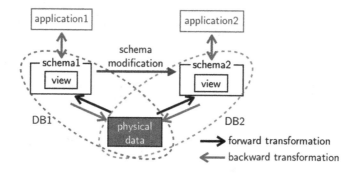

Fig. 1. Co-existence of relational schemas

Note that forward and backward transformations realize an implementation of SMO and its strategy. Not to cause side effects, transformations must satisfy the round-tripping property.

(**Round-tripping property**) Given a target data, transforming it to a source data by a backward transformation, and retransforming it to a target data by a forward transformation should return the same target data. It is the same the other way around.

2.2 Bidirectional Transformation

For the implementation of our idea, we utilize bidirectional transformation (BX for short). BX [12] is a mature technique synchronizing updates between heterogeneous data models. It is applied to a classical view update problem of relational schema [2,8] in the following manner [3,9,10].

Suppose a source schema in which components are base tables and a target schema in which components are view tables. BX consists of a pair of forward and backward transformations between these two schemas. Given an instance of source schema S (source) and instance of target schema T (target), a forward transformation $get(S) = T$ accepts source S and produces target T. A backward transformation $put(S, T') = S'$ accepts the original source S and a changed target T', and produces a changed source S'. Note that we do not need global id because put is allowed to access the original source. Instead of having one-to-one correspondence between source and target, put takes the original source in addition to a changed target and produces a changed source. To ensure consistency between source and target, BX must satisfy the following round-tripping laws, called GETPUT and PUTGET:

$$put(S, get(S)) = S \qquad \text{(GETPUT)}$$
$$get(put(S, T')) = T' \qquad \text{(PUTGET)}$$

The GETPUT ensures an unchanged target corresponds to an unchanged source. The PUTGET ensures an update of a target is reflected to a source such that the updated target can be computed again by get giving the updated source.

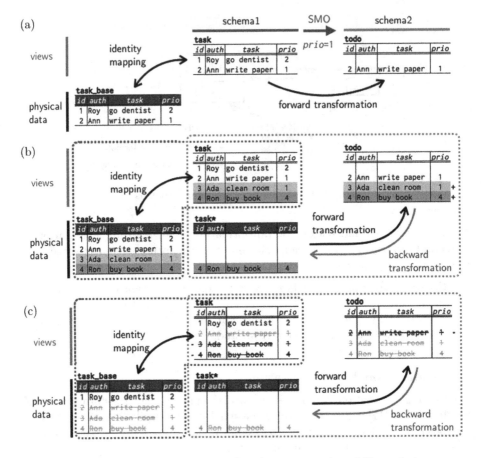

Fig. 2. Schema modification and update propagation of Example 1

3   Overview

We present our central idea and relation with the later sections before we discuss our approach in detail.

3.1   The View-Embedding Methodology

Our goal is to provide a programming framework; a user intentionally describes a co-existence strategy, and an implementation is automatically derived. We propose the view-embedding methodology to describe a co-existence strategy. It describes how to embed a view update on a target schema into a source schema against a static relationship f (a functional correspondence) from a source to a target schema. There are four cases.

– **Two-way:** An insertion to a target schema occurs in the range of f and is embedded into a source schema in one-way. If this embedding occurs as a direct insertion over a source schema, f computes the inserted tuple of a target schema from a source schema in another one-way. The same behavior is applied to a deletion.

– **One-way:** An insertion to a target schema occurs out of range of f and is embedded into a source schema in one-way. Even if this embedding occurs as a direct insertion over a source schema, f does not compute the inserted tuple of a target schema from a source schema. The same behavior is applied to a deletion. When a deletion directly occurs against an embedded tuple in a source schema, the inserted tuple in a target schema is not deleted.

– **One-way/two-way:** A behavior of insertion is the same as the one-way. However, a behavior of deletion is different from the one-way. When a deletion directly occurs against an embedded tuple in a source schema, the inserted tuple in a target schema is deleted in another one-way.

– **No-embedding:** An insertion to a target schema occurs out of range of f and is not embedded into a source schema. The same behavior is applied to a deletion.

In this paper, we describe a co-existence strategy as a combination of view-embedding classes: the two-way, the one-way/two-way, and the no-embedding. Since these three cover existing SMO strategies and can design more, we put view-embedding of the one-way into a future work.

Example 2. From Example 1 and Fig. 2, an insertion/deletion of (3, Ada, clean room, 1) in which $prio=1$ corresponds to the two-way because it is in the range of a static relationship, i.e., selection by $prio=1$. An insertion/deletion of (4, Ron, buy book, 4) in which $prio=4$ corresponds to the one-way/two-way because it is out of range of a static relation and a deletion from a source schema is reflected to a target schema. There does not exist the no-embedding in Example 1 because view-embedding by the two-way and the one-way/two-way cover all cases, namely, ensure arbitrary updates on a target schema.   □

We assume a source schema has more information than a target schema so that any update can be embedded. If a source schema has less information than a target schema, a co-existence strategy can be oppositely described, i.e., from a source schema to a target schema. In Sect. 4, we introduce a Datalog based language to describe a co-existence strategy by view-embedding of the two-way and the one-way/two-way. The no-embedding is complementarily defined from them by a mechanism mentioned later in Sect. 5.

3.2 Framework Design

We shall realize a co-existence of relational schemas by implementing a co-existence strategy onto RDBMS. Recall the implementation revealed in Example 1 consists of a pair of a forward transformation (as view definition) and a backward transformation (as trigger) by satisfying the round-tripping property. We implement them by BX consisting of get_{total} and put_{total}. Global id is not

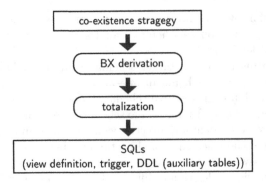

Fig. 3. A framework design

necessary. Without one-to-one correspondence, BX produces consistent instances of source and target schemas by reflecting updates from each side.

Figure 3 shows a framework design. An input is a user-written co-existence strategy that describes view-embedding of the two-way and the one-way/two-way. An output is SQLs representing a BX of get_{total} and put_{total} that realizes arbitrary update on a target schema and data sharing with a source schema. We design a derivation by two steps. The first step is the BX derivation. It derives a BX from a co-existence strategy by adding auxiliary tables. The derived BX realizes data sharing with a source schema. The second step is the totalization. The derived BX is defined for data sharing through the view-embedding. Thus the BX might be partially defined against arbitrary updates on a target schema, i.e., updates of the no-embedding are not covered. The second step derives a totalized BX of get_{total} and put_{total} from the derived BX by adding another auxiliary table to cover the no-embedding. Finally, SQLs (view definition, trigger, and DDL to define auxiliary tables of physical data) are generated from get_{total} and put_{total}. In each step, we utilize the bidirectionalization engine, BIRDS [20]. In Sect. 5, we propose a novel mechanism to systematically add auxiliary tables in the BX derivation step (Sect. 5.1) and the totalization step (Sect. 5.2).

4   Schema Co-existence Strategy Description

Our language is to describe a co-existence strategy by view-embedding methodology. The language is similar to BIRDS language which is a fragment of Datalog and defines *put* function. Our language follows its syntax and gives more predicates to express view-embedding classes. In the rest of this section, we explain how a strategy is described.

4.1 View-Embedding of the Two-Way

We describe a co-existence strategy of the two-way in the same manner as BIRDS language. Its Datalog form with atoms $H, L_1, ..., L_j, ..., L_m$ is as follows:

$$H :- L_1, ..., L_j, ..., L_m. \tag{1}$$

Suppose view tables $s_1(X_1), ..., s_i(X_i), ..., s_n(X_n)$ of a source schema and a view table $t(Y)$ of a target schema, where X_i and Y are sets of variables representing attributes. H is a rule head expressing a set of insertion/deletion into a view $s_i(X_i)$ denoted by $+s_i(X_i)/-s_i(X_i)$. L_j in a rule body takes view tables of a source schema $s_i(X_i)$, a view table of a target schema $t(Y)$, arithmetic comparison predicates (e.g., $>$, $=$), or their negation.

Example 3. From Example 1, suppose a view task(*auth, task, prio*) of the source schema and a view todo(*auth, task, prio*) of the target schema by excluding *id*. Its co-existence strategy as the two-way is described with predicates +task and -task as follows:

$$+\text{task}(A, T, P) :- \text{todo}(A, T, P), \neg\text{task}(A, T, P), P = 1. \tag{2}$$
$$-\text{task}(A, T, P) :- \text{task}(A, T, P), \neg\text{todo}(A, T, P), P = 1. \tag{3}$$

The rule (2) expresses that tuples existing in todo of the target schema but not in task of the source schema are insertions over todo and are embedded into task when the predicate $P = 1$ is satisfied. The rule (3) oppositely expresses that tuples which exist in task but not in todo are deletions over todo and are to be embedded into task when the predicate $P = 1$ is satisfied. □

4.2 View-Embedding of the One-way/two-way

For this class, we introduce predicates $\oplus s_i(X_i)/\ominus s_i(X_i)$ of a rule head to denote a set of insertions/deletions to $s_i(X_i)$. A rule body is described in the same manner as the two-way.

Example 4. From Example 1, an inserted/deleted tuple of *prio* $\neq 1$ over todo is embedded to task as the one-way/two-way. Its co-existence strategy is described with predicates $\oplus$task and $\ominus$task as follows:

$$\oplus\text{task}(A, T, P) :- \text{todo}(A, T, P), \neg\text{task}(A, T, P), P \neq 1. \tag{4}$$
$$\ominus\text{task}(A, T, P) :- \text{task}(A, T, P), \neg\text{todo}(A, T, P), P \neq 1. \tag{5}$$

They express $\oplus$task and $\ominus$task are computed in the same manner as rule (2) and (3) by replacing the predicate $P = 1$ to $P \neq 1$. □

5 Implementation

To implement a co-existence strategy as BX, we derive get_{total} and put_{total} from a user-written strategy by our language. A derivation process composes two steps: the BX derivation and the totalization. In this section, we propose a method to add relevant auxiliary tables systematically in each step.

5.1   BX Derivation

This step derives a BX of $get_{partial}$ and $put_{partial}$ from a co-existence strategy. A user-written strategy is rewritten to BIRDS language to define $put_{partial}$. Then the bidirectionalization engine, BIRDS, derives $get_{partial}$ as Datalog program.

The two-way: A rule of this class is written in the same manner with BIRDS language. Rewriting is not necessary for a rule which head is $+s_i(X_i)$ or $-s_i(X_i)$.

The one-way/two-way: A rule which head is $\oplus s_i(X_i)$ or $\ominus s_i(X_i)$ is rewritten to BIRDS language by adding an auxiliary table $s_{one.i}(X_i)$ of physical data. $s_{one.i}(X_i)$ stores embedded tuples into a view $s_i(X_i)$ of a source schema so that insertions/deletions of the one-way/two-way is distinguished from insertions/deletions of the two-way. Suppose rules of this class as following form:

$$\oplus s_i(X_i) :- L_{i.1}^+, ..., L_{i.k}^+. \tag{6}$$

$$\ominus s_i(X_i) :- L_{i.1}^-, ..., L_{i.l}^-. \tag{7}$$

where $L_{i.1}^+, ..., L_{i.k}^+, L_{i.1}^-, ..., L_{i.l}^-$ are atoms in a rule body taking predicates defined in Sect. 4.1. Rules are rewritten to consistently embed insertion/deletion into $s_i(X_i)$ and $s_{one.i}(X_i)$ as follows:

$$+s_i(X) :- L_{i.1}^+, ..., L_{i.k}^+. \tag{8}$$

$$-s_i(X) :- L_{i.1}^-, ..., L_{i.l}^-, s_{one.i}(X_i). \tag{9}$$

$$+s_{one.i}(X_i) :- L_{i.1}^+, ..., L_{i.k}^+, \neg s_{one.i}(X_i). \tag{10}$$

$$-s_{one.i}(X_i) :- L_{i.1}^-, ..., L_{i.l}^-, s_{one.i}(X_i). \tag{11}$$

Rewritten rules define $put_{partial}$. The bidirectionalization engine derives Datalog program of $get_{partial}$ from $put_{partial}$ by satisfying GETPUT and PUTGET.

Example 5. Rewriting of a co-existence strategy from Example 3 and 4 (rules (2)–(5)) results in a following BIRDS program of $put_{partial}$ by adding an auxiliary table, task_one($auth, task, prio$).

$$+\text{task}(A, T, P) :- \text{todo}(A, T, P), \neg\text{task}(A, T, P), P = 1. \tag{12}$$

$$-\text{task}(A, T, P) :- \text{task}(A, T, P), \neg\text{todo}(A, T, P), P = 1. \tag{13}$$

$$+\text{task}(A,T,P):-\text{todo}(A,T,P),\neg\text{task}(A,T,P), P \neq 1. \tag{14}$$

$$-\text{task}(A,T,P):-\text{task}(A,T,P), \neg\text{todo}(A,T,P), P \neq 1, \text{task\_one}(A,T,P). \tag{15}$$

$$+\text{task\_one}(A,T,P):-\text{todo}(A,T,P), \neg\text{task}(A,T,P), P \neq 1, \neg\text{task\_one}(A,T,P). \tag{16}$$

$$-\text{task\_one}(A,T,P):-\text{task}(A,T,P), \neg\text{todo}(A,T,P), P \neq 1, \text{task\_one}(A,T,P). \tag{17}$$

The bidirectionalization engine derives $get_{partial}$ of Datalog program from them:

$$\text{todo}(A,T,P) :- \text{task}(A,T,P), P = 1. \tag{18}$$

$$\text{todo}(A, T, P) :- \text{task}(A, T, P), \text{task\_one}(A, T, P), P \neq 1. \tag{19}$$

Rule (18) expresses selection of tuples in task by the predicate $P=1$. Rule (19) expresses selection of tuples in both task and task_one by the predicate $P \neq 1$, where tuples in task_one exist just by a view-embedding of the one-way/two-way. Thus even when a tuple satisfying the predicate $P \neq 1$ is directly inserted to task, it is not propagated to todo.   □

5.2   Totalization

This step derives get_{total} and put_{total} from $get_{partial}$ and $put_{partial}$ to cover the no-embedding. We exploit our previous work to make put a total function [18]. To make $put_{partial}$ total, a new auxiliary table $t_{ttl}(Y)$ of physical data is added. When a tuple is inserted into a view $t(Y)$ but rules of $put_{partial}$ do not compute an insertion or even a deletion to any views $s_i(X_i)$ ($i = [1, n]$) in a source schema, this insertion to $t(Y)$ is embedded into the auxiliary table $t_{ttl}(Y)$. When this tuple is deleted from $t(Y)$, it is also deleted from $t_{ttl}(Y)$. Rules of the no-embedding are defined with rule head, $+t_{ttl}(Y)/-t_{ttl}(Y)$, expressing a set of insertions/deletions to $t_{ttl}(Y)$ as follows:

$$+t_{ttl}(Y) :- +t(Y), \neg+s_1(X_1), ..., \neg+s_n(X_n), \tag{20}$$
$$\neg-s_1(X_1), ..., \neg-s_m(X_m), F_{X_j} = X_k.$$
$$-t_{ttl}(Y) :- -t(Y), \neg+s'_1(X_1), ..., \neg+s'_n(X_n), F_{X_j} = X_k. \tag{21}$$
$$+t(Y) :- t(Y), \neg t_{tmp}(Y). \tag{22}$$
$$-t(Y) :- \neg t(Y), t_{tmp}(Y). \tag{23}$$
$$t_{tmp}(Y) :- t_{get}(Y) \tag{24}$$
$$t_{tmp}(Y) :- t_{ttl}(Y). \tag{25}$$

where $F_{X_j} = X_k$ is a predicate of foreign key if it exists in a strategy, each $+s'_i(X_i)$ expresses a rule which body is composed by rule body of $+s_i(X_i)$ excluded $t(Y)$ and $F_{X_j} = X_k$, $+t(Y)/-t(Y)$ are intermediate tables of insertion/deletion over $t(Y)$, $t_{get}(Y)$ expresses rules of a derived $get_{partial}$, and $t_{tmp}(Y)$ is an intermediate table expressing a temporary $t(Y)$. Now combined rules of $put_{partial}$ and the no-embedding define put_{total}. The bidirectionalization engine derives Datalog program of get_{total} from put_{total} by satisfying GETPUT and PUTGET. Because Example 5 does not have the no-embedding, we show the modified example.

Example 6. Suppose a co-existence strategy of the two-way by rules (2) and (3), $put_{partial}$ defined by (12) and (13), and derived $get_{partial}$ of (18). The rules of the no-embedding with an auxiliary table todo_ttl is defined as follows:

$$+\text{todo\_ttl}(A, T, P) :- +\text{todo}(A, T, P), \neg+\text{task}(A, T, P), \neg-\text{task}(A, T, P). \tag{26}$$
$$-\text{todo\_ttl}(A, T, P) :- -\text{todo}(A, T, P), \text{task}(A, T, P). \tag{27}$$
$$-\text{todo\_ttl}(A, T, P) :- -\text{todo}(A, T, P), \neg(P = 1). \tag{28}$$
$$+\text{todo}(A, T, P) :- \text{todo}(A, T, P), \neg\text{todo\_tmp}(A, T, P). \tag{29}$$
$$-\text{todo}(A, T, P) :- \neg\text{todo}(A, T, P), \text{todo\_tmp}(A, T, P). \tag{30}$$

$$\text{todo\_tmp}(A, T, P) :- \text{task}(A, T, P), P = 1. \tag{31}$$

$$\text{todo\_tmp}(A, T, P) :- \text{todo\_ttl}(A, T, P). \tag{32}$$

Then rules (14)–(17), (26)-(32) define put_{total}. The bidirectionalization engine derives Datalog program of get_{total} as follows:

$$\text{todo}(A, T, P) :- \text{task}(A, T, P), P = 1. \tag{33}$$

$$\text{todo}(A, T, P) :- \text{todo\_ttl}(A, T, P), P \neq 1. \tag{34}$$

$$\text{todo}(A, T, P) :- \text{task}(A, T, P), \text{todo\_ttl}(A, T, P). \tag{35}$$

Rule (33) expresses $get_{partial}$ of the two-way. Rules (34) and (35) express the no-propagation by transform tuples in todo_ttl to todo when they satisfy the predicate $P \neq 1$ or when the same tuples exist in task.   □

6   Experimental Evaluation

We have constructed a prototype of the framework in OCaml. It adds auxiliary tables to a user-written co-existence strategy, invokes BIRDS, derives Datalog programs of put_{total} and get_{total}, and generates SQLs as trigger and view definition. To show effectiveness, we performed two experiments: replicating predefined strategies of SMOs [13,14] and defining a new strategy. All experiments are run with PostgresSQL 10.5 on a Core i5 machine 2.3 GHz and 8 GB memory.

6.1   Replication of SMOs Strategies

We perform replication of predefined strategies from three SMOs out of six for schema modification. SMO consists of a pair with its inverse SMO, e.g., DROP COLUMN and ADD COLUMN. We experiment strategies of SMOs in which source schema has more information than target schema because other strategies of paired SMOs are replicated by describing a strategy oppositely. Table 1 shows experimental results. In each, source schema is derived by a co-existence strategy expressing identity mapping between its views and base tables of physical data. Then a co-existence strategy to replicate SMO's strategy derives target schema from source schema. Note that our method replicates inner/outer join on primary key without totalization to manage key uniqueness between source and target schema. Outer join on foreign key restricts foreign key as $F = B$ and does not update $s_2(F, B)$ by generating a new key.

The program size of inner/outer join on a primary key by our method is larger than SMOs' strategies because of a description of a primary key constraint. Execution time is measured on write/read of 10,000 tuples over each schema and shows an average of 10 trials. The results shows writing on target schema costs than doing on source schema because an update on a view of target schema updates views of source schema, and then updates base tables of physical data.

Table 1. Experimental results

SMO	Description	Source schema	Target schema	LOC (SMO strategy)	LOC (co-existence strategy)	write on source/read on target [s]	write on target/read on source [s]	Inverse SMO
DROP COLUMN	by projection	$s(A,B)$	$t(A)$	4	2	0.87/0.07	2.24/0.01	ADD COLUMN
MERGE TABLE	by union (forward) and selection (backward)	$s_1(A,B)$, $s_2(A,B)$	$t(A,B)$	14	10	0.79/0.06	4.91/0.01	PARTITION TABLE
JOIN TABLE	by inner join on primary key	$s_1(P,A)$, $s_2(P,B)$	$t(P,A,B)$	7	11	0.79/0.03	2.50/0.01	DECOMPOSE TABLE
	by outer join on primary key	$s_1(P,A)$, $s_2(P,B)$	$t(P,A,B)$	5	13	0.85/0.11	4.20/0.03	
	by outer join on foreign key	$s_1(A,F)$, $s_2(F,B)$	$t(A,B)$	11	6	0.97/0.11	1.91/0.09	

6.2 A New Strategy

Consider a new strategy modifying Example 1. Suppose one selection condition of the two-way $(B = 1)$ and another condition of the one-way/two-way $(B = 2)$. $B \neq 1$ or $B \neq 2$ becomes the no-embedding. A strategy is described as follows:

$$+s(A,B) :- t(A,B), \neg s(A,B), B = 1. \tag{36}$$
$$-s(A,B) :- s(A,B), \neg t(A,B), B = 1. \tag{37}$$
$$\oplus s(A,B) :- t(A,B), \neg s(A,B), B = 2. \tag{38}$$
$$\ominus s(A,B) :- s(A,B), \neg t(A,B), B = 2. \tag{39}$$

where source schema is $s(A,B)$ and target schema is $t(A,B)$. Our framework derives Datalog program of get_{total} as follows:

$$t(A,B) :- s(A,B), B = 1. \tag{40}$$
$$t(A,B) :- s(A,B), s_{one}(A,B), B = 2. \tag{41}$$
$$t(A,B) :- t_{ttl}(A,B), \neg(B = 1), \neg(B = 2). \tag{42}$$
$$t(A,B) :- t_{ttl}(A,B), s_{one}(A,B), s(A,B). \tag{43}$$
$$t(A,B) :- t_{ttl}(A,B), s(A,B), \neg(B = 2). \tag{44}$$

An experiment is performed in the same manner. Write on source/ read on target takes 0.77/0.44 [s] and write on target/read on source takes 2.34/0.01 [s]. A result shows that the framework is practical to program not only SMOs strategy but also a new user-intended strategy.

7 Related Work

The co-existence of relational schemas starts from a demand for high elasticity of relational schema in a database's practical problems. The database refactoring [1] summarizes a design pattern of small changes to define a new schema by SQL scripts. Flyway [11] and Liquibase [15] are valuable tools to organize a series of small changes and sequentially execute SQL scripts. To efficiently support these manual-based works, a database community has widely researched the schema evolution [5,17]. Curino et al. [6,7] propose PRISM/PRISM++. They enable schema modification by SMOs and automatically translate query and update issued against an old schema to run on a new schema. Moon et al. [16] propose PRIMA. It also provides SMOs and translates query and update on the latest schema to access data of legacy schemas. These works set a new database for a new schema, and data is not shared across schemas. Against this limitation, Herrmann et al. propose MSVDB [13,14]. It achieves the co-existence of schemas and data sharing by SMOs and their co-existence strategies. However, strategies are limited to predefined cases. In contrast, our work proposes a programmable co-existence strategy which achieves more expressive power.

A co-existence strategy is for data sharing or no sharing between schemas. Its theoretical background is data transformation between heterogeneous data models [19]. A database community has treated this topic as the view update problem [2,8], and a programming language community has studied in the bidirectional transformation. Foster et al. [12] propose the first bidirectional programming languages, lenses. It prepares primitive operators of bidirectional transformation. A large bidirectional transformation is constructed by concatenating them. Bohannon et al. [3] propose lenses for view update in relational database. Its expressive power is limited to the predefined primitive operators. To overcome this limitation, Tran et al. [20] propose BIRDS to make view update strategy programmable based on the bidirectional transformation technique [9,10]. Our prior work [18] proposes to program a co-existence strategy as bidirectional transformation and make it to handle arbitrary updates on a view of a target schema. In contrast, this paper proposes a new programming framework by the view-embedding methodology for three classes. It realizes more expressing power than bidirectional transformation. Predefined strategies of SMOs and a new strategy are programable.

8 Conclusion

In this paper, we present the framework to give full control over deciding how to propagate updates across schemas for a co-existence strategy of relational schemas. We propose a language to describe a strategy based on classes of view-embedding even without global id. By systematically giving auxiliary tables and utilizing the bidirectionalization engine, BIRDS, all equipments for implementation are derived. As future works, we consider to work for a class of the one-way, further foreign key handling, totalization of join, and performance improvement.

Acknowledgement. This work is partially supported by the Japan Society for the Promotion of Science (JSPS) Grant-in-Aid for Scientific Research (S) No. 17H06099.

References

1. Ambler, S.W., Sadalage, P.J.: Refactoring Databases: Evolutionary Database Design (paperback). Pearson Education, London (2006)
2. Bancilhon, F., Spyratos, N.: Update semantics of relational views. ACM Trans. Database Syst. (TODS) **6**(4), 557–575 (1981)
3. Bohannon, A., Pierce, B.C., Vaughan, J.A.: Relational lenses: a language for updatable views. In: Proceedings of the twenty-fifth ACM SIGMOD-SIGACT-SIGART Symposium on Principles of Database Systems, pp. 338–347 (2006)
4. Brodie, M.L., Liu, J.T.: The power and limits of relational technology in the age of information ecosystems. In: On The Move Federated Conferences and Workshops (2010)
5. Cauruccuio, L., Polese, G., Tortoga, G.: Synchronization of queries and views upon schema evolutions: a survey. ACM Trans. Database Syst. (TODS) **41**(2), 1–41 (2016)
6. Curino, C.A., Moon, H.J., Deutsch, A., Zaniolo, C.: Update rewriting and integrity constraint maintenance in a schema evolution support system: prism++. Proc. VLDB Endowment **4**(2), 117–128 (2010)
7. Curino, C.A., Moon, H.J., Zzniolo, C.: Graceful database schema evolution: the prism workbench. Proc. VLDB Endowment **1**(1), 761–772 (2008)
8. Dayal, U., Bernstein, P.A.: On the correct translation of update operations on relational views. ACM Trans. Database Syst. (TODS) **7**(3), 381–416 (1982)
9. Fischer, S., Hu, Z., Pacheco, H.: "putback" is the essence of bidirectional programming. Technical report, GRACE Center, National Institute of infomatics (2012)
10. Fischer, S., Hu, Z., Pacheco, H.: A clear picture of lens laws. In: Hinze, R., Voigtländer, J. (eds.) MPC 2015. LNCS, vol. 9129, pp. 215–223. Springer, Cham (2015). https://doi.org/10.1007/978-3-319-19797-5_10
11. Flayway: Flyway by redgate (2020). https://flywaydb.org/
12. Foster, J.N., Greenwald, M.B., Moore, J.T., Pierce, B.C., Schmitt, A.: Combinators for bi-directional tree transformations: a linguistic approach to the view update problem. ACM SIGPLAN Not. **40**(1), 233–246 (2005)
13. Herrmann, K., Voigt, H., Behrend, A., Rausch, J., Lehner, W.: Living in parallel realities: co-existing schema versions with a bidirectional database evolution language. In: Proceedings of the 2017 ACM International Conference on Management of Data, pp. 1101–1116 (2017)
14. Herrmann, K., Voigt, H., Pedersen, T.B., Lehner, W.: Multi-schema-version data management: data independence in the twenty-first century. VLDB J. **27**(4), 547–571 (2018). https://doi.org/10.1007/s00778-018-0508-7
15. Liquibase: Liquivase by datical (2020). https://www.liquibase.org/
16. Moon, H.J., Curino, C.A., Deutsch, A., Hou, C.Y., Zanilo, C.: Managing and querying transaction-time databases under schema evolution. Proc. VLDB Endowment **1**(1), 882–895 (2008)
17. Roddick, J.F.: A survey of schema versioning issues for database systems. Inf. Softw. Technol. **37**(7), 383–393 (1995)
18. Tanaka, J., Tran, V.D., Kato, H., Hu, Z.: Toward co-existing database schemas based on bidirectional transformation. arXiv preprint arXiv:1910.10959 (2019)
19. Terwilliger, J.F., Cleve, A., Curino, C.A.: How clean is your sandbox? In: Hu, Z., de Lara, J. (eds.) ICMT 2012. LNCS, vol. 7307, pp. 1–23. Springer, Heidelberg (2012). https://doi.org/10.1007/978-3-642-30476-7_1
20. Tran, V.D., Kato, H., Hu, Z.: Programmable view update strategies on relations. Proc. VLDB Endow. **13**(5), 726–739 (2020)

Data Integration Models
and Architectures for Service Alliances

Yasuhito Asano[1(✉)], Zhenjiang Hu[2], Yasunori Ishihara[3], Makoto Onizuka[4], Masato Takeichi[5], and Masatoshi Yoshikawa[6]

[1] INIAD, Toyo University, Tokyo, Japan
yasuhito.asano@iniad.org
[2] Peking University, Beijing, China
[3] Nanzan University, Nagoya, Japan
[4] Osaka University, Suita, Japan
[5] The University of Tokyo, Tokyo, Japan
[6] Kyoto University, Kyoto, Japan

Abstract. In recent years, providers offering similar services have increasingly formed alliances to increase their opportunities for matching customers. Moreover, it is no longer uncommon for one provider to participate in multiple alliances. It is important that providers participating in such multiple alliances integrate their data automatically, easily, and flexibly. Several view-based data integration architectures have been proposed, but they nevertheless present difficulties for multiple service alliances. Actually, two novel view-based data integration architectures have been developed in recent years to tackle these issues. They are the Dejima architecture and the BCDS architecture. No work of the relevant literature has discussed whether these architectures meet the requirements of multiple service alliances. The analyses presented herein clarify this point. First, three models of multiple service alliances using views are presented. Then these architectures are assessed for their capability of resolving the issues presented above. Finally, models implementing these architectures are summarized.

Keywords: Bidirectional transformation · Data integration · Distributed data management · Ridesharing · Service alliance

1 Introduction

As development of computer network technology progresses, providers offering similar services have increasingly formed alliances to increase their opportunities for matching customers. For instance, a marketplace platform such as e-Bay or Amazon marketplace can be regarded as an alliance of companies providing shopping services. Companies participating in the alliance can display

This work is partially supported by Japan Society for the Promotion of Science (JSPS) Grants-in-Aid for Scientific Research (S) No. 17H06099, (A) No. 18H04093, and (C) No. 18K11314.

L. Qin et al. (Eds.): SFDI 2020/LSGDA 2020, CCIS 1281, pp. 152–164, 2020.
https://doi.org/10.1007/978-3-030-61133-0_12

their products to customers through the marketplace platform. A customer can choose a preferred product among those provided by the participant companies. Another example is ridesharing alliances. Ridesharing services allow non-professional drivers to provide taxi services using their vehicles. Each driver (or vehicle) usually belongs to a single ridesharing company such as Uber or Didi. As the ridesharing market size increases, several ridesharing service providers have formed partnerships with other providers to increase chances of matching providers to customers [12]. Actually, Uber and Didi have merged their China operations. Also, Ola Cabs and GrabTaxi are in talks to join a global taxi alliance. In fact, in recent years, it is no longer uncommon for one provider to participate in multiple alliances. For example, several shopping service companies are listing their products on both Amazon and Rakuten in Japan, although they also have their own shopping sites on the web.

As Asano et al. [2] have described, even a single alliance can raise distributed data management issues. A simple method of implementing an alliance is an applicationroach by which a single representative provider manages global data of all the participant providers and each provider manages local data by itself. As one illustration of that idea regarding the Amazon marketplace, Amazon's global database manages all products. Each provider sends Amazon relevant product information. Such an applicationroach might lead to inconsistency between the global database of Amazon and the local database of each provider if some provider is unable to write appropriate code for updating its local database when its product is sold on Amazon.

Multiple alliances present additional severe issues. For example, one can consider a ridesharing service provider publishing data of one vehicle to two alliances. What will happen when a request to the vehicle from one alliance comes almost simultaneously as that from the other alliance? This provider must write code appropriately for controlling concurrency among its local databases and the two global databases of the alliances, although that would constitute a difficult task for such a provider. But the related tasks are difficult in other ways: because this code depends on the provider's data scheme and the alliance's data scheme, slightly different codes must be prepared for each provider and alliance pair. Therefore, some novel architecture is necessary for integrating such distributed databases easily and flexibly. Although distributed data integration architectures using views have been studied in the field of databases by Piazza [5,6] and ORCHESTRA (CDSS) [8,9], they are known to present three difficulties for integration with distributed databases: (1) read-only view issue, (2) single global schema issue, and (3) global consistency issue. Section 2 presents details of these issues. However, Bidirectional Information Systems for Collaborative, Updatable, Interoperable, and Trusted Sharing (BISCUITS) project[1] has tackled these issues and presented novel architectures based on bidirectional transformation (BX, for short) techniques over the last several years. One architecture

---

[1] http://www.biscuits.work/.

is that of Dejima[2] proposed by Ishihara et al. [1,7]. That architecture enables a peer to share data with another peer symmetrically using a view called Dejima. Section 2 presents a more concrete explanation. Another architecture is Bidirectional Collaborative Data Sharing (BCDS) architecture proposed by Takeichi [11]. Actually, BCDS enables peers to share data asymmetrically by allowing each peer to create a view for exporting its data and a view for importing the data from another peer. Section 2 presents a more concrete explanation.

No report of the relevant literature has described an earlier study addressing that point sufficiently. Therefore, the objective of this paper is clarification of whether these architectures meet the requirements of multiple service alliances. To do so, we must consider models of multiple service alliances using views for distributed data management. Several questions arise to consider such a model. For example, what data should be shared in an alliance? Should they be data of services or data of customers? Who should manage the shared data? Each peer or a mediator other than peers? To organize these questions, we first present three models of multiple service alliances: (a) mediator view model, (b) provider view model, and (c) customer view model. We then discuss whether the Dejima and BCDS architectures are useful for implementing these models. For this discussion, we specifically address two issues that arise in relation to implementation of these models: (4) update privilege issue, and (5) virtual view issue. Section 4 presents related details. Then, by examining whether the architectures described above can resolve these issues, we summarize which models can be implemented using these architectures. Our discussion is expected to give a perspective on what the data integration architecture should aim for and how multiple service alliances should be implemented.

The remainder of this paper is organized as follows. First we summarize features of the Dejima and BCDS architectures and their approaches to resolve issues (1)–(3) in Sect. 2. Then we present the three models of multiple service alliance in Sect. 3. In Sect. 4, we explain issues (4) and (5), which arise when considering these models. In addition, by solving the issues (1)–(5), we can elucidate whether the Dejima and BCDS architectures are useful for implementing multiple service alliances. Important conclusions are presented in Sect. 5.

2   Related Work

View-based data integration architectures have been studied actively, as summarized by Doan, Halevy, and Ives [3]. However, these architectures present the following issues: (1) They assume that views are read only (i.e. direct update of views can not be done by just anyone) because of the view update problem [10]. Although details of the view update problem are not explained herein, any conventional approach that makes a view for integrating distributed databases, including these architectures and Extract/Transform/Load (ETL)

---

[2] Dejima was a small, artificial island located in Nagasaki, Japan. All trade between Japan and foreign countries was conducted through Dejima during 1641–1854. This architecture is named based on its resemblance to Dejima in terms of functionality.

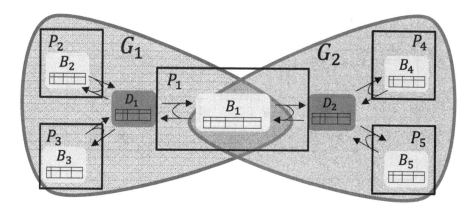

Fig. 1. Example of Dejima architecture.

tools, is adversely affected by this shortcoming. For example, one can consider that a mediator wants to collect data of available vehicles on several ridesharing service providers and wants to assign a passenger to some vehicle in the collected data represented as a view. It is preferable that the mediator be able to update the tuple corresponding to the vehicle on the view and that the update propagate automatically to the local databases of the providers while maintaining consistency between the view and the local databases. This is impossible, however, because of the view update problem. (2) Because they usually rely on the assumption that a single global scheme is shared by all peers [4,14], they are not sufficiently flexible to address local databases of providers that have mutually differing schemata. (3) They lack global consistency among local databases of peers [8,9].

Recently, an architecture named Dejima was proposed to tackle with these issues [1,7]. Recently, the so-called Dejima architecture was proposed to address these issues [1,7]. Figure 1 portrays an example of data integration using Dejima. Peers P_1, P_2, and P_3 have their respective base tables of B_1, B_2, and B_3. They share view D_1, Dejima of them. It is noteworthy that each shared view can have data extracted from multiple base tables in a peer, whereas we present only a single table for each peer in the figure for simplicity. For example, a Dejima can have data of the natural joining of two base tables in a peer.

Each peer can decide which part of its base tables should be published to their Dejima by writing code in Datalog language. This code actually defines how base tables should be updated when the corresponding Dejima is updated. For example, each of P_1, P_2, and P_3 in Fig. 1 should write a code for their Dejima D_1. Then, BX between each base table and the Dejima maintains their consistency; if some peer updates its base table, then it is propagated to the Dejima. The update of Dejima is propagated automatically to the base tables of the other peers. For example, when P_1 inserts a tuple into B_1, then the tuple might be inserted into D_1; but it might be inserted into B_2 and B_3 if the codes accept

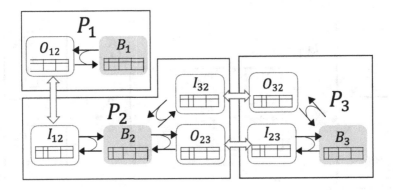

Fig. 2. Example of BCDS architecture.

the update. In this way, they form a group of integrated data corresponding to G_1 in the figure. Therefore, the Dejima architecture allows the view update and solves the read-only view issue (1), in contrast to conventional view-based data integration architectures.

The code written in Datalog is also used for converting the schema of base tables into that of the view. In other words, it absorbs the difference between the local schema and the global schema. Therefore, the Dejima architecture solves the single global schema issue (2).

Furthermore, this architecture allows a single peer to participate in multiple groups. For example, P_1 publishes its data to two groups G_1 and G_2 in the figure. Dejima architecture is intended to support distributed transactions to hold global consistency between multiple Dejima groups. It is therefore expected to resolve issue (3) and enable us the data integration of multiple service alliances. We discuss this expectation further later.

During the last year, Takeichi [11] proposed another architecture, designated as BCDS, to address the issues presented above. Figure 2 presents an example of data integration using BCDS. It is noteworthy that each P_i and B_i in this figure is unrelated to those in Fig. 1. Each peer can create an "OPort" to provide another peer with a part of its data and can define an "IPort" to receive the data provided through the OPort of another peer. Each peer can have multiple OPorts and IPorts to share data with multiple peers. For example, P_2 receives data from P_1 through O_{12} and I_{12}. The OPort of P_1 created for P_2. The IPort of P_2 defined for P_1. Because these ports absorb the difference between the data schemata of peers, BCDS solves issue (2) above.

Although the Dejima architecture shares data among peers symmetrically (i.e. peers share the same view as their Dejima), the BCDS architecture shares data asymmetrically. For example, the data provided by P_2 to P_3 and the data provided by P_3 to P_2 are distinctive in the Figure. The former is represented as a path using O_{23} and I_{23}; the latter is represented as a path using O_{32} and I_{32}. In this way, the BCDS is able to infer the ownership of each tuple in the shared data without a complicated provenance analysis.

In the BCDS architecture, an update is executed on the base table of a peer propagates to its all OPorts; it also propagates its all IPorts unless the update is not derived from one of its IPorts. For instance, an update on B_1 might propagate to B_2 and B_3 along the path using O_{12}, I_{12}, B_2, O_{23}, I_{23}, and B_3, whereas the propagated update on B_2 does not propagate to I_{32}. In this way, a peer can update a tuple owned by it and propagate the update to other peers. Furthermore, according to the policy of the peer, the BCDS enables each peer to dismiss the update propagated from its OPort. One can consider that P_3 updates a tuple in B_3, which is obtained originally from I_{23}. This update propagates to B_2 through O_{23}, although P_2 can dismiss the update if it violates its policy. Such a case might occur frequently if the tuple includes data that were created originally by P_2, and if P_2 does not appreciate unintended changes of data. In this way, each peer can prohibit other peers from updating data owned by the peer if the update violates its policy. Therefore, BCDS resolves issue (1) above.

Although the BCDS architecture does not support distributed transactions, it can be useful for data integration for multiple service alliances. We explain that point later.

Asano et al. [2] describe a similar topic to that addressed herein. They clarify desired properties for the data integration for a service alliance and propose an idea for implementing a ridesharing alliance using the Dejima architecture. They mainly describe a single-service alliance, although they could insufficiently discuss requirements for various models of multiple service alliances. As described herein, we specifically examine data integration for multiple service alliances as claimed above.

3 Models of Multiple Service Alliances

As described above, numerous elements must be considered for models of multiple service alliances. However, herein, we specifically examine who should manage the shared data of providers. For elements of other kinds, we adopt decisive assumptions. For example, whereas several candidates of answers to question of which data should be shared, we assume that data of services are shared by providers. Our discussion based on such an assumption would not lose much generality. Moreover, it is applicable to other kinds of data, including data of customer requests.

3.1 Concrete Example: Ridesharing

As a concrete example of models of multiple service alliances, we can present ridesharing alliances as described below. Consequently, the providers are companies which manage their own vehicles as services. The customers are passengers who request vehicles. A simple example includes three providers A, B, and C, with A and B forming Alliance 1 and B and C forming Alliance 2. Figure 4 presents an example of the local databases of these providers. Each table includes vehicle data of a provider, although their local schemata differ. We first explain

Provider A

vid	location	rid
v_1	Demachi	r_1
v_2	Kyoto Station	r_2
v_3	Shijo	0

Provider B

vid	location	rid	sharable
v_4	Demachi	0	TRUE
v_5	Gion	r_3	TRUE
v_6	Kitayama	0	FALSE

Provider C

vid	location	rid	type
v_7	Gion	0	sedan
v_8	Demachi	r_4	SUV
v_9	Kyoto Station	0	wagon

Fig. 3. Vehicle databases.

their common schema. In each table, `vid` denotes the ID of each vehicle; `rid` denotes the ID of each request that is currently assigned to each vehicle. An empty vehicle has `rid` = 0, for illustration, although a NULL value is used instead of 0 in a DBMS. That is, when the passenger corresponding to a request gets off a vehicle, `rid` of the tuple corresponding to the vehicle is updated to 0. Here we use unique `vid` and `rid` among all providers in this example for simplicity, although their uniqueness need only be guaranteed on each provider in practice. Furthermore, for representative places in Kyoto, we use their names, although coordinates are used more often in practice, as an attribute `location` to denote the current location of the respective vehicles. Next we explain the schema of each provider's own. Provider B has an attribute `sharable` representing whether each vehicle is available in the alliance to which it belongs. Provider C has an attribute `type` of each vehicle. As described above, these schemata constitute a simplified example. Perhaps some provider has multiple tables to store vehicle information, and desires to publish the joining of the tables to an alliance. In actuality, such a case is problematic in conventional view-based data integration architectures, in contrast to the Dejima and BCDS architectures, as discussed for issues (1) and (2) in the preceding section.

Figure 4 presents an example of shared data in each alliance. Attribute `pid` denotes the provider to which the vehicle corresponding to `vid` belongs. Presumably, each provider publishes data of available vehicles to other providers in the alliance. Although only empty vehicles are currently available, each provider can ascertain another condition under which its vehicles are available to others. For example, provider B decides to publish vehicles that are empty and sharable (i.e. `sharable` is TRUE) to Alliance 1 and Alliance 2. Then provider C decides to publish vehicles that are empty and not wagon type (i.e `type` is not wagon) to Alliance 2.

(a) Shared data for Alliance 1

vid	location	rid	pid
v_3	Shijo	0	A
v_4	Demachi	0	B

(b) Shared data for Alliance 2

vid	location	rid	pid
v_4	Demachi	0	B
v_7	Gion	0	C

Fig. 4. Shared data for two alliances.

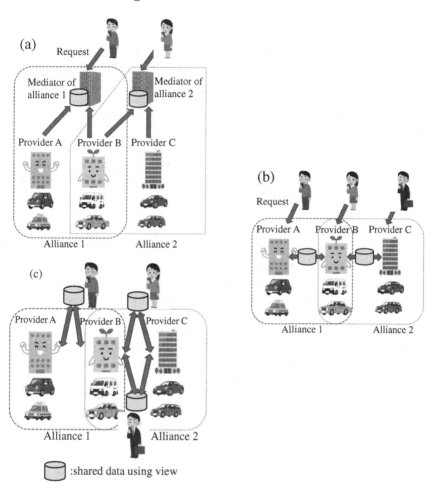

Fig. 5. Models: (a) mediator view, (b) provider view, and (c) customer view.

3.2   Three Models of Multiple Service Alliances

Figure 5 portrays three models that specifically examine who should manage the shared data as a view. In this subsection, we continue the concrete examples for ridesharing services above. Using these models, we assess how customers (passengers) request services (vehicles). Of course, an implementation of ridesharing alliances is expected to support operations of several kinds, such as reservation, canceling requests, and carpooling. However, we specifically examine the request operation here to clarify important properties for service alliances. Our discussion is applicable to operations of other kinds.

Mediator View Model. The mediator, assumed to be a trusted third party, manages the view for its alliance. A passenger requests to the mediator as presented in Fig. 5(a). Then the mediator ascertains which vehicle should be assigned to the passenger.

We explain below how a request should be processed using the example given in Figs. 3 and 4. One can consider a new passenger for whom rid is r_5 and who is close to Shijo. The passenger sends a request to Alliance 1. It is noteworthy that r_5 does not appear in Figs. 3 and 4 because it is a new passenger and is not assigned to any vehicle. Then, the mediator of the alliance will assign r_5 to vehicle v_3. The update of the tuple having v_3 should be propagated to the corresponding provider A which has v_3.

A salient advantage of this model is that it readily preserves provider and customer privacy. The passenger request is sent only to the mediator and the provider who has the assigned vehicle. The vehicle information of a provider is known only by the mediator and passengers who have been assigned to it. An important shortcoming is that finding such a mediator for each alliance is difficult; moreover, the mediator might be able to coerce or persuade providers.

Provider View Model. In this model, every provider in each alliance has a view for the alliance. A passenger makes a requests to some provider, as presented in Fig. 5(b). The provider then assigns a vehicle in its local database or the view.

We explain how a request should be processed using the example presented above. Presumably the current status of vehicle data is given in Figs. 3 and 4. The request explained for the mediator view model above is not considered. A new passenger is considered, for whom rid is r_6, who is close to Demachi, and who sends a request to provider A. It is noteworthy that r_6 does not appear in Figs. 3 and 4 because it is a new passenger and is not assigned to any vehicle. Vehicle v_1 of A is full. Therefore, A will assign r_6 to vehicle v_4 in the view for Alliance 1. The update of the tuple having v_4 should be propagated to B.

This model requires no mediator. Therefore, providers who mutually agree might be able to form an alliance by themselves. However, because the information of requests and vehicles is published to providers in an alliance, it is difficult to preserve the privacy of providers and customers.

Customer View Model. Current ridesharing providers provide smartphone applications. By those services, a passenger can send a query to the provider to find nearby vehicles. The customer view model allows passengers to have a view corresponding to a query to an alliance, as presented in Fig. 5(c).

Using the example presented above, one can explain how a request should be processed, assuming that the current status is given in Figs. 3 and 4. A newly considered passenger, for whom rid is r_7, sends a query to Alliance 2 to find empty vehicles close to Gion. It is noteworthy that r_7 does not appear in the figures because it is a new passenger and not assigned to any vehicle currently. Then, only the first tuple having v_4 in Fig. 4(b) is received as a view by the passenger. Consequently, the passenger will assign r_7 to v_4. This update should be propagated to the provider C.

Although the request of a passenger is assigned by others (i.e. the mediator or a provider) in the other models presented above, the passenger can choose a proper vehicle by changing queries in this model. Application developers might be able to develop smartphone applications similar to those used for conventional ridesharing applications. Therefore, this is more convenient than the other models for passengers and application developers. This model might be more difficult than other models to be implemented; when the number of providers in the alliance is fixed, the number of views for an alliance is fixed in the other models, although the number in this model can be numerous as queries of passengers increase. Furthermore, preserving the privacy of passengers and providers in this model is difficult.

4 Discussion of Architectures and Models

All three models described in the previous section require solution of two issues, (1) read-only view issues and (2) single global schema issues, as described in Sect. 2. That is, the update of the base table of a provider should be reflected in the view corresponding to shared data. The base tables of providers might have mutually different schemata, as shown in Fig. 3. In contrast to conventional architectures, the Dejima and BCDS architectures have resolved these issues using BX. For example, the Dejima architecture enables providers to write Datalog rules [13] for defining an updatable view for shared data in an alliance.

Issue (3) related to global consistency is crucially important for all the models of the multiple alliances, as explained in Sect. 2. For example, in Fig. 4, a request to v_4 in the Alliance 1 can occur along with one to Alliance 2 almost simultaneously because v_4 is published to both alliances. One should avoid double-booking caused by the timing of these requests. Generally speaking, such updates of the same data on the views on different peers can be propagated to a local database almost simultaneously. A distributed transaction is desired to control such concurrent updates. The Dejima architecture is going to support distributed transactions. It is expected to solve this issue. The current implementation of the BCDS architecture does not support distributed transactions. Therefore, strict concurrency control is not available. However, when a tuple on a view is updated, the update eventually propagates to the base table of the peer which created the tuple originally. The peer can determine whether the update is dismissed. Therefore, double-bookings can be avoided by dismissing a request to a vehicle that has already been assigned to another request.

Another issue (4) related to update privilege is raised by data sharing in an alliance. Whereas each peer can manage update privilege on its local database by DBMS, it might be unable to manage update privilege on a view that includes its data but which exists on another peer. As a result, an unexpected update on

Table 1. Issues to be resolved in models for multiple alliances.

	(1)	(2)	(3)	(4)	(5)
Mediator view	✓	✓	✓	-	-
Provider view	✓	✓	✓	✓	-
Customer view	✓	✓	✓	✓	✓

the view in another peer can be propagated to its local database. The mediator view model presents a simple solution to this issue. The mediator assumes a trusted third party. It should have update privilege on the view that collects service data of providers. Each provider has no view containing data of other providers. In the provider or customer view models, the issue becomes even more severe. A view containing data of a provider exists with another provider or a customer. If they are careless or malicious, then an unexpected update cannot be prevented in the current implementation of the Dejima architecture. However, in the BCDS architecture, when a provider (or a customer) attempts to update data obtained by its IPort from the OPort of another provider that created the data originally, the update becomes valid only if the latter provider approves it. Therefore, a careless unexpected update would not be approved. It would be dismissed. Addressing malicious updates is left as future work for data integration architectures using views.

We have explained that the customer view model incorporates the assumption of numerous views. These views are created or deleted frequently by user queries. Therefore, virtual views would be more appropriate than materialized views for this model. Unfortunately, the Dejima and BCDS architectures assume materialized views. Data integration through virtual views, designated as issue (5) in Tables 1 and 2, is left as another subject to be addressed in future work.

Table 2. Issues to be resolved using data integration architectures.

	(1)	(2)	(3)	(4)	(5)
Conventional	-	-	-	-	-
Dejima	✓	✓	✓	-	-
BCDS	✓	✓	△	✓	-

Tables 1 and 2 present salient points of our discussion above. In these tables, as one might expect, (1)–(5) denote issues (1)–(5). Table 1 shows issues of the respective models for multiple service alliances. For example, to implement the provider view models, issues (1)–(4) must be resolved. Table 2 presents issues that can be resolved for each architecture. "Conventional" represents the conventional architectures described in Sect. 2. The triangle symbol in the "BCDS" row signifies that the BCDS architecture has a mechanism to solve the consistency problem for the provider view model, although it does not support distributed transactions.

5   Conclusion

For this study, have investigated three models of data integration using views for multiple service alliances. Furthermore, we have discussed how state-of-the-art data integration architectures based on bidirectional transformation, the Dejima and BCDS architectures, satisfy the requirements for the three models. Although we have examined ridesharing alliances herein, the salient features of our discussion are expected to be applicable and useful for implementing service alliances of other kinds because several essential features are common among them.

References

1. Asano, Y., et al.: Flexible framework for data integration and update propagation: system aspect. In: Second Workshop on Software Foundations for Data Interoperability (2019)
2. Asano, Y., Hu, Z., Ishihara, Y., Kato, H., Onizuka, M., Yoshikawa, M.: Controlling and sharing distributed data for implementing service alliance. In: Second Workshop on Software Foundations for Data Interoperability (2019)
3. Doan, A., Halevy, A.Y., Ives, Z.G.: Principles of Data Integration. Morgan Kaufmann, Burlington (2012)
4. Halevy, A.Y.: Answering queries using views: a survey. VLDB J. **10**(4), 270–294 (2001). https://doi.org/10.1007/s007780100054
5. Halevy, A.Y., Ives, Z.G., Madhavan, J., Mork, P., Suciu, D., Tatarinov, I.: The Piazza peer data management system. IEEE Trans. Knowl. Data Eng. **16**(7), 787–798 (2004)
6. Halevy, A.Y., Ives, Z.G., Mork, P., Tatarinov, I.: Piazza: data management infrastructure for Semantic Web applications. In: WWW, pp. 556–567 (2003)
7. Ishihara, Y., Kato, H., Nakano, K., Onizuka, M., Sasaki, Y.: Toward BX-based architecture for controlling and sharing distributed data. In: Second Workshop on Software Foundations for Data Interoperability (2019)
8. Ives, Z., Khandelwal, N., Kapur, A., Cakir, M.: ORCHESTRA: rapid, collaborative sharing of dynamic data. In: CIDR, pp. 107–118 (2005)
9. Karvounarakis, G., Green, T.J., Ives, Z.G., Tannen, V.: Collaborative data sharing via update exchange and provenance. ACM Trans. Database Syst. **38**(3), 19:1–19:42 (2013)
10. Keller, A.M.: Choosing a view update translator by dialog at view definition time. In: VLDB, pp. 467–474 (1986)
11. Takeichi, M.: BCDS agent: an architecture for bidirectional collaborative data sharing. Technical report, March 2020. http://takeichimasato.net/blog/?p=1200
12. Tom, M.: A visual guide to the twisted web created by the Uber/Didi merger (2016). https://pitchbook.com/news/articles/a-visual-guide-to-the-twisted-web-created-by-the-uberdidi-merger

13. Tran, V.D., Kato, H., Hu, Z.: Programmable view update strategies on relations. PVLDB **13**(5), 726–739 (2020)
14. Ullman, J.D.: Information integration using logical views. In: Afrati, F., Kolaitis, P. (eds.) ICDT 1997. LNCS, vol. 1186, pp. 19–40. Springer, Heidelberg (1997). https://doi.org/10.1007/3-540-62222-5_34

Towards Smart Data Sharing
by Updatable Views

Makoto Onizuka[1(✉)], Yasunori Ishihara[2], and Masato Takeichi[3]

[1] Osaka University, Osaka, Japan
oni@acm.org
[2] Nanzan University, Nagoya, Japan
yasunori.ishihara@nanzan-u.ac.jp
[3] University of Tokyo, Tokyo, Japan
takeichi@acm.org

Abstract. We consider a problem of collaborative data sharing among multiple peers through updatable views each of which provided with the use of the bidirectional transformation in the peer.

We propose a novel framework *Smart Data Sharing* for developing versatile data integration systems based on collaborative data sharing.

1 Introduction

Considerable research for data integration has been carried out from various viewpoints [4]. Data integration problems in the context of peer data management are discussed in Piazza [5,6]. Although most of these research and systems assume to use data set for sharing with read-only permission, enabling the shared data set to be updatable, i.e, with read-write mode, enhances the flexibility of data integration and system interoperability in collaborative data-sharing systems as in ORCHESTRA [8,9], Dejima [2,3,7], and BCDS Agent [10]. An excellent methodology based on the *bidirectional transformation* has been established for the *view-updating* problem. However, it lacks functions to deal with view-updating properly across peers in *collaborative data sharing*.

We propose a novel framework *Smart Data Sharing* for developing such systems with the use of the bidirectional transformation in each peer and *updatable views* for data exchange between peers. Each view of the peer is produced from the peer's *source* table by the forward transformation and the update on the *view* is to be reflected in the source by the backward transformation. These forward and backward transformations comprise a bidirectional transformation which maintains consistency between the source table and the view.

2 Preliminaries and Understandings

We first take up a few concepts specific to our Smart Data Sharing and recall previously developed tools of our interest for use.

This work was partly supported by JSPS Kakenhi 17H06099 and 18H04093.

L. Qin et al. (Eds.): SFDI 2020/LSGDA 2020, CCIS 1281, pp. 165–171, 2020.
https://doi.org/10.1007/978-3-030-61133-0_13

Updatable View. A read-only view could be obtained from source tables by a database query in the same way as in the traditional data integration. As an extension to this basic scheme, we could consider data sharing through views where updates of shared data are allowed. This is called *collaborative data sharing* [8].

In collaborative data sharing, the update of the view in each peer should be reflected in the corresponding source table. We will refer to these views facing to each other between peers as *updatable views*.

We will see later in Sect. 3 how to configure the updatable view.

Bidirectional Transformation. To describe the relationship between the source S and the view V, we will use the *bidirectional transformation* comprised of two functions $get : S \rightarrow V$ and $put : S \times V \rightarrow S$.

For every source instance $s \in S$, corresponding view instance $v \in V$ is defined as $v = get(s)$ by the forward transformation get. And this view instance $v \in V$ could be updated by some view-updating operation to yield a new view instance $v' \in V$ from v, which in turn causes the update of s resulting $s' \in S$ by the backward transformation. This backward transformation from the view to the source is defined by put which takes $s \in S$ and $v' \in V$ to yield $s' = put(s, v')$. Note that the function put takes the (old) source instance $s \in S$ as well as the updated view $v' \in V$. Without the source, the backward transformation is defined only for a limited class of view-updating operations.

Round-Tripping Property. The *round-tripping property* [1] says that the data are kept consistent through the trip to and from the source and the view by get and put. This property is described using two conditions:

> GET-PUT Condition For any $s \in S$, $put(s, (get(s))) = s$ holds.
> PUT-GET Condition For any $s \in S$ and $v \in V$, $get(put(s, v)) = v$ holds.

The condition GET-PUT is the most fundamental one of the bidirectional transformation. And as such any bidirectional transformation must satisfy the GET-PUT condition; the source remains unchanged unless the update is made on the view. We might consider that the PUT-GET condition is also appropriate to most of the bidirectional transformation. This property clarifies whether get and put are considered well-behaved for our purposes. We assume the round-tripping property of the bidirectional transformation throughout this paper.

Conformity Between Updatable Views. When talking about view-updating in general, we presuppose that the round-tripping property holds for keeping the consistency between the source and the view. In collaborative data sharing through updatable views, however, the above story goes true only in each participating peer. We call the updatable views which are facing each other be *conformable* if they satisfy the round-tripping condition respectively in each peer and both share the same superficial view consisting of common values. We will discuss in Sect. 3 how conformable updatable views are formed for our use.

Before discussing details about updatable views, let us consider how updates proceed between these views.

Collaborative Update by Updatable Views. Assume that a peer P and another peer Q share data of the column A of their source tables S_p and S_q through the updatable views V_p and V_q. And the peers P and Q produce instances of updatable views $v_p = get_p(s_p)$ and $v_q = get_q(s_q)$ respectively by the forward transformation get_p and get_q as SQL statements

CREATE VIEW V_p AS SELECT A FROM S_p WHERE $even$(A), and
CREATE VIEW V_q AS SELECT A FROM S_q,

where $even$ is the predicate for the number being even. In short, P expects the shared data being even while Q permits any (Fig. 1).

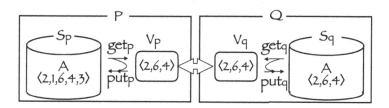

Fig. 1. Data Sharing through Updatable Views

How can we make V_p and V_q conformable?

To be concrete, take a case that P and Q share the data set $\{2, 6, 4\}$ as a common instance of v_p and v_q of the updatable views, and consider what happens if Q makes update on the column A of s_q so that $v_q = get_q(s_q)$ becomes $\{2, 5, 4\}$.

Our data sharing presupposes that the data instances of V_p and V_q are made be equal to the newest whenever either of them is updated. Hence, the view $v_p \in V_p$ seems to become $\{2, 5, 4\}$ in our case. But if we observe closely with conditions, it is not possible for v_p to have odd numbers since it should contain only even numbers of the column A extracted from s_p.

If we admit this as a temporary instance of V_p before updating S_p after the update by Q, another problem comes up in processing the backward transformation put_p of the peer P. This is because the backward transformation may reject odd numbers in $v_p \in V_p$.

If we are more generous to accept odd numbers to update $s_p \in S_p$ and to get the final view instance in V_p to be shared with Q, yet another problem arises. What is the update for the odd number 5? We may ignore the update for the record corresponding to 5 and make v_p become $\{2, 6, 4\}$ again, or may replacing the record 6 with 5 in s_p and make an instance $\{2, 4\}$ in V_p.

Any trials of the remedy on the inspiration for these problems have gone into the definition of the bidirectional transformation. In our collaborative data sharing, we expect each peer to work autonomously and independently each other with its own bidirectional transformation. Moreover, each peer has its own *updating policy* on how to deal with the update by the partner peer.

Our *Smart Data Sharing* solves these problems through reinforcement of the updating policy.

3   Smart Data Sharing

Even though the round-tripping property of the bidirectional transformation assures us of consistent view-updating between the view and the source in each peer, why are we confronted with incompatible updates across peers? The cause leading to this problem comes from potential differences in data types, or SQL schemas of the facing updatable views of participating peers.

Types and Values of Updatable View. Consider first the updatable view V_p in P associated with a type (schema) derived from the type of the source S_p. As a matter of course, the forward transformation get_p takes both types of S_p and V_p into account. When we do an update on $v_p \in V_p$, we have to follow the type of V_p. Such an updated view $v'_p \in V_p$ will be reflected in the source S_p correctly by the backward transformation put_p thanks to the round-tripping property. We understand that this is true in the peer P.

In collaborative data sharing, if updatable views facing each other always have the same type, updating either of the views proceeds as above in each peer. It is impractical, however, in that each peer of our collaborative data-sharing system behaves autonomously with its policy, and more than that the source table differs from peer to peer, and so does the view.

Although as they are, updatable views facing each other should be *conformable* to exchange data for sharing. For the views V_p and V_q to be conformable, they should consist of the same *surface values* of their supertype T satisfying $V_p \subseteq T$ and $V_q \subseteq T$[1]. That is, we can have conformable updatable views if we set up them for the surface value. We sometimes omit to specify the supertype T when it can be understood from the context. And we do so here in this paper.

In contrast to the surface value of the updatable view, we refer to the original data of the source S and the view V as *deep values* when considering in a peer. As far as surface values concerned, data of the updatable views can be considered to be equal. However, if we take deep values in each peer, they may be different in that they consist of different values. Note that the bidirectional transformation provided in each peer deals with the deep value.

Next we give the process of updating the source upon update on the view in our Smart Data Sharing instead of redefining the round-tripping property.

---

[1] We do not say anything about the operation associated with the type and use $\subseteq$ instead of $<:$ for the type hierarchy.

Designing Smart Data Sharing. For the collaborative data-sharing system with updatable views across peers, our *Smart Data Sharing* enforces the peer's updating policy during the process of view-updating in each peer.

Since our bidirectional transformation takes the deep value as the argument, we need to extend the function *put* to deal with exceptional cases for surface values which are out of the domain of the original functions. We assume that *put* produces Maybe values Just a and Nothing[2]. If the original *put* gives a value $s \in S$, this extended *put* gives Just s. And the extended *put* gives Nothing when the original *put* gives values out-of-range of S. We intentionally overload the function names *put* for the extended version. We do not need to extend *get*.

Assume that the updatable view $v \in V$ is updated to $v' \in V$ in surface values and we are to reflect the update in the source $s \in S$ by *put* to possibly yield new $s' \in S$. We may need to confirm that the view instance stays the same after updating the source by comparing $v'' = get(s')$ with v'. After this process completes, we reach a new state of the source $s^* \in S$ and the view $v^* \in V$ with the *result code* Accepted, Rejected, etc. as the reply to the partner peer.

Such an updating task is described as:

```
(s*, v*, reply) =
  case put(s, v') of      -- ① Apply the backward transformation to the updated view
    Just s' ->            -- ② Acceptable as the update of deep values
      let v''=get(s') in   -- ③ Apply the forward transformation to the new source
        case v'' == v' of   -- ④ Is the new view same as the updated view?
          True -> (s', v', Accepted)      -- ⑤ Round-tripping holds for the update
          False -> enforce_policy(s, s', v, v', v'')    -- ⑥ See below
    Nothing -> (s, v, Rejected)    -- ⑦ The deep value obtained is out of S
```

It should be noted that $v''{==}v'$ in ④ compares the view of deep values v'' and the updatable view of surface values v'.

Consider the example in the previous section: the source table of P is $s_p = \{2, 1, 6, 4, 3\}$ and get_p extracts only even numbers from s_p as the view v_p. Updatable views are $v_p = v_q = \{2, 6, 4\}$ of type integer and Q is about to update v_q to $v'_q = \{2, 5, 4\}$. After the update v'_p shares the surface values of v'_q, i.e., $v'_p = v'_q$.

Assume here that put_p is defined to accept only even values, then the final result becomes $(s_p, v_p, \mathtt{Rejected})$ because v'_p contains an odd value and it falls in Case ⑦.

Otherwise, if put_p is defined so that $put_p(s_p, v'_p) = \{2, 1, 5, 4, 3\}$ which leads s_p to $s'_p = \{2, 1, 5, 4, 3\}$. Then, $v''_p = get_p(s'_p) = \{2, 4\}$ consisting of deep values and hence $v'_p \neq v''_p$, which invokes enforce_policy as Case ⑥ to give $(s'_p, v''_p, \mathtt{Surmised})$, for example.

---

[2] We follow the notation of Haskell here for conciseness.

Thus, we could have typical results of the update using put_p associated with `enforce_policy` as:

- $(s_p, v_p, \text{Rejected})$: P keeps the old s_p and v_p, and tells Q that v'_q is rejected.
- $(s'_p, v''_p, \text{Surmised})$: P updates instances of S_p and V_p to become s'_p and v''_p, respectively, and tells Q that the update $v'_q \in V_q$ is surmised (i.e., partially accepted) and the new instance v''_p has been produced to be shared.

The function `enforce_policy` is a programmable part of Smart Data Sharing and the returned value may be other than above.

Implementing Peer's Updating Policy. There would be other opportunities for responding to the update of the partner peer. Our Smart Data Sharing realizes a tool for implementing strategies according to the peer's updating policy.

Examples of these approaches are:

- Source similarity approach. We introduce a similarity metric between source tables, and enforce the policy by selecting s^* among the source tables s' so that the similarity between s' and $put(s, v')$ is at least given threshold θ_S.
- View similarity approach. We introduce a similarity metric between views, and enforces the policy by selecting s^* among the source tables s' such that the similarity between $get(s')$ and v' is at least given threshold θ_V.
- Combined approach. Both source similarity and view similarity are taken into account, using some weight parameter.

Thus, our Smart Data Sharing generalizes the decisive updating policy of the peer as in these approaches.

4   Conclusion

We have proposed *Smart Data Sharing* for collaborative data sharing.

Our Smart Data Sharing enhances the collaborative work by exchanging both the data to be shared and the reply to the participant peer. This could be used for enabling the peers to agree on the way with the reply code of their own as well as default `Accepted` and `Rejected`. Although the agreement before starting data sharing would be preferable, such a *static agreement* seems impractical in collaborative systems with autonomous peers that behave independently with each other. One of the reason has been discussed in Sect. 3 on the type of updatable views. Another difficulty of making a static agreement would be the problem of correct and concise specification of the updating policy. A *dynamic agreement* reached by Smart Data Sharing with proper reply code may open the door to strategic policymaking as examples shown in the last part of Sect. 3. We have to work further on these topics.

References

1. Abou-Saleh, F., Cheney, J., Gibbons, J., McKinna, J., Stevens, P.: Introduction to bidirectional transformations. In: Gibbons, J., Stevens, P. (eds.) Bidirectional Transformations. LNCS, vol. 9715, pp. 1–28. Springer, Cham (2018). https://doi.org/10.1007/978-3-319-79108-1_1

2. Asano, Y., et al.: Flexible framework for data integration and update propagation: system aspect. In: 2019 IEEE International Conference on Big Data and Smart Computing (BigComp), pp. 1–5. IEEE (2019)

3. Asano, Y., Hu, Z., Ishihara, Y., Kato, H., Onizuka, M., Yoshikawa, M.: Controlling and sharing distributed data for implementing service alliance. In: 2019 IEEE International Conference on Big Data and Smart Computing (BigComp), pp. 1–4. IEEE (2019)

4. Doan, A., Halevy, A.Y., Ives, Z.G.: Principles of Data Integration. Morgan Kaufmann, Elsevier (2012)

5. Halevy, A.Y., Ives, Z.G., Madhavan, J., Mork, P., Suciu, D., Tatarinov, I.: The piazza peer data management system. IEEE Trans. Knowl. Data Eng. **16**(7), 787–798 (2004)

6. Halevy, A.Y., Ives, Z.G., Mork, P., Tatarinov, I.: Piazza: data management infrastructure for semantic web applications. In: Proceedings of the 12th International Conference on World Wide Web, pp. 556–567 (2003)

7. Ishihara, Y., Kato, H., Nakano, K., Onizuka, M., Sasaki, Y.: Toward BX-based architecture for controlling and sharing distributed data. In: 2019 IEEE International Conference on Big Data and Smart Computing (BigComp), pp. 1–5. IEEE (2019)

8. Ives, Z.G., Khandelwal, N., Kapur, A., Cakir, M. ORCHESTRA: rapid, collaborative sharing of dynamic data. In: CIDR, pp. 107–118 (2005)

9. Karvounarakis, G., Green, T.J., Ives, Z.G., Tannen, V.: Collaborative data sharing via update exchange and provenance. ACM Trans. Database Syst. **38**(3), 19:1–19:42 (2013)

10. Takeichi, M.: BCDS Agent: An Architecture for Bidirectional Collaborative Data Sharing (http://takeichimasato.net/blog/?p=1200). Technical report, March (2020)

Integration of Fast-Evolving Data Sources Using a Deep Learning Approach

Zijie Wang, Lixi Zhou, and Jia Zou[✉]

Arizona State University, Tempe, USA
{zijiewang,lixi.zhou,jia.zou}@asu.edu

Abstract. Data scientists spent 80–90% of their efforts in data integration and there is still no end-to-end automatic integration and wrangling pipeline working for a large number of data sources. This work proposes a data integration system that transforms fast-evolving raw data sources to user desired tables. Based on a set of pre-trained models, a user only needs to specify the schema of the outcome feature vector as well as a few examples of rows, the system will automatically generate the outcome table from the raw data sources. The training process is automatically injected with provisioned schema evolution so that the model is resistant to data source changes. Our experiments show that the proposed approach is particularly effective for the integration of data with fast evolving schemas.

Keywords: Data integration · Schema evolution · Deep learning

1 Introduction

Data scientists spent 80–90% efforts in the data integration and wrangling process [7,35,38]. Although there exist a lot of works trying to facilitate or accelerate this process, including the automation in entity matching [15,21,24,25,30,37,42], schema discovery and matching [16,17,31,32,43,44], and so on, however there is still no end-to-end automatic data integration pipeline that directly drives features from raw data without much human intervention [7,35,38].

Given the vast variety of data integration requirements of different machine learning applications, it is challenging to provide one end-to-end system for all heterogeneous data integration problems. While domain-specific systems seem more reasonable to support automatic data integration, they suffer from the fast evolution of data schemas, which may easily break an automated pipeline. Taking the coronavirus disease 2019 (COVID-19) data repository [4] maintained by the Johns Hopkins University (JHU) for example, not only the data contents are updated at an hourly basis, the data schema also changes frequently. For example, their data collected in March, 2020 has used at least five different formats at different time points of that month [4].

In this paper, we focus on automating the process of driving features from fast evolving raw data sources. We argue that if the feature vectors required

© Springer Nature Switzerland AG 2020
L. Qin et al. (Eds.): SFDI 2020/LSGDA 2020, CCIS 1281, pp. 172–186, 2020.
https://doi.org/10.1007/978-3-030-61133-0_14

by an application is relatively stable compared to the varieties and dynamics in both data schemas and contents, a deep learning approach performs better in accuracy, latency, and storage overhead than a baseline approach that uses traditional techniques such as locality sensitive hashing (LSH) [18, 20].

The targeting use scenario is that given a set of fast evolving data sources for a data science application, because the data content updates fast, the application may need to periodically integrate data from the data sources to keep its timeliness. However, because the schema also evolves (e.g. dimension pivoting (Fig. 1), attribute name changes, attribute addition/removal, key expansion/contraction (Fig. 2), etc.), it may happen that previous versions of codes that extract feature vectors from the data sources cannot work correctly anymore. It will incur huge burden on the data scientist if s/he needs to tweak the data integration code every time. Next we provide a motivating example as following:

A data scientist wants to train a machine learning model to predict COVID-19 global outbreak. S/he needs features including date, country/region, subregion, population, confirmed COVID-19 cases, deaths, mobility to grocery, parks, restaurants, workplaces, and so on. Each time s/he may specify a range of dates and locations, and the row-keys (i.e. date, country/region/subregion) in the outcome table can be automatically populated correspondingly. Then the first question is that given two initially known and matching data sources, such as the daily updated Google mobility data [3] and JHU COVID-19 cases data [4], of which the data is updated at daily basis and the schemas evolve at weekly basis, how to efficiently fill in the outcome table each time without much human intervention? An extended and more interesting problem is that the users are given a large set of unknown data sources. Some data sources may be dead, which were once used for past data integration tasks, but is now outdated for new data integration requests. In the same time, new data sources are added dynamically. Then, how to automatically discover relevant data sources and fill in the user specified outcome table with minimum human manual efforts?

Another motivating example is the internet of things applications where different types of sensors, devices or machines may have diversified schemas and the data integration process needs to be adaptive to various devices deployed in different locations or upgraded overtime.

We observe that while a dataset may be represented in different ways at different time points, we can always map these different representations into an abstracted key-value based data model. Then if the features required by an application are relatively stable compared to the data sources, it is feasible to learn a mapping between the abstract data model and the features. As illustrated in Fig. 1, in a lot of cases of schema evolution, the mapping from the data model to the user desired integrated table is constant, and can be easily learned.

Based on above observation, we formalize the data model as a list of quadruples in the form of (`key_array`, `key_type_array`, `value`, `value_type`). We then train a deep learning model that learns the mapping between the abstract data model and the user-desired table for each unique data integration request. The trained model can be used to transform raw data collected from fast-evolving

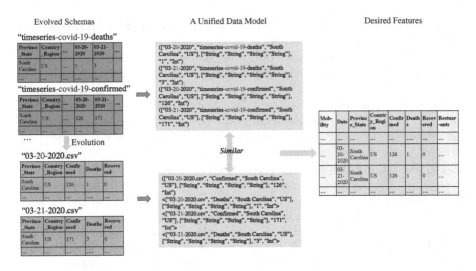

Fig. 1. Mappings among source data (with dimension-pivoting applied), abstract data model and user-desired output table.

sources into user-desired features with good adaptivity to schema evolution. First, each raw dataset, is decomposed into a stream of quadruples based on the abstract data model. Second, each quadruples serves as features, for which the model should predict its position in the outcome table (i.e. column id and row id), and an aggregation mode that specifies how this value should be aggregated with other values mapped to this table. We support aggregation modes like +, max, min, replace, concat, discard, and so on. Based on this idea, we design an end-to-end system that automates the data integration process. The system provides interfaces for (1) registering new data sources; (2) issuing a data integration request by specifying the schema of the desired outcome table; (3) training and managing models. We compare two types of model architecture in this work. In both types, the first layer is an embedding layer, and the last layer is a fully connected layer. The difference is that in the first type, we use three Conv2D and pooling layers in middle, but in the second type, we use long short-term memory (LSTM) as the second layer. We find in our preliminary results that the convolutional neural network (CNN)-based model can achieve better accuracy than the LSTM-based model.

Through experiments, we also observe that compared to a baseline data integration approach that requires to store LSH signatures for each column, our proposed approach incurs merely constant storage overheads, which may save significant amount of storage space, particularly for wide tables. In addition, for integrating wide and/or sparse datasets, we also observe a computational advantage in the deep learning approach. Additionally, our approach can seamlessly handle heterogeneous data sources and schema evolution without any additional LSH computation and storage overheads.

Usually a major concern over a deep learning approach is that the training process may take a lot of domain experts' efforts in labeling data. However, we argue that in our targeting scenario, the data labeling process can be largely automated if human experts are able to find a bootstrapping high-level mapping between the initial data source and the target outcome table. Then, the labeling can be fully automated and even the schema changes can be automatically injected. Once the models are trained, they can handle most of schema evolution without any human/tool intervention.

We summarize our key contributions as following:

- We propose and formalize a deep-learning approach to address the problem of end-to-end automatic data integration of the fast-evolving CSV files.
- We share experiences of the system design and model training.
- We implement a prototype of the system and give a preliminary evaluation with detailed analysis for the proposed approach.

In the rest of the work, we will first introduce related works in Sect. 2. Then we will formalize the problem in Sect. 3. Following that, we will propose a baseline approach and a deep learning approach in Sect. 4. Finally, we will present our preliminary experimental results in Sect. 5 and conclude the paper.

2   Background and Related Works

2.1   Handling Schema Evolutions

Schema evolution in relational database, XML, JSON and ontology has been an active research area for a long time [14,33]. One major approach is through model (schema) management [8,9] and to automatically generate executable mapping between the old and evolved schema [27,39,41]. While this approach greatly expands the theoretical foundation of relational schema evolution, it requires application maintenance and may cause undesirable system downtimes [12]. To address the problem, Prism [12] is proposed to automate the end-to-end schema modification process by providing database admins (DBAs) a schema modification language (SMO) and automatically rewriting users' legacy queries. However, Prism requires data migration to the latest schema for each schema evolution, which may not be practical for today's Big Data era. Other techniques include versioning [23,29,34], which avoids the data migration overhead, but incurs version management burden and significantly slows down query performance.

Most of these works are mainly targeting at enterprise data integration problems and require that relational schema must be available for each source dataset. However the open data sources widely used by today's data science applications are often lacking schemas or metadata information [26]. A deep learning model, once trained, can handle most schema evolution without any human intervention, and does not require any data migration, or version management overhead. Moreover, today's data science applications are more tolerant to data errors compared to traditional enterprise transaction applications, which makes a deep learning approach promising.

2.2   Data Discovery

Data discovery is to find related tables in a data lake. Aurum [16] is an automatic data discovery system that proposes to build enterprise knowledge graph (EKG) to solve real-world business data integration problems. In EKG, a node represents a set of attributes/columns, and an edge connects two similar nodes. In addition, a hyperedge connects any number of nodes that are hierarchically related. They propose a two-step approach to build EKG using LSH-based and TFIDF-based signatures. They also provide a data discovery query language SRQL so that users can efficiently query the relationships among datasets. Aurum [16] is mainly targeting at enterprise data integration. In recent, numerous works are proposed to address open data discovery problems, including automatically discover table unionability [32] and joinability [43,44], based on LSH and similarity measures. Nargesian and et al. [31] propose a Markov approach to optimize the navigation organization as a DAG for a data lake so that the probability of finding a table by any of attributes can be maximized. In the DAG, each node of navigation DAG represents a subset of the attributes in the data lake, and an edge represents a navigation transition. All of these works provide helpful insights from an algorithmic perspective and system perspective for general data discovery problems. Particularly, Fernandez and et al. [17] propose a semantic matcher based on word embeddings to discover semantic links in the EKG.

Our work proposes to integrate data discovery and schema matching into a deep learning model inference process. We argue that in our targeting scenario, the approach we propose can save significant storage overhead as we only need store data integration models which are significantly smaller than the EKG, and can also achieve better performance for wide and sparse tables. We will prove in the paper that the training data generation and labeling process can be fully automated.

2.3   Schema Matching

Traditionally, to solve the data integration problem for data science applications, once related datasets are discovered, the programmer will either manually design queries to integrate these datasets, or leverage a schema matching tool to automatically discover queries to perform the data integration.

There are numerous prior-arts in schema matching [19,22,27,36], which mainly match schemas based on metadata (e.g. attribute name) and/or instances. Entity matching (EM) [11], which is to identify data instances that refer to the same real-world entity, is also related. Some EM works also employ a deep learning-based approach [15,21,24,25,30,37,42]. Mudgal and et al. [30] evaluate and compare the performance of different deep learning models applied to EM with three types of data: structured data, textual data, and dirty data (with missing value, inconsistent attributes and/or misplaced values). They find that deep learning doesn't outperform existing EM solutions on structured data, but it outperforms them on textual and dirty data.

In addition, to apply schema matching to heterogeneous data sources, it is important to discover schemas from semi-structured or non-structured data. We proposed a schema discovery mechanism for JSON data [40], among other related works [13, 28].

Our approach proposes a key-value-based data model to unify open CSV datasets. We train deep learning models to learn the mappings between the data items in source datasets (key-value pairs) and their positions as well as aggregation modes in the target table. As mentioned, the mappings can be learnt by parsing and training only a small portion of data items to optimize the online inference overhead.

2.4   Other Related Works

Thirumuruganathan and et al. [38] discuss various representations for learning tasks in relational data curation. Cappuzzo and et al. [10] further propose an algorithm for obtaining local embeddings using a tripartite-graph-based representation for data integration tasks such as schema matching, and entity matching on relational database. We are mainly targeting at open data in CSV format and choose to use a key-value based representation. We will compare different representations in our future works.

3   Problem Formulation

In this section, we will formalize the data integration problems we are targeting at.

3.1   Data Model/Representation

Now, we start formalizing the targeting problems by abstracting representations for the raw data sources. We mainly consider following data models:

Key-Value Representation: Suppose there are m raw datasets stored in the system to form a data repository, represented as $D = \{d_i\}(0 \leq i < m)$, each raw dataset is modeled as a set of n_i data items (or cells), denoted as $d_i = \{c_{ij}\}(0 \leq i < m, 0 \leq j < n_i)$. We further describe each data item $c_{ij} \in d_i$ as a typed key-value pair, represented as $c_{ij} = \langle \boldsymbol{key}_{ij}^{T_{key_{ij}}}, value_{ij}^{T_{value_{ij}}} \rangle$. For a CSV field, the key is represented as an alphabetically ordered string array of the file name, column name, row-keys; and the value can be simply the value of the field. Figure 1 gives an example of CSV files. We can further define a super set to describe the current state of the entire data repository: $C = \{c_{ij} \in d_i | \forall d_i \in D\}$. In this work, we mainly use key-value representation.

Column-based Representation: For d_i in the type of CSV files, we can further define that d_i also has p_i attributes (i.e. columns), denoted as $d_i = \{A_{i0}, ..., A_{ip_i}\}$ and each attribute corresponds to a set of values that share the same attribute. A cell is often relevant with other attributes in the same tuple, and such linking gets lost in the column-based representation. So we only use this representation when defining the baseline solution on structured data as described in Sect. 4.1. Also compared to the key-value representation, the column-based representation is more difficult to extend to semi-structured and non-structured data.

Graph representation: Cappuzzo and et al. [10] propose to use a tripartite graph-based representation to describe relational data and capture all row-wise, column-wise, and table-wise linkings. While it will be interesting to apply this representation to describe heterogeneous open data, without the relational schema information, constructing a heterogeneous graph in open data is very expensive and challenging. We will leave this to future work.

3.2   Problem Definition

Given a fast evolving data repository D, for the t-th data integration request, the user input should specify the schema of the expected outcome table represented as $V^{A^t \times R^t} = \{v_{kl}\}(0 \leq k < p, 0 \leq l < q)$. The schema includes a list of p attributes denoted as $A^t = \{a_k\}(0 \leq k < p)$, where a_k represents the k-th attribute, as well as a list of q possible row keys, denoted as $R^t = \{r_l\}(0 \leq l < q)$. Then we need find a model $f_t^{D \rightarrow (A^t \cup \{NULL\}) \times (R^t \cup \{NULL\})}$ that assigns a label denoted as $(a_k, r_l), a_k \in (A^t \cup \{NULL\}), r_l \in (R^t \cup \{NULL\})$ to each data item $c_{ij}(0 \leq i < m, 0 \leq j < n_i)$. It means that for each data item decomposed from the candidate raw datasets, the system needs to determine $a_k \in A^t$, and $r_l \in R^t$, so that $c_{ij}.value_{ij}^{T_{value_{ij}}}$ should be put into the cell indexed by the row r_l and the column a_k in the outcome table or it doesn't belong to the outcome table and should be discarded, for which case we define that $r_l = NULL$ and $a_k = NULL$.

4   Solution

In this section, we will first present a baseline approach that applies existing data discovery techniques for a simplified data integration problem and analyze its limitations. Then we will propose an end-to-end deep learning approach as a more general and more automated solution to our targeting data integration problem.

4.1   A Baseline Data Integration Approach

We first simplify the problem by assuming that all raw datasets are structured datasets. Then $d_i \in D$ can be represented as a list of columns, denoted as $d_i = \{a_{ik}\}(0 \leq k < p_i)$, where a_{ik} is the k-th column in d_i.

For this simplified problem, we can apply existing data discovery techniques [43,44] based on LSH to discover the most similar column in the raw data repository to each column specified in the user desired output. First, the algorithm computes locality sensitive hash (LSH) signatures for each column in the source raw datasets and the user-provided example of the target dataset, then it identifies matching columns, and formulates queries over these matching datasets to create the output integrated dataset.

First, for each column in the structured raw datasets $a_{ik} \in d_i$, we create L LSH signatures using a family of L hash functions, denoted as $H^s_{ik} = (h^s_{ik1}, ..., h^s_{ikL})$ and insert each signature into its corresponding hashmap.

Then, for each column $a'_k \in A^t(0 \leq k' < p)$ in the example of the expected outcome table $V^{A^t \times R^t}$) as specified by the user in its data integration request), we also create L LSH signatures, denoted as $H^t_{k'} = (h^t_{k'1}, ..., h^t_{k'L})$.

After that, every pair of $\langle H^s_{ik}, H^t_{k'} \rangle$ for $\forall d_i \in D$ will be compared, if they match, we insert the pair of target column and source column $\langle a_{k'}, a_{ik} \rangle$, into the hashmap that stores all mapping from target column to candidate columns.

Next, it searches for a minimal subset of raw datasets $D' \subset D$ so that for $\forall a_{k'} \in A^t$, $\exists d_i \in D$, satisfying that $\langle a_{k'}, a_{ik} \rangle$ exists in the hashmap.

Finally it performs join and filter operations over D' to create and output the outcome integrated table.

Analysis. For the baseline algorithm, the computational overhead is mainly incurred by generating LSH signatures for all columns in the raw datasets, of which the complexity is $O((p + \sum_0^m p_i) \times L)$, which can be carried out in offline style. The online overhead mainly includes the matching of all raw columns to each of the target columns, of which the complexity is $O(p \times \sum_0^m p_i)$.

In case of schema evolution and data updates, it requires to generate and store LSH signatures for each updated/newly-added column. This could be a prohibitive overhead for fast-evolving data sources.

In addition, the baseline algorithm also requires to store $(p + \sum_0^m p_i) \times L$ signatures, which could be quite significant if the raw datasets are dominated by wide tables.

Moreover, because the baseline algorithm is constrained by the simplifying assumptions that we mentioned earlier, it cannot be easily extended to semi-structured and unstructured raw datasets, and raw datasets that spread target feature values as column/attribute names, as illustrated in Fig. 1.

4.2   An End-to-End Deep Learning Approach

To provide a more flexible and efficient solution to handle integration of heterogeneous and fast evolving data, we further propose a novel approach based on deep learning.

1. Feature Representation. For each raw dataset $d_i \in D = \{c_{ij}\}$, a data item is modeled as a key-value pair $c_{ij} = \langle \boldsymbol{key}_{ij}^{T\,key_{ij}}, value_{ij}^{T\,value_{ij}} \rangle$. Therefore, it is easy to store each raw dataset as a set of quadruples, in the form of (`key_array`, `key_type_array`, `value`, `value_type`) as illustrated in Fig. 1. Each field in the quadruple is encoded based on a dictionary and can be decoded based on the type information. This transformation process that parses raw data into key-value representation is conducted offline at storage time. We will describe a few techniques to accelerate this process, such as data scheduling and sampling.

2. Label Representation. On the other hand, the label to predict is formulated as a (`row_key(s)`, `column_attribute`, `aggregation_mode`) tuple that specifies the position $(a_k, r_l), a_k \in A^t, r_l \in R^t$ in the outcome table $V^{A^t \times R^t}$ as well as how values assigned to the same cell in the output table should be aggregated. We support multiple aggregation modes, such as arithmetic addition (+), string concatenation (`concat`), replace of the old value using the new value (`replace`), keep the old value and discard the new value (`discard`), and so on. The labeling process is illustrated in Fig. 2. In our implementation and experiments for this work, the label is represented as a one-hot vector.

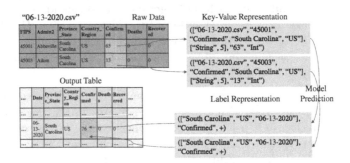

Fig. 2. Illustration of the labeling process for the schema evolution with key expansions

3. Model Architecture. We propose a three-layer neural network model architecture to learn the function (i.e. $f_t^{C \rightarrow (A^t \cup \{NULL\}) \times (R^t \cup \{NULL\})}$) that maps the input feature quadruple ($c_{ij} \in d_i, \forall d_i \in D$) to its position in the outcome table ($(a_k, r_l), a_k \in A^t, r_l \in R^t$). The first layer is a word embedding layer. As advocated in DeepMatcher [30], using an existing character embedding trained with large corpus like Wikipedia data may improve the accuracy. We will consider such approach in our future works, and the last layer is a fully connected layer. For the middle layers, we try both RNN (LSTM) and CNN, and find that due to the locality (i.e. key array is irrelevant with value) is critical, CNN can achieve better accuracy. We find that CNN performs better than LSTM in our preliminary experiments (Sect. 5).

4. Training Data Preparation. To train the data integration model, the user needs to create a set of labeled training samples. The candidate training datasets and their mappings to the target outcome table can be manually determined, or automatically determined by leveraging existing data discovery and schema matching approaches. But once these are determined, due to the mappings are usually a finite set of rules, the labeling process can be easily automated by developing a python script to transform the datasets into a series of key-value pairs and corresponding labels. In addition, we automatically inject schema changes into the training data by pivoting dimensions, expanding keys, changing attribute names and so on. We inject key expansion changes based on hierarchical entity relationships, while attribute name changes are injected based on the synonym entity relationships extracted from the Google knowledge graph.

5. Model Training Process. We observe that it only takes up to several seconds' time for training in commodity hardware with GPU, and the training process only needs to be performed once. Despite of the schema changes of most types, a trained model can be reused many times to integrate updated or new data sources. Therefore, if the application is relatively stable compared to the data sources, the training overhead gets well amortized over multiple integration processes.

6. Output Table Assembling. For each prediction, a data dispatcher is responsible to assemble a triple (`row_id`, `column_id`, `value`) from it to describe $(a_k, r_l, value_{ij}^{T_{value_{ij}}})$, buffer it in local, and dispatch the tuples to users' registered deep learning workers once the buffer is full. At each deep learning worker, a client of our system is responsible to receive tuples and assemble tuples into tensors. In addition, if user has registered a number of workers to form a distributed cluster, the output table will be partitioned in a way to guarantee load balance and ensure the independent identical distribution (i.e. iid) to avoid introducing bias. Finally, if user hasn't registered any deep learning workers, the data will be written to local.

Analysis. For the deep learning approach, the offline overhead includes the transformation and storage of all raw datasets into key-value pairs, as well as the training expense. The online overhead is mainly in model inference, which can be accelerated by advanced hardwares, like GPU, FPGA, and ASIC.

The overall storage overhead is mainly caused by the storage of pre-trained models, which is linear to the number of different applications. However we find that the storage overhead for a single model is merely up to several to tens of kilobytes. One thing to note is that the proposed key-value model can also significantly reduce intermediate processing overhead for sparse data. In the future, we may consider to cache the key-value representation for reuse.

Once a data integration model is trained, there is almost no need for human intervention, despite of newly added or updated data sources, which also distinguishes it from the baseline approach and other existing works.

Finally the performance of the deep learning approach can be further optimized by using an early stopping mechanism. Instead of parsing all data items in the source datasets, we can parse only n_k sampled items for each column, and we will skip the parsing of the rest of the column for testing if most of the sampled items are discarded. n_k is determined by the number of values in the column.

5 Preliminary Results

5.1 Environment Setup

We implement the deep learning approach using TensorFlow version 1.14, CUDA version 10 and python, and the baseline approach also in python using pandas APIs. We deploy the system in a desktop installing Intel i7 CPU, 32 GB memory, and Nvidia RTX 2070 Super GPU with 8 GB Memory.

We mainly evaluate our system in two COVID-19 data integration scenarios that are close to the example in Sect. 3. In the first scenario, we predict COVID-19 death using daily and regional information regarding number of confirmed cases and a mobility factor. From a set of raw data sources, we need create a time-series 2-dimensional array, where each row represents data for a state/province on a specific date, and each column represents date, state, country, the number of confirmed cases, and the value of mobility factor, which can be used as inputs to various curve-fitting techniques [1,2] for COVID-19 death prediction. In the second scenario, we use regional information including total population, male population, female population, number of hospitals, number of ICUs and so on for COVID-19 death prediction.

We assume the user specifies/recommends a small set of initial data sources. For the first scenario, the user specifies the John Hopkins University's COVID-19 github repository [4] and Google mobility data [3]. For the second scenario, a dataset from Kaiser Health News [6] and a dataset from Harvard dataverse COVID-19 repository [5] are used. In the first scenario, both of the two source datasets are updated at daily basis and observed with frequent schema changes. The statistics about the above source tables are illustrated in Table 1.

For both models, we use 256 neurons for the first layer and the third layer respectively. For the last layer, we use 512 neurons for LSTM, and for CNN, we use three conv2D and pooling layers, each of which uses 100 3×3, 4×4, and 5×5 filters respectively and 1 stride. We use learning rate of 0.001 and batch size of 256.

We then evaluate the accuracy and the end-to-end latency of the trained models for synthetic data with schema changes applied (we do not consider column expansion and contraction in preliminary experiments) and data that is irrelevant with the target tables that are synthesized from real-world COVID-19 data as illustrated in Table 2. The accuracy of the data integration model is defined as the ratio of the number of correctly classified data cells to the total tested classified data cells.

5.2 Testing Accuracy Analysis

The model testing accuracy for the first scenario with time series and regional information is illustrated in Table 3. In total, the training dataset includes 28751 automatically labeled training samples. We observe that using CNN achieves significantly higher accuracy in various testing cases, particularly for testing

Table 1. Statistics of relevant data sources.

	numRows	numCols
JHU-COVID-19	310	66
Google-Mobility	477322	11
KHN-COVID-19	3142	11
Harvard-COVID-19	3143	459

Table 2. Statistics of open CSV COVID-19 data that we've collected in the data repository.

numFiles	avgNumAttributes (Width)	avgNumRows (Depth)
2306	65	3422

Table 3. Testing accuracy comparison.

Testing cases	LSTM	CNN
Relevant data with no schema changes	98.76%	99.29%
Relevant data with schema changes	98.13%	99.92%
Totally irrelevant data	99.96%	99.04%
Partially irrelevant data	67.16%	98.41%

with partially irrelevant data cells. This is mainly because CNN considers the locality of features while sequence is less important for this case.

For the second scenario with only regional information, we only try the LSTM model and it can achieve 100% accuracy for relevant data with no schema changes, and we didn't test with other cases, which we will leave to future works.

We see an obvious advantage of our proposed deep learning approach compared to the baseline approach. For example, the baseline approach cannot handle the first scenario as illustrated in Fig. 1 where the time-series dimension is pivoted and can be hardly mapped to any column in the target table. However, in the second scenario, the baseline approach can correctly identify all related attributes and map attributes in the source datasets to the target table.

5.3 Latency Analysis

We also test and compare the end-to-end latency including training and testing of the deep learning approach to the baseline approach. The results are illustrated in Table 4.

5.4 Storage Overhead Analysis

We find that the deep learning approach has an obvious benefit in saving storage overhead compared to the baseline approach. Each LSTM model has 1000

Table 4. Latency break-down and comparison (Unit: second).

	Latency	Measurement details
Data-decomposition-scenario1	7.47	JHU and Google mobility datasets
Training-latency-LSTM-scenario1	11.37	for 28751 training samples
Testing-latency-LSTM-scenario1	6.3	for 30000 testing samples
Training-latency-CNN-scenario1	7.52	for 28751 training samples
Testing-latency-CNN-scenario1	3.66	for 30000 testing samples
Data-decomposition-scenario2	8.14	Harvard and KHN datasets
Training-latency-LSTM-scenario2	6.93	for 5000 training samples
Testing-latency-LSTM-scenario2	0.17	for 1000 testing samples
Baseline-approach-creating-LSH-scenario2	14.65	for 11 columns in KHN data and 459 columns in Harvard data
Baseline-approach-matching-LSH-scenario2	23.21	for 11 columns in KHN data and 459 columns in Harvard data
Baseline-approach-join-scenario2	0.04	using pd.DataFrame.merge()

parameters in total, which is 16 KB in size, and the CNN model has 5500 parameters, which is 88 KB. However, for the baseline approach, we store 512 MinHash LSH signatures [20] for each column and each signature has 4 bytes, so it takes 154 KB for the JHU COVID-19 dataset and the Google mobility dataset in the first scenario, and 940 KB for the Harvard and KHN COVID-19 datasets in the second scenario. If consider all 2306 CSV files (Table 2, it requires 300 MB of storage overhead in total, while the deep learning approach only needs to store the model that is smaller than 100 KB.

6   Conclusion

In this work, we propose an end-to-end approach based on deep learning for periodical extraction of user expected tables from fast evolving data sources of open CSV files. We further propose a relatively stable key-value based representation to embody the fast-evolving source data and to generate training data by automatically injecting schema changes (e.g. dimension pivoting, attribute name changes, attribute addition/removal, key expansion/contraction, etc.). We formalize the problem and conduct preliminary experiments on open COVID-19 data. The initial results show that our proposed approach can achieve better accuracy and latency, with significantly reduced storage overhead, compared to the baseline approach, and that using deep learning to handle schema evolution is a promising research direction.

References

1. Caltech covid-19 modeling. https://github.com/quantummind/caltech_covid_19_modeling
2. Cdc covid-19 death forecasting models. https://www.cdc.gov/coronavirus/2019-ncov/covid-data/forecasting-us.html
3. Community mobility reports. https://www.google.com/covid19/mobility/
4. Covid-19 data repository by the center for systems science and engineering (CSSE) at johns hopkins university. https://github.com/CSSEGISandData/COVID-19

5. Harvard covid-19 data: county_age and sex_with_ann. https://dataverse.harvard.edu
6. Kaiser health news data repository. https://khn.org/news/as-coronavirus-spreads-widely-millions-of-older-americans-live-in-counties-with-no-icu-beds/#lookup
7. Abadi, D., et al.: The seattle report on database research. ACM SIGMOD Rec. **48**(4), 44–53 (2020)
8. Bernstein, P.A.: Applying model management to classical meta data problems. In: CIDR, vol. 2003, pp. 209–220. Citeseer (2003)
9. Bernstein, P.A., Rahm, E.: Data warehouse scenarios for model management. In: Laender, A.H.F., Liddle, S.W., Storey, V.C. (eds.) ER 2000. LNCS, vol. 1920, pp. 1–15. Springer, Heidelberg (2000). https://doi.org/10.1007/3-540-45393-8_1
10. Cappuzzo, R., Papotti, P., Thirumuruganathan, S.: Creating embeddings of heterogeneous relational datasets for data integration tasks. In: Proceedings of the 2020 ACM SIGMOD International Conference on Management of Data, pp. 1335–1349 (2020)
11. Christen, P.: Data Matching: Concepts and Techniques for Record Linkage, Entity Resolution, and Duplicate Detection. Springer Science & Business Media, Berlin (2012)
12. Curino, C.A., Moon, H.J., Zaniolo, C.: Graceful database schema evolution: the prism workbench. Proc. VLDB Endowment **1**(1), 761–772 (2008)
13. DiScala, M., Abadi, D.J.: Automatic generation of normalized relational schemas from nested key-value data. In: Proceedings of the 2016 International Conference on Management of Data, pp. 295–310 (2016)
14. Doan, A., Halevy, A.Y.: Semantic integration research in the database community: a brief survey. AI Mag. **26**(1), 83–83 (2005)
15. Ebraheem, M., Thirumuruganathan, S., Joty, S., Ouzzani, M., Tang, N.: Deeper-deep entity resolution. arXiv preprint arXiv:1710.00597 (2017)
16. Fernandez, R.C., Abedjan, Z., Koko, F., Yuan, G., Madden, S., Stonebraker, M.: Aurum: a data discovery system. In: 2018 IEEE 34th International Conference on Data Engineering (ICDE), pp. 1001–1012. IEEE (2018)
17. Fernandez, R.C., et al.: Seeping semantics: linking datasets using word embeddings for data discovery. In: 2018 IEEE 34th International Conference on Data Engineering (ICDE), pp. 989–1000. IEEE (2018)
18. Gionis, A., et al.: Similarity search in high dimensions via hashing. Vldb **99**, 518–529 (1999)
19. Gottlob, G., Senellart, P.: Schema mapping discovery from data instances. J. ACM (JACM) **57**(2), 1–37 (2010)
20. Indyk, P., Motwani, R.: Approximate nearest neighbors: towards removing the curse of dimensionality. In: Proceedings of the Thirtieth Annual ACM Symposium on Theory of Computing, pp. 604–613 (1998)
21. Kasai, J., Qian, K., Gurajada, S., Li, Y., Popa, L.: Low-resource deep entity resolution with transfer and active learning. arXiv preprint arXiv:1906.08042 (2019)
22. Kimmig, A., Memory, A., Miller, R.J., Getoor, L.: A collective, probabilistic approach to schema mapping using diverse noisy evidence. IEEE Trans. Knowl. Data Eng. **31**(8), 1426–1439 (2018)
23. Klein, M.C., Fensel, D.: Ontology versioning on the semantic web. In: SWWS, pp. 75–91 (2001)
24. Konda, P., et al.: Magellan: toward building entity matching management systems. Proc. VLDB Endowment **9**(12), 1197–1208 (2016)

25. Meduri, V.V., Popa, L., Sen, P., Sarwat, M.: A comprehensive benchmark framework for active learning methods in entity matching. In: Proceedings of the 2020 ACM SIGMOD International Conference on Management of Data, pp. 1133–1147 (2020)
26. Miller, R.J.: Open data integration. Proc. VLDB Endowment **11**(12), 2130–2139 (2018)
27. Miller, R.J., Haas, L.M., Hernández, M.A.: Schema mapping as query discovery. VLDB **2000**, 77–88 (2000)
28. Mior, M.J., Salem, K., Aboulnaga, A., Liu, R.: Nose: schema design for nosql applications. IEEE Trans. Knowl. Data Eng. **29**(10), 2275–2289 (2017)
29. Moon, H.J., Curino, C.A., Deutsch, A., Hou, C.-Y., Zaniolo, C.: Managing and querying transaction-time databases under schema evolution. Proc. VLDB Endowment **1**(1), 882–895 (2008)
30. Mudgal, S., et al.: Deep learning for entity matching: a design space exploration. In: Proceedings of the 2018 International Conference on Management of Data, pp. 19–34 (2018)
31. Nargesian, F., Pu, K.Q., Zhu, E., Ghadiri Bashardoost, B., Miller, R.J.: Organizing data lakes for navigation. In: Proceedings of the 2020 ACM SIGMOD International Conference on Management of Data, pp. 1939–1950 (2020)
32. Nargesian, F., Zhu, E., Pu, K.Q., Miller, R.J.: Table union search on open data. Proc. VLDB Endowment **11**(7), 813–825 (2018)
33. Rahm, E., Bernstein, P.A.: An online bibliography on schema evolution. ACM Sigmod Rec. **35**(4), 30–31 (2006)
34. Sheng, Y.: Non-blocking Lazy Schema Changes in Multi-Version Database Management Systems. PhD thesis, Carnegie Mellon University Pittsburgh, PA (2019)
35. Stonebraker, M., Ilyas, I.F.: Data integration: the current status and the way forward. IEEE Data Eng. Bull. **41**(2), 3–9 (2018)
36. Ten Cate, B., Kolaitis, P.G., Tan, W.-C.: Schema mappings and data examples. In: Proceedings of the 16th International Conference on Extending Database Technology, pp. 777–780 (2013)
37. Thirumuruganathan, S., Parambath, S.A.P., Ouzzani, M., Tang, N., Joty, S.: Reuse and adaptation for entity resolution through transfer learning. arXiv preprint arXiv:1809.11084 (2018)
38. Thirumuruganathan, S., Tang, N., Ouzzani, M., Doan, A.: Data curation with deep learning [vision]. arXiv preprint arXiv:1803.01384 (2018)
39. Velegrakis, Y., Miller, R.J., Popa, L.: Preserving mapping consistency under schema changes. VLDB J. **13**(3), 274–293 (2004)
40. Wang, L., Zhang, S., Shi, J., Jiao, L., Hassanzadeh, O., Zou, J., Wangz, C.: Schema management for document stores. Proc. VLDB Endowment **8**(9), 922–933 (2015)
41. Yu, C., Popa, L.: Semantic adaptation of schema mappings when schemas evolve. In: Proceedings of the 31st International Conference on Very Large Data Bases, pp. 1006–1017. VLDB Endowment (2005)
42. Zhao, C., He, Y.: Auto-EM: end-to-end fuzzy entity-matching using pre-trained deep models and transfer learning. In: The World Wide Web Conference, pp. 2413–2424 (2019)
43. Zhu, E., Deng, D., Nargesian, F., Miller, R.J.: Josie: overlap set similarity search for finding joinable tables in data lakes. In: Proceedings of the 2019 International Conference on Management of Data, pp. 847–864 (2019)
44. Zhu, E., Nargesian, F., Pu, K.Q., Miller, R.J.: LSH ensemble: internet-scale domain search. arXiv preprint arXiv:1603.07410 (2016)

Towards Guaranteeing Global Consistency for Peer-Based Data Integration Architecture

Kota Miyake[(⊠)], Yusuke Wakuta, Yuya Sasaki, and Makoto Onizuka

Osaka University, 1-1 Yamadaoka, Suita-shi, Osaka 565-0871, Japan
miyake.kouta@ist.osaka-u.ac.jp

Abstract. Dejima is a peer-based data integration architecture that peers share their data in updatable views. Since peers in Dejima are distributedly deployed to manage their database, update in a peer may propagate to other peers. A transaction management method is necessary to guarantee global consistency. This paper analyzes the characteristics of Dejima from the perspective of transaction management and proposes a transaction management method for efficiency and autonomy of peers.

Keywords: Data integration · Distributed transaction management · Concurrency control

1 Introduction

Data integration is the process of providing the user a unified view of data residing at different databases. Since each user's schema is designed based on their purposes, these databases have different schemas. Most of the conventional frameworks for data integration first gather data from multiple databases and then provide an integrated view of these data as a single global schema [6]. Recently, as a large amount of generated data increases the cost of transferring data, the conventional frameworks would be not appropriate. In our preliminary work, we proposed Dejima [1,2], an architecture for data integration. Dejima is influenced by ORCHESTRA [5]. It adopts the decentralized structure and preserves the autonomy of each peer in a peer network. In Dejima, an update in a peer propagates to other peers through updatable views. One of the big differences between Dejima and ORCHESTRA is that Dejima guarantees global consistency.

Dejima needs a transaction management to guarantee global consistency. A naive solution is locking all the records in all peers at the same time, but this is not efficient and significantly decreases the throughput. As for recent advances in distributed transaction management, Spanner [4] applies multi-version two-phase locking in a distributed environment and uses the true time API to get the correct timestamps despite the difference between each database server's clock; Megastore [3] guarantees global consistency in well-grained partitioned

© Springer Nature Switzerland AG 2020
L. Qin et al. (Eds.): SFDI 2020/LSGDA 2020, CCIS 1281, pp. 187–193, 2020.
https://doi.org/10.1007/978-3-030-61133-0_15

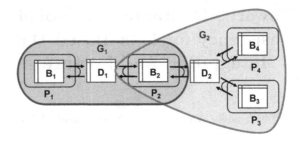

Fig. 1. An example of the Dejima architecture deployment.

databases; Calvin [7] determines a unique serializable schedule from issued transactions before performing. Since Calvin can handle databases deterministically
(i.e., the orders of transactions are not affected by other elements such as OS
scheduling), it can reduce communication costs because each database can know
the orders of transactions by time stamps. However, these methods were designed
for data replication environments instead of peer-to-peer environments. Hence
we cannot directly adopt these methods to Dejima.

In designing a transaction management method for Dejima, besides efficiency and scalability, another challenge is not to compromise the autonomy of
peers and data propagation. In this paper, we design a transaction management
method for Dejima by taking into consideration the characteristics of the Dejima
architecture. For the sake of efficiency and autonomy of peers, we propose the
concept of *family record set* and regard federated databases as a *single virtual
view*. Then we can perform two-phase locking on the virtual view to guarantee
a serializable schedule. We provide an implementation and evaluation plan for
our techniques.

2   Dejima Architecture

We introduce an overview of Dejima. The Dejima architecture consists of two
components: *peers* and *Dejima groups*. A peer P represents a client, such as
a company or service, which participates in Dejima to share data. Each peer
has its own database and its local schema. We call the tables in each peer's
database *base tables* (denoted by B). A Dejima group G is a set of peers to share
a part of records in their databases. We say that P participates in G if P is
contained by G. In a Dejima group, the peers share a view derived from their base
tables, called *Dejima table D*. One of the significant differences between Dejima
and other architectures is that Dejima makes view *updatable* via bidirectional
transformation [8]. In other words, each peer can convert updates in a Dejima
table to the updates in their base tables and vice versa. In doing so, updates in a
peer's base table can be propagated to the Dejima table and then to other peers'
base tables. We denote updated records of table X as ΔX. We assume that a
Dejima table is defined by four common types of queries: Selection, Projection,

Join, and Union (SPJU query). Note that although JOIN queries may result in the ambiguity of view update for Dejima tables, bidirectional transformation [8] can be utilized to resolve the ambiguity.

We illustrate an example of data integration in Dejima. Figure 1 shows an example of the Dejima architecture deployment, which consists of four peers and two Dejima groups. Each peer P_i has its base table B_i. P_1 and P_2 participate in G_1 and share Dejima table D_1. P_2, P_3 and P_4 participate in G_2 and share Dejima table D_2. The Black arrows in the figure represent bidirectional transformations. Consider a query at P_1 inserts records to B_1. The update ΔB_1 is converted to records inserted into D_1 by incremental view maintenance, and then the ΔD_1 is sent to P_2. After receiving ΔD_1, P_2 transforms this update to ΔB_2 via bidirectional transformation and updates B_2. ΔB_2 is converted to ΔD_2 and further propagated to P_3 and P_4. This example is an insertion case. We can process deletions in the same way. We can also translate an update with a pair of insertion and deletion.

We summarize four characteristics of Dejima that we need to consider for developing distributed transaction management methods.

Autonomy of Peer: Dejima preserves the autonomy of peers because it does not demand a specific database management system. Each peer may use an arbitrary database management system and manages its own local schema. Their local concurrency control methods may also differ. Thus, Dejima requires a transaction management method which can prevent any anomalies despite these differences. Dejima also integrates databases in a decentralized manner, so it is not suitable to employ a single global transaction management component.

Deadlock: To guarantee global consistency in Dejima, we can leverage locking protocols. In Dejima, updates are propagated to other peers, which may cause deadlocks frequently. When a deadlock happens, we need to abort transactions to resolve it. Since a transaction incurs communication between peers, aborting transactions renders previous communications of this transaction invalid. Therefore, we need to reduce deadlocks as much as possible to achieve high throughput.

Dejima Table Defined with JOIN Query: Dejima table can be defined by JOIN queries. This poses additional challenges compared to selection, projection, and union queries. We explain an example to show the difficulty of updates of Dejima tables by JOIN queries. Consider D, a Dejima table defined by the query that joins base tables A and B. We express D as $D = A \bowtie B$. We suppose that two transactions T_A and T_B are issued at the same time. Transaction T_A inserts records into A, while T_B inserts records into B. To satisfy global consistency, ΔD after committing two transactions should be $\Delta D = A \bowtie \Delta B + \Delta A \bowtie B + \Delta A \bowtie \Delta B$ as if T_A and T_B are executed serially. If the local concurrency control prevents transactions from reading uncommitted records by other transactions, each transaction cannot refer to updates in an opposite ongoing transaction. Therefore, both of the two transactions cannot acquire $\Delta A \bowtie \Delta B$. Inconsistency occurs in this case. Thus, we need to ensure that $\Delta A \bowtie \Delta B$ can be obtained by either of two transactions for ensuring global consistency. Note that such inconsistency may occur not only for insertions but also deletions and updates.

Update Propagation via Multiple Paths: When a transaction propagates to some peer via multiple paths, the databases may become an inconsistent state because different bidirectional transformations on the paths may convert to different updated records. There are two cases of propagating via multiple paths: 1) the paths cross at the same peer; 2) a propagated transaction returns to a peer which the transaction has already gone through. In case 1, the propagated updates at this peer may be different on each path. In case 2, An inconsistent propagation cycle may form (e.g., an inserted record is eventually deleted after the propagation).

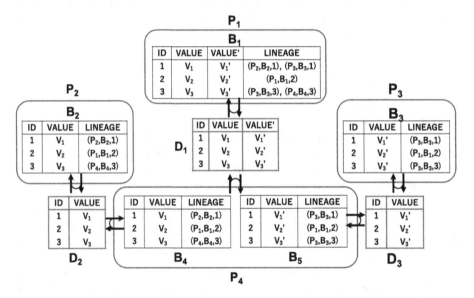

Fig. 2. An example of the Dejima with the concept of FRS. Records with the same lineage belong to the same FRS. An update to a record may propagate to other records in the same FRS. The update never propagates to other records in a different FRS.

3   Transaction Management in Dejima

We propose a transaction management method for the Dejima architecture. Our key idea is to regard the whole base tables as a single virtual view. We propose a concept of *Family Record Set* (FRS) and perform a *Conservative Two-Phase Locking* (C2PL) on this virtual view.

3.1   Family Record Set

To manage transactions and guarantee global consistency, we find out what records will be updated by an update and what peers have these records. To this end, we introduce a concept of FRS, which represents a set of all records affected by an update. The FRS of an update contains the following records: (1) *original records*, which are the records updated in the base tables where the update occurs, and (2) *derived records*, which are the records updated through the update propagation.

Since Dejima tables are defined by SPJU queries, for each update, the FRS forms an atomic unit for update propagation. We can treat the integrated databases as a single virtual view. An FRS represents a single record in this virtual view.

In an FRS, we define the original record set for a particular derived record as lineage. Since a derived record can be generated by joining multiple records, the lineage may not be a single original record but a set of records. Figure 2 shows an example of Dejima with the concept of FRS. We express records in each lineage by (peer ID, base table ID, record ID). We can use each record's lineage to distinguish which FRS a record belongs to. Consequently, acquiring locks of records with a particular lineage is equivalent to obtaining locks of the corresponding record in the virtual view. Next, we present our transaction management algorithm.

3.2   Algorithm

A transaction acquires locks before it is executed. So we can reduce the number of aborts of ongoing transactions and prevent the deadlock. Our algorithm works as follows.

1. We first obtain the lineages of records that are to be updated.
2. The local transaction acquires shared locks of the records that the transaction reads.
3. All peers are notified with the lineages obtained in step 1. The transaction requires exclusive locks of the records whose lineage is obtained at step 1.
   (a) If all locks are acquired successfully, the transaction is executed by a two-phase commit through peers in a tree-formed network structure.
   (b) If the transaction cannot acquire all locks, release the locks, and abort the transaction.

When a transaction includes insertion queries, we shall propagate the transaction with the lineages of the inserted records. According to the propagated lineages, each peer attach the lineages to the derived records.

Since all peers are notified with the requests for exclusive locks, it is sufficient to acquire shared locks locally at peer P where the transaction is issued. When another peer requests an exclusive lock for the record, peer P blocks the request.

Communication Tracing Tree Structure Of The Network. Considering the autonomy of peers in Dejima, we assume that each peer is only aware of the peers with which it shares data. Hence the communication in Dejima needs to be performed in a tree structure of the network.

Combined FRS. Because of the Dejima table may be defined by JOIN queries, multiple FRSs may be combined and form a new FRS by join operations. Consider two FRSs F and F', which contain records R and R', respectively. If there is a record derived by joining some record in R and some record R', this join record forms a new FRS, which is a joint set of F or F'. When we require exclusive locks of records in F, we should acquire additional exclusive locks for records in F' to achieve consistent update propagation. This additional exclusive locks eliminate the situation where a transaction updates records in F and another transaction updates records in F' at the same time. Thus, we can successfully obtain $\Delta A \bowtie \Delta B$ mentioned in Sect. 2.

Detection of Update Propagation via Multiple Paths. To detect the propagation via multiple paths, we attach a globally unique ID to every transaction. This ID is represented as a pair (peer ID, local transaction ID). Propagating a transaction with this ID enables a peer to detect whether its base table is updated by the same transaction through multiple paths. When such an update is detected, the peer aborts the transaction immediately.

4   Implementation and Evaluation Plan

We discuss our implementation and evaluation plan[1]. We use PostgreSQL for the local database at each peer. Update propagation is implemented using DBMS triggers and virtual views. The triggers and the virtual views are generated via bidirectional transformations, which are implemented using BIRDS [8]. We first plan to implement our proposal method and evaluate the consistency and availability of the Dejima for several real-world applications. Then we plan to evaluate the efficiency by measuring the throughput, latency, and scalability of the Dejima. The scalability will be investigated by testing workloads with varying degrees of contention and a varying number of peers or peer groups. Other transaction management protocols such as optimistic concurrency control will be compared.

5   Conclusion

We proposed a transaction management method for Dejima. This method handles distributed base tables as a single virtual view with a new concept FRS and then perform C2PL on this view. C2PL acquires locks before performing a transaction, reducing the number of aborts of ongoing transactions. As future work, we plan to implement this method on Dejima and evaluate scalability and efficiency.

---

[1] The source code is available at https://github.com/ekayim/dejima-prototype.

References

1. Asano, Y., et al.: Flexible framework for data integration and update propagation: system aspect. In: 2019 IEEE International Conference on Big Data and Smart Computing (BigComp), pp. 1–5. IEEE (2019)
2. Asano, Y., et al.: Making view update strategies programmable-toward controlling and sharing distributed data. arXiv preprint arXiv:1809.10357 (2018)
3. Baker, J. et al.: Megastore: providing scalable, highly available storage for interactive services. In: CIDR (2011)
4. Corbett, J.C., et al.: Spanner: Google's globally distributed database. ACM Trans. Comput. Syst. TOCS **31**(3), 1–22 (2013)
5. Karvounarakis, G., Green, T.J., Ives, Z.G., Tannen, V.: Collaborative data sharing via update exchange and provenance. ACM Trans. Comput. Syst. TODS **38**(3), 1–42 (2013)
6. Lenzerini, M.: Data integration: a theoretical perspective. In: Proceedings of the twenty-first ACM SIGMOD-SIGACT-SIGART symposium on Principles of database systems, pp. 233–246 (2002)
7. Thomson, A., Diamond, T., Weng, S.C., Ren, K., Shao, P., Abadi, D.J.: Calvin: fast distributed transactions for partitioned database systems. In: Proceedings of the 2012 ACM SIGMOD International Conference on Management of Data, pp. 1–12 (2012)
8. Tran, V., Kato, H., Hu, Z.: Programmable view update strategies on relations. Proc. VLDB Endow. **13**(5), 726–739 (2020)

Author Index

Printed in the United States
By Bookmasters